D. H. Lawrence

Novelist, Poet, Prophet

D. H. LAWRENCE

Novelist, Poet, Prophet

Edited by
Stephen Spender

HARPER & ROW, PUBLISHERS
NEW YORK, EVANSTON, SAN FRANCISCO, LONDON

Contents

Lawrence and the Movements
of Modern Culture
Diana Trilling

Among the major writers of the first half of this century Lawrence is, I think, unique for the ambiguous response he receives from his readers. Not alone today, as we try to fit him to a world which is so much changed from his, but even while he was alive and even among his admirers his reception was always a qualified one. James, Proust, Kafka, Yeats, Joyce, Eliot: most of the figures of Lawrence's time, once they were recognized or at least where they were recognized, were accepted with sufficient single-mindedness – even James, who probably comes closest to Lawrence in the ability to create an unsure response in his public, is eventually more successful than Lawrence has ever been in persuading his readers to subdue their reservations to their appreciation. It is a striking fact of Lawrence's career that he had to wait scarcely at all for recognition; although his books never sold in enormous quantity his genius was acknowledged almost from the start. But his admirers, or at any rate the more sober of them as distinct from the fans and idolators, would seem always to have proceeded with some caution in assessing the work, separating Lawrence's sheer literary gift, the energy of his communication, from his message and trying to sort out what was relevant and useful in the doctrine from what was overcharged and excessive even as poetic statement.

But our opinion of what is useful or not useful, relevant or irrelevant in a writer's work changes of course from generation to generation as our modes of feeling and perception alter and while Lawrence has continued to be received equivocally, the ground for acceptance or rejection of his books, the very order in which we rank them, has regularly and significantly shifted. Indeed it is possible to trace certain of the major developments in culture over the last forty years on the basis of how people have read him or what they have chosen to take from his work.

Thus, remarkable as it seems today, in the 1930s what was thought to be at

1

the centre of Lawrence's doctrine was an appeal – as simple as that – for the release of sexuality, and the book of his which was most fully responded to was one which, if it is now discussed at all, is assigned a relatively minor place in the canon, *Lady Chatterley's Lover*. It was *Lady Chatterley*, not *Women in Love* or *The Rainbow* or even *Sons and Lovers*, which was regarded as his most impressive accomplishment, also as his chief doctrinal pronouncement, and it was read as a rousing call to sexual freedom from a writer who had perhaps too often wandered in the dark bypaths of myth and metaphor but who had at last, near the close of his career, emerged into the clearer atmosphere of human actuality. It was of great point that the book had been suppressed: the public charge of indecency underwrote its worth as a document of the serious life – just as a few years earlier it had been one's high literary duty to bootleg a copy of Joyce's *Ulysses* and struggle with its innovative techniques, now it became one's high moral duty to acquire a copy of *Lady Chatterley* and put oneself to its sexual schooling. This was a period in which sexologies were coming to be widely and openly read: mistakenly, Lawrence's novel was taken to offer a similar if more elevated instruction although, in fact, far from providing a manual of eroticism, Lawrence drew a curtain on his single scene of sexual excursion or improvisation, leaving the reader to guess what had gone on, and dealt with the detailed physiology of intercourse only insofar as he wished to describe the possibility of failure, which he then went on to blame on the female partner. But women in the 1930s and 1940s, almost in the degree that they thought of themselves as culturally advanced and surely in the degree that they were available to Freudian doctrine, were quite prepared to accept the accusation that they were lacking in proper submissiveness to men and therefore at fault in most situations of unhappiness. Lawrence's harshness to women, instead of alienating his female readers, would seem to have fed their well-stimulated appetite for blame.

In venturing to be as outspoken as he was about sex, Lawrence had been solemnity itself; he never intended *Lady Chatterley* to be fun nor was it taken by his readers as anything except a thoroughly no-nonsense business. Despite his insistence on a language of love-making which would rid sex of its shames and shams and present it in its naked purity, the sexuality of *Lady Chatterley* could not have been more cloaked than it was in portentous emotion – Lawrence's erotic manifesto had little or nothing to do with the investigation of pleasure, everything to do with the deeper connections of body and spirit and the subtle resonances of love. But the 1930s were of course the era not only of the great Depression but also of the rising tide of totalitarianism; in a world of deprivation and fear the abrogation of the pleasure principle in favour of a new emotional economics, a new dialectic of male-female relations, was not particularly noteworthy – whatever proposed a personal transcendence of material circumstance was a gift of and to the imagination. In *Lady Chatterley* Lawrence offered his readers a world which, actual as it was, with the actuality of explicit sex, yet led one beyond the banal universe of economic and political necessity. Under circumstances in which politics, at least the politics of intellectuals, had become so egregiously moral an enterprise, it was an undertaking licensed only by the fact that Lawrence similarly charged the erotic life with morality, to the point indeed – as was eventually said – of puritanism.

When his critics of the 1950s accused Lawrence of puritanism they meant something other than this would mean today. The word is now seldom used but when it is it refers to any view of sexuality which proposes a hindrance to the pursuit of sexual gratification; in the 1950s it meant a view of sexuality in which freedom was circumscribed, perhaps even defined, by those values of love and responsibility which had traditionally been supposed to curb and direct our sexual instincts. With the war and most immediately in response to the atomic bomb, a mood of profound if unchannelled despair had come to prevail in the advanced sections of culture; the young in particular were seized with the sense of having destinies already arranged for them, of being governed by governments in which they were unable to make themselves heard and of being implicated in decisions in which they had no voice. It was this sense of fatedness, of having lost all freedom of social will, of social choice, which was now to be corrected, or at any rate countered, by a new and unlimited freedom of the sexual will – in the advanced fiction of the period, as almost ever since, only a single expression of purposiveness is permitted for the characters who speak for their authors, that of their sexual urgency.

But if an unconditioned sexuality, which is to say a sexuality with no goal except its own fulfilment, was the reply of the 1950s to a society which had created conditions so coercive that nothing was left to the individual save his existential self, so long as that was allowed to last, then clearly Lawrence provided small comfort. It required no exigent reading to understand that the sexuality for which Laurence spoke was nothing if not conditioned, and not merely by the full-scale emotions which he insisted upon both as its source and justification but also by the larger social purpose to which he thought that sexuality must minister. No more than Lady Chatterley's affair with her game-keeper was to be read as an essay in pleasure was her escape from her crippled and impotent husband, who represents our modern civilization, to be read as the negation of society as such; it is only the society which produces a Clifford Chatterley which has been refused. Because, as his work progresses, there is less and less of the paraphernalia of society in Lawrence's novels and because the social ideal becomes increasingly more abstract, the 1930s and 1940s commonly thought of his work as anti-social in its intention. Indeed, in the 1930s, this may largely have accounted for the emphasis that was put upon his sexual doctrine – if one thought of Lawrence as only an advocate for sexual freedom one could the more readily forgive his neglect of its social context. The 1950s were more accurate in their comprehension of his work. They recognized that behind the demand that we surrender to the dark imperative of the blood and return to a more primitive consciousness than that of the contemporary world there lay not the wish for the annihilation of society but Lawrence's vision of social regeneration. A renovated state of personal being would issue in a renovated state of social being.

For the 1950s, however, the fact that Lawrence looked to sex as an instrument of social revision was not the sole evidence of his retrograde stance. For readers who came to his books from, say, Henry Miller, or even from Colette, the ultimate proof of Lawrence's puritanism and of his willingness to accept a regressive social authority was the extraordinary stress he put upon marriage. 'Your most vital necessity in this life,' Lawrence had written in 1914 to Thomas Dunlop, British consul at Spezia, 'is that you shall love your wife completely and implicitly and in entire nakedness of body and spirit. . . . You asked me once what my message was . . . this that I tell you is my message as far as I've got any.' Obviously at another moment Lawrence might have put the matter less simplistically or made more of the connection between personal and social modes of feeling. This does not alter the truth of his brief prescriptive summary. In the first instance Lawrence was always in search of some transcendent meeting of man and woman: *a* man, *a* woman. Except as seen in its metaphoric meaning which is also its largest social dimension, the whole of his doctrine, whatever its transmutation into religion or politics or anthropology, boils down to Lawrence's imagination of the perfect embodiment of woman in wife.

Two short decades after Lawrence's death in 1930, the Wagnerian heroism with which he had invested this quest had lost its splendid overtones of moral grandeur and become only embarrassing. As I have said, the importance which Lawrence gave to the relation of man-woman or husband-wife, the generation which had come of age in the war years gave to a quite other sort of relation, that of self and society. In the face of society's manifest ascendancy over the self, withdrawal and passivity became the order of the day in politics – witness the fact that McCarthyism, instead of being at once resisted and destroyed, as surely it might have been, was allowed to run its unrestricted course for several disastrous years – while in the more personal sphere the call went out, fundamentally different in kind from Lawrence's, for attainment to a new consciousness through drugs, on the one hand, and on the other hand through a reversion to the polymorphous perversity of infant life, before civilization makes its claim

4

on the body and its instincts. Throughout his writing Lawrence had frequently used the phrase 'lapsing back' to describe the process by which mankind must regenerate itself. The concept was always and only a figurative one, however fiercely he might insist upon its actuality. What was the precise intention of the writing of Norman Mailer or Norman O. Brown, of Allen Ginsberg or William Burroughs, whether their work too was chiefly to be understood as figure of speech or whether a new generation of writers was issuing a literal summons to a more primitive way of life, might be open to argument. But one thing was certain: the resounding entrance upon the literary scene of these writers and others of like view heralded a new era in culture and yet another assessment of Lawrence.

At no time in Lawrence's life or since his death had there been so sharp a swing away from the established culture and from the priorities of modern competitive society as developed in the late 1950s and 1960s – although this movement perhaps shows signs of abatement as we advance into the 1970s, many of its effects, particularly in the sphere of sexual conduct, are probably irreversible. Casual or merely companionable sex, sexual experience as an end in itself, indulgence of the desire for sensation: all of these had of course been distasteful to Lawrence and we can suppose that he would especially have loathed a culture which encouraged them in the name of radical progress. But the rejection by the young of the values and ambitions and rewards of modern industrial society should, in logic, have been sympathetic to him – the imperative of logic must be emphasized, however, because it is difficult to imagine Lawrence acceding in any attitude or principle unless he had himself formulated it.

But then even the logical connection between Lawrence's views and those of a present generation of readers is perhaps not as firm as at first appears. To be sure, the part played by Lawrence's hatred of the first world war in his rejection of modern life is closely paralleled by the part played by the Vietnam war in the rejection of the power-structure of the state by so many of the present-day young. Indeed, in the force with which it announces the difference between that which increases and that which diminishes life, the slogan 'Make love, not war' is close to the heart of Lawrence's doctrine. But Lawrence never made slogans nor, had he been offered one, would he have been willing to rest in it, – which is an oblique way of saying that he had no instinct for the facile and indolent. More directly to the point, the love-making to which one is being encouraged in our contemporary use of this slogan, although it is presumably dedicated to the same social goal as Lawrence's, is of a very different order of personal experience than anything Lawrence had in mind; thus it is bound to propose a different social outcome. The sexuality which Lawrence celebrated was mating. What a present generation means by love-making is coupling. Coupling can be understood in various ways; it can mean anything from the unimpeded satisfaction of the sexual appetites to an escape from singleness, from isolation. But one thing it does *not* mean is ultimate or transcendent emotion such as Lawrence was proposing when he spoke of loving your wife 'completely and implicitly and in entire nakedness of body and spirit'. Therefore, while it can put itself in opposition to the established society, it cannot regenerate it in any way that would accord with Lawrence's moral vision.

Aware of Lawrence's antagonism to Freud one hesitates to adduce a Freudian concept, that of the superego, to explain what is surely the chief difference between Lawrence's view of sex and the view which has become increasingly salient in our contemporary culture, connected though the two may seem to be by their common aversion from the kind of eroticism which, to borrow Auden's famous line, has built our cities. If we accept Freud's definition of the superego as the sum and source of our ideals, our conscience, our guilts, the repository of the parental teachings in obedience to, or defiance of which we shape the character of our mature lives, then Lawrence must be recognized as one of the most superego-ridden people who yet managed to be a literary genius. The sexuality preached by Lawrence, attached as it was to idealism and to high social purpose, was but minimally a function of the Freudian *id* and even less a reversion to the polymorphous perversity of infancy. It was a clear product of the superego, which in fact is why it was so perfectly tailored to the 1930s when any diminution of confidence in the efficiency of the existent social organization was so well compensated for by faith in the ability of man to solve all his social problems through highminded and selfless social action. The revolutionary ardour of the 1930s, optimistic, orderly, submissive to idea and discipline, is much more accurately described as an impetus than an impulse. It found its corollary in the disciplined and ideology-bound sexual ardour of Lawrence. In fact, as was being demonstrated in Soviet Russia at the very time, the responsible mating for which Lawrence was a spokesman was far more appropriate to the continuing effort of radical social change than the earlier Communist promise of free love, free abortion, free divorce had been, for it represented a reassertion in the personal life of the rigours which are always involved in political as distinct from cultural revolution.

For much the same reason that ours is a time of revolutions in and through culture and not of political revolution, it is a time when there is also likely to be a considerable resistance to any view of the world which, like Lawrence's, is heavily charged with superego, that is to say with ideals and stern ideas and discipline. While there was often a kind of grandiosity in Lawrence's projection of the social scene which consorted with his Wagnerian vision – his vision, that is, of a supernal quest – and which probably underlay his fascination with proto-fascist posturings, actually one is misled in supposing that his image of the hero was itself larger than life. He was a slight man and much given to domestic occupations, and he always entrusts his doctrine to men of similar stature and temperament, also to men of more or less the same class as his: his leading male characters are regularly slight, wiry, fierce, home-centered men of the working class. These protagonists nevertheless stand full in the heroic tradition: they think of life as a test, a challenge to be faced up to and overcome. Even the clothes in which Lawrence dresses them or in which he would ideally wish them to be dressed make *figures* of them, moulding their bodies, encouraging the swagger of masculinity. The young today love swagger and costume too, but they love the clothes of masquerade and deception, which Lawrence would have despised. More important, they have scorn for the defined maleness, the defined womanliness which led Lawrence to a concern with outward appearance and which made for him a first condition of the heroic. There is a way to put the difference, finally, which while it may seem unflattering to the contemporary young is surely not an unqualified judgement on Lawrence: whereas the representatives of the advanced culture of our present decade would find it difficult to bring sex into conjuction with character, for Lawrence it was impossible to separate the two.

Memoir of
D.H.Lawrence
Barbara Weekley Barr

Much of what Lawrence said to me over twenty years ago is still quite clear in my memory, chiefly because he was so direct himself. He never hummed and hawed or offered the usual kind of cautionary advice which is supposed to bene-fit young people.

'The only thing worth living for is life itself,' he said. His strong influence on many people was due to the fact that he profoundly altered their sense of values. 'I shall change the world for the next thousand years,' he once said to Frieda, his wife. I believed him.

Although it was as a young woman that I really came to know Lawrence, I first met him when I was seven. My father was Professor of Modern Languages at Nottingham University, and Frieda was then his wife. There were three children: Monty, the eldest, Elsa, my sister, and I, the youngest.

In the early spring of 1912 Lawrence, who had at one time attended my father's evening classes, went to see him at the college to ask for a letter of recommendation for a post in Germany. He was invited to the house and so met Frieda. She had heard my father speak of him earlier, when he had said to her: 'I have got a genius in my evening class.'

One day, Frieda, Elsa, and I were walking along a country lane outside Nottingham when we met a tall, pale, cross-looking young man, who took us to Holbrook's Farm. My mother obviously knew him. It was Lawrence. A sister of Jessie Chambers, the Miriam of *Sons and Lovers*, had married the farmer. Mr Holbrook showed Elsa and me over the farm, and gave us a ride on a horse. I remember that, as it reared up, I slipped off and was caught by Mr Holbrook.

When we went into the farmhouse, Elsa and I found that everyone else had gone out. There was a plate of rock cakes on which Lawrence had printed a notice, 'Take One'.

Later on we joined the others again in the parlour, where Frieda was standing by a piano, singing. Lawrence, still pale and preoccupied, was sitting near her.

The story of their going away together has been told before. To Monty, Elsa, and me, it was a mystery for many years.

We left Nottingham and went to stay with relatives in London. My father kept his post in Nottingham, travelling to and fro once or twice in the week. He did not speak of Frieda until one day, about three years later, when, sitting on a tombstone in a country churchyard, he asked me, 'Would you like to see Mama?'

'Not very much,' I answered, apprehensively. She had become rather an unreal figure by then.

'I have arranged for you to see her; Monty and Elsa too.' he told me.

Before this, my mother had made several attempts to see us, once waiting outside the dame school Elsa and I attended at Bedford Park, London, to snatch a few minutes' talk with us. This was stopped at once. Thereafter, we were escorted to school, and told to run away if we saw our mother. I remember scampering along in fear and excitement to the safety of Miss Dollman's school at the sight of Frieda's disquieting, solitary figure. Then, looking over my shoulder, I would see that she was still smiling in a bewildered way, not wishing, perhaps, to leave any sting.

She at last won her plea to see us. An interview, timed to last half an hour, was arranged at a lawyer's office. We were all nervous when we went there. Monty took charge. Frieda came in looking excited, but in tears, with an open box of sweets in her hand. Monty talked quite cheerfully with her, but we were all relieved when the lawyer's clerk diffidently entered to say that the half hour was over.

After another interval we saw our mother again. She came up from the country, where she and Lawrence had a cottage. It was during the 1914 war. We met her at the station. Monty, then a correct schoolboy of fifteen or sixteen, was embarrassed to see that she was carrying branches of apple blossom. She took us to *Figaro*, which Beecham was conducting, and then to tea at Lyons, where she gave us each ten shillings. Afterwards, in the ladies' room, Elsa said to me, anxiously, 'You are not to *like* Mama, you know, just because we have got ten shillings.' This money was formally returned to Frieda by my father.

There were a few other meetings after this.

In the winter of 1923-4, Elsa and I met Lawrence again. It may have been Catherine Carswell who had something to do with it, because her house in Hampstead was the meeting place. Middleton Murry was there that evening as well.

My childhood feeling about Lawrence had been that he was a fairly ordinary young man. This encounter gave me a very different impression altogether. I had not seen anyone like him before; nor have I since. He was tall and fragile – a queer, unearthly creature. He had a high-pitched voice, a slight Midlands accent, and a mocking, but spirited and brilliant manner. I liked his eyes. They were blue, wide apart, in cave-like sockets, under a fine brow. But they could be soft, and were kindly in the extreme. He had high cheekbones, a clubby Midlands nose, and a well-shaped jaw. His skin and hair were fair, and his beard red. When he was excited, or looking well, his cheeks had a delicate colour. He seemed beyond being human and ordinary, and I felt at once that he was more like an element – say a rock or rushing water. Lawrence talked to Elsa and me with great friendliness. Secretly I much preferred Middleton Murry, who sat near, dark, smiling and inscrutable, but more like the other men we had known.

Lawrence had just come back from America. 'Why is everyone over here so kind and loving?' he enquired derisively. 'If I get the porter to carry my bag, he wants to love me as well! I don't like it.' I thought Lawrence a queer fish.

In Hollywood, he told us, a friend had taken him to the house of a famous British film star. This man had made a typical entry into the gorgeous lounge, dressed in a sort of polo outfit, accompanied by baying dogs. In a few minutes the wife appeared, prettily leading their two children. All three were groomed to perfection. Lawrence thought the actor a buffoon. Hollywood he described as a huge lunatic asylum.

Frieda was lighthearted that evening, Murry a little embarrassed, and Lawrence very friendly. But Elsa and I did not know what to make of him. He talked to me about my art school, but was highly critical of it – and of me. Shortly afterwards, he remarked to Elsa, 'Barby is not the stuff of which artists are made.'

In February 1924, when he and Frieda went to visit her mother in Germany, Lawrence said of us to our grandmother: 'They are just little suburban nobodies.'

By the time Lawrence and Frieda had returned from America the second time (30 September 1925), I had become engaged. I took the man to dine with them at Garland's Hotel, where they sometimes stayed. He was considerably older than I was, a lazy, philandering sort.

In a black suit, looking frail and distinguished, Lawrence talked politely to the man. So did my mother. Afterwards we went to see *The Gold Rush*.

It did not take Lawrence long to make up his mind about the engagement. 'We shall have to laugh her out of this,' he told Frieda. 'Where is Barby's *instinct*?' A little while after this I saw him at his sister Ada's house at Ripley,

Childhood

A collier's house at Eastwood: 'ugliness, ugliness, ugliness . . .'. ('Nottingham and the Mining Country')

Left 8A Victoria Street, Eastwood, where David Herbert Lawrence was born on 11 September 1885.

Opposite, top A collier's kitchen in Eastwood: 'On the right side of the fireplace, in the recess . . ., a long narrow window, and below it, a low brown fixed cupboard . . .' (*A Collier's Friday Night*)

Opposite, bottom Brinsley Colliery where Lawrence's father, Arthur Lawrence, worked. 'When I was a boy . . . I thought the Lord was always at the pit-top.' (*Sons and Lovers*)

Below The view from Victoria Street. In spite of his criticism of Eastwood, Lawrence felt, as a young boy, that it was 'the real England – the hard pith of England'. ('Nottingham and the Mining Country')

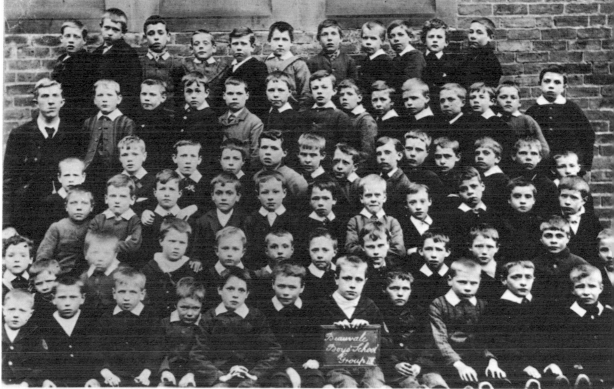

Above Group IV at Beauvale Boys' School, *c.* 1895. Lawrence, 'a delicate brat with a snuffy nose', is second from the left, third row down.

Above, top Beauvale Boys' School at Eastwood, where Lawrence was a pupil from 1893 to 1898.

Opposite Moorgreen Colliery. 'He found his eternal and his infinite in the pure machine principle of perfect co-ordination into one pure, complex, infinitely repeated motion, like the spinning of a wheel. . . . It was pure organic disintegration and pure mechanical organisation. This is the first and finest state of chaos.' (*Women in Love*)

Above The Lawrence family group: from left to right, top row: Emily, George and Ernest. Bottom row: Ada, Mrs Lawrence, David Herbert and Mr Lawrence.

Opposite, top The house on Walker Street, which Lawrence nicknamed 'Bleak House'. At the end of the street one could see 'Crich on the left, Underwood in front – High Park woods and Annesley on the right: I lived in that house from the age of 6 to 18, and I know that view better than any in the world.' (Letter to Rolf Gardiner, 3 December 1926)

Opposite, bottom Nottingham High School which Lawrence left at sixteen.

just outside Nottingham. This was the first time Lawrence had a chance to talk to me about my 'young man'.

I met both his sisters there. Emily, older than he, was a fair, stolid-looking Midlands type. Her husband, Sam, and she had not been getting on since he had been through the war, though at first they had been a devoted pair. Lawrence had been lecturing Emily in an effort to act as peacemaker.

Ada, the other sister, was two or three years younger than Lawrence. She was a handsome, dark version of Lawrence and had a rather unhappy adoration for him.

When I saw my mother in this house, I thought she seemed a little out of place. I do not think Ada ever liked her, or forgave her for going off with her favourite brother.

Lawrence had a cold. Sitting up in bed in Ada's spotless room, he talked to me about my 'young man'. 'You see,' he explained patiently, 'he hasn't enough *life*. Your father with his books and so on has some life; this man hasn't *any*. The fight that every man knows he has to make against the world . . . he just shirks, using you as an escape from his life responsibility. He's a cadging dog, and he'll be much happier, really, if you kick him off . . . they always are. He's a bit inferior somehow. One feels a bit ashamed of him sneaking up the street.

'No, don't marry him, unless you feel divorce is a light business. Just shake him off, like a dog shakes off his fleas.'

I sat feeling woebegone during all this. To defend a weak position, I said, 'Well, he seems *stronger*, somehow, than I am.' It was a lie, and Lawrence looked mystified.

'Stronger'? I simply don't see it,' he remarked, 'unless it is in being outside the pale . . . alien to society. Maybe he is in that way.' I began to be won over at this point. 'You can't play with life,' he told me. 'The only thing worth having, anyhow, is courage.'

Lawrence then came downstairs. We had a pleasant meal at Ada's. It was suggested that I should spend the night.

I telephoned my hostess, wife of a Nottingham professor. When she told her husband, he was very much alarmed. The idea of my spending a night under the same roof as Lawrence horrified him. Supposing he should happen to meet my father, who was in Nottingham, too? Presently his wife telephoned, imploring me to go back to their house. I reluctantly agreed and then went to tell the others.

Lawrence sprang to his feet, white with rage. 'These mean, dirty little insults your mother has had to put up with all these years!' he spat out, gasping for breath.

Opposite 'The Streets were like visions of pure ugliness . . . a flat succession of wall, window and door, a new-brick channel that began nowhere and ended nowhere.' (*The Rainbow*)

I was dismayed, not knowing how to act. The others were silent, Ada looking a little scornful.

Feeling something like a criminal, I crept dejectedly back to my Nottingham friends in the dark.

Lawrence and Frieda went abroad again a few days later, first to Baden, then on to Spotorno, in Italy.

In 1926, I spent a very happy spring with Lawrence and Frieda on the Italian Riviera.

This visit caused a certain amount of fuss and trouble at home, but eventually I reached Alassio, a few miles from the village of Spotorno, where they had rented the Villa Bernarda.

For reasons of family decorum, I was to stay at Alassio in a *pensione*, excellently managed by a Miss Hill and a Miss Gould. Miss Hill, a colonial and the niece of an archbishop, was romantic and ethereal. Miss Gould, a chubby Englishwoman doggedly devoted to Miss Hill, was a feminine replica of a vicar uncle of mine.

Lawrence came over with Frieda to lunch and made himself very agreeable to the two spinsters. He rather liked taking a look at new people. 'One of those women's marriages,' he remarked amusedly afterwards.

Italy seemed a kind of paradise to me, though Alassio, once just a fishing village, had now become a sort of retreat for English gentlefolk living there to benefit from the favourable exchange rate. Many of them were Anglo-Indians – army people or civil servants – who looked on the Italians as a slightly improved kind of 'native'.

I tried to paint at Alassio and once when I was working out of doors, an English admiral came up, admired my painting, and took me out to tea.

Lawrence disapproved of this escapade. There was a curious streak of conventionality in him which cropped up now and then and which he no doubt inherited from his hardworking, puritanical mother. 'You want to be very careful of that kind of man,' he warned me severely.

He was also shocked to hear that I travelled third class in Italy and said, 'An English girl doing that here gives the impression that she is looking for an "adventure".' Fortunately, I was able to assure him that my worst experience had been drinking out of a bottle which was handed round a compartment by Italians with the friendly invitation 'Come on, don't be fussy.'

Before long I went to stay at the Villa Bernarda at Spotorno.

I remember so well walking in darkness up the narrow streets of the village, enthralled by its romantic ancient feeling and the wonderful foreign smell.

From the villa, a little way up the hill, I saw the light of an upstairs balcony window shine out towards the sea. The house was in two stories, connected by an outside stone staircase. Built on a slope, the villa had a still lower part, intended for storing wine and oil.

When I knocked, Frieda flung the door open joyfully. I saw Lawrence sitting up in bed against the sitting room wall.

'Why did you come so late?' he asked, crossly.

Talking endlessly over the chicken, which she had cooked on the charcoal fire, and the red wine, Frieda and I were very happy. Lawrence, in his nearby bed, took in every word. I went to bed in one of the downstairs rooms.

The next morning I was awakened by loud bumping noises overhead. I was half prepared for this, as I had heard that the Lawrences threw saucepans or plates at each other. However, I hurried upstairs to intervene.

Frieda, her neck scratched, was in tears. 'He has been horrid,' she said with a glare at the glum, pale man sitting on the edge of his bed. She had told him that, now I was with her at last, he was to keep out of our relationship and not interfere. This had infuriated Lawrence. I was exhilarated, rather than shocked.

It soon blew over, but a few days later the sparks flew again when Lawrence, after inveighing bitterly against Frieda, flung his wine in her face. This time I joined in, shouting, 'She's too good for you; it's casting pearls before swine!'

After Frieda had gone out of the room in anger, I asked Lawrence, 'Do you care for her?'

'It's indecent to ask,' he replied. 'Look what I've done for your mother! Haven't I just helped her with her rotten painting?'

In spite of his independent mind, Lawrence felt the need of sympathy. He was trying to sort out his feelings and values, and find a balance. He wanted Frieda to do the same, but she resisted him, somehow.

'Why does your mother want to be so *important*?' he demanded. 'Why can't she be simple and talk to me naturally, as you do, like a woman?.

I listened to his complainings. The incident was trivial, but his feelings seemed really shattered.

Afterwards when someone told me that he had said, 'Frieda's daughter tried to flirt with me,' I thought it mean of him.

He and I liked to go for long walks. At Spotorno, and afterwards at Scandicci, we often went off in the afternoons and walked up the mountains. We talked a lot, mostly about people. Then we would forget about them, and just enjoy looking at the lovely Italian scene.

I began to paint the landscape. Lawrence, who had learned how to paint in oils, perhaps from Dorothy Brett in New Mexico, was a discerning critic. At first he was disparaging about my 'studio stuff'. '*Play* with the paint,' he urged me. 'Forget all you learned at the art school.'

One day, after spending the morning up the mountain, I came in and flung down a canvas despondently. 'It's good . . . there's air in it,' said Lawrence, jumping up. His judgement was sound, for this was the first picture I sold when I got back to London.

'Screw the tops on your paint-tubes afterwards,' Lawrence said. 'It just takes courage. You'll never get a husband if you are too untidy.'

Sometimes he took a hand in my painting, putting figures of peasants in the landscape, saying that it needed them to give it life. A picture of mine called *Peasants Building a House* was the most successful of these. Lawrence put in a black-haired young man drinking out of a Chianti bottle, and an old man holding a trowel, standing up in the half-built house.

The creative atmosphere of the Lawrence household was like a draught of life to me. I painted away assiduously at Spotorno.

'She might be an artist if she finds herself,' Lawrence told Frieda.

Sometimes he talked of his childhood, proudly saying that there had been more life and richness in it than in any middle-class child's home. Ada was his favourite sister. When they has been youngsters, he had once said to her, 'Let's go away, and find a better life together somewhere.' But Ada had been too timid; not having his gifts, she had perforce to stay where she was.

Lawrence had formerly hated his drunken father, but at this time had swung in sympathy towards him, away from his mother. She had been a sensitive woman, who, added to her hard lot, had endured the extra strain of having a self-indulgent, violent man as her husband.

When Lawrence was sixteen, he had a serious illness. His mother could not afford the medicines he needed, or even good food. This illness probably sowed the seed of the tuberculosis which killed him.

His mother died in her fifties of cancer, a disease Lawrence told me 'usually caused by fret'.

I believe the Lawrences had some Irish blood in them. There was a story, too, that as a child his great-grandfather had been found wandering on the field of Waterloo after the battle, and brought home by English soldiers.

His elder sister Emily would recite sentimental poetry at great length to Lawrence when he was small. 'I used to pull her hair till she cried, but she went on and on, the tears streaming down her face.' He chuckled. So did I. I could just picture the plain Midlands face of the persistent, weeping Emily.

In the grounds of the Villa Bernarda were the ruins of an old castle. The villa itself was a haphazard sort of house. You could sit upstairs or downstairs and do as you pleased.

One afternoon, Lawrence was downstairs reading the autobiography of Mabel Dodge Luhan.

'It's terrible, the will to power of this kind of woman,' he exclaimed. 'She destroys everybody, herself included, with her really frightful kind of will.' The manuscript seemed to fascinate him with horror. 'Read it, and let it be a lesson to you!' he said.

Lawrence must have read a great deal, though I did not often see him with a book. The only serious writer I heard him speak of with respect was Hardy. He didn't like Dickens, and said his people were 'frowsty'. Charlotte Bronte repelled him. He thought *Jane Eyre* should have been called *Everybody's Governess*. At that time he had just read *Gentlemen Prefer Blondes* with amusement. The part about Germans and eating reminded him of my German grandmother.

'Two hours after supper she has a few snails. Then at bedtime some honey-cake, with Schnapps. Really, I don't know *how* she can do it,' he told us, laughing.

Lawrence had been learning Russian, and would often turn up with a Russian dictionary. For some time he had wanted to visit Russia, believing there was a spark there which had been quenched in the rest of Europe. 'It seems to sink into a soupy state – Europe today,' he said. 'That's why I would like to be back at the ranch.'

Lawrence detested Bolshevism. Fascism was not to his taste either. While we were at Spotorno, an Englishwoman, Violet Gibson, shot at Mussolini. The Italians referred politely to the incident to us, and seemed almost sympathetic to the 'poor mad lady', whose bullet had passed through the cartilage of their bovine dictator's nose.

'Put a ring through it,' Lawrence advised a lieutenant of the Bersaglieri who happened to visit us the next day.

Some of *Mornings in Mexico* was written at the Villa Bernarda. In it he mentions Giovanni, the gardener who lived in the lower part among his chickens and wine bottles. Lawrence was indulgent towards the old man, but Frieda and I didn't care for him, because he would get drunk and frighten us.

Lawrence hardly ever wrote for more than four or five hours a day. His writing flowed off the end of his pen. 'If it doesn't, my writing is no good,' he said. He never discussed his writings with me, and advised me not to read his books till I was older. 'By the time you are forty, you will be able to understand them.' After Lawrence had finished a novel, he seldom wanted to look at it again.

Lawrence was quite clever with his hands. He could cook, sew, and was even good at embroidery.

In early February, my sister Elsa came for a brief visit. She flew to Paris, then still quite an enterprising thing to do. Lawrence was surprised that anyone should want to fly. 'I hate those artificial sensations,' he commented.

Elsa was better disciplined. Unlike me, she hated 'rows'. At the Bernarda she lectured Frieda about them, being concerned to see, after one of their quarrels, that Lawrence had tears in his eyes, a rare thing for him.

Elsa liked Spotorno, and joined in our afternoon walks, but more in disagreement with us than in accord. 'You and Lawrence encourage each other to be spiteful about everyone,' she said. There was some truth in this, though Lawrence thought that I was much worse than he was.

'You always have a vendetta against someone,' he exclaimed one day. 'I wouldn't marry you, Barby, if you had a million pounds.' 'You'll never care about anybody,' he told me another time. 'You with your everlasting criticisms! If the Archangel Gabriel came down from Heaven and asked you to marry him, you'd find fault.' The idea seemed to amuse him.

One day he talked to Elsa about the stars, the millions of other universes, and the endlessness of space, saying, 'So you see our little lives aren't so very important after all.'

This reminder of human insignificance must have made Elsa reckless, because that evening she drank too much wine at supper, and talked wildly.

Seeing her tipsy, and listening to her haranguing Lawrence, I laughed hilariously, as did Frieda. Lawrence was amused too, but with reservations. 'The contrast from her usual self is too sharp, it frightens me,' he observed fastidiously.

Also in February, Lawrence's sister Ada came with a friend to stay at the Bernarda, so Elsa and I moved to the tiny Hotel Ligure. As we breakfasted on the balcony over the sea, Frieda appeared looking angry and upset. Ada and the friend had been 'bossy', she said. They had tried to oust her from her kitchen, where she managed so well.

Elsa and I both gave her advice. The situation disturbed us. When I went up to the Villa, I was very chilly to Ada.

'I don't trust Barby; she's too clever,' Lawrence told my mother resentfully. His feelings were hurt as well. The atmosphere was unpleasant for a few days until Lawrence went off to Florence with Ada, later going on alone to Rome and Capri where he stayed with the Earl Brewsters.

When he returned from his journey, Lawrence told me: 'Ada depresses me; I have to get away. She doesn't *believe* in me. She loves me . . . oh, yes!'
Young then, and enthusiastic, I believed in him.

Lawrence thought that Elsa had more sense than I had. 'She is wise, and will make the best of life,' he wrote to me once. 'You are too inclined to throw everything away because of one irritating factor. There's been too much of that in all lives. You throw your soup at the waiter because it's too hot, or set fire to your bed, because there's a flea in it. Well, then can you lie on the ground.'

There was a quality in Elsa that he liked. Beyond her conventional autocratic exterior, he found a wistfulness.

'She rather makes a man feel he would like to put her in his pocket. Your pathos is unreal,' he said to me, discouragingly. 'Your troubles are all your own fault.'

Towards the latter part of April, Elsa and I were returning to England. Before we left Italy, Lawrence and Frieda took us to see Florence where we stayed at the Pensione Lucchesi, on the Arno. Lawrence showed us round Florence. At the Uffizi we stood in front of Botticelli's Venus *Rising from the Sea*, which he said was full of air. It was true: the figure seemed to float in sea air.

We met Norman Douglas, Pino Orioli, and many of the Florentine eccentrics too, all of whom were very friendly to Frieda's daughters.

I saw the Misericordia go to the scene of an accident. This is the voluntary ambulance service for which young men are chosen from noted Florence families. It was begun in the Middle Ages, and it has always been the tradition that the men who serve it wear masks, so that their charity has no personal significance. Florence did not cast its spell over me on this first visit, perhaps because it rained, and we were going back to England.

That spring in Florence, Lawrence met the Aldous Huxleys again. They became great friends. Sometime after my return, I had a letter from Aldous Huxley's Belgian wife, Maria, asking me to go and see her at the flat where they were staying in London. Lawrence and Huxley had first met in 1915, but they did not form a friendship until after their third meeting in Florence in that year, 1926.

Maria, with her charming face and large blue eyes, interested me very much, but we were both a little shy of each other.

The Lawrences' relationship had been an enigma to me, but Maria made me see its significance. 'A great passion' was how she described it. 'Frieda is silly. She is like a child, but Lawrence likes her *because* she is a child,' she said.

The Villa Mirenda on a hill at Scandicci, a few miles from Florence, was an old white house, more dignified than the Villa Bernarda.

Two large chestnut trees were in flower in front of it when I went there in the spring of 1927. (I also visited the Lawrences at the Villa Mirenda the following spring, 1928.) It had oil lamps, and a stove to light with pine logs in the evenings. There was a piano, hired from Florence, in the big whitewashed sitting room. The floor was covered with fine woven rush. On the wall hung the big *Holy Family* which Lawrence had painted on one of the canvases Maria Huxley had given him. His *Eve Re-entering Paradise* was in another room, as well as the

Nuns with the Gardener and a picture of naked men among autumn willows. He painted many others as well. Later an exhibition was arranged at the Warren Gallery which so shocked the prigs that the pictures were removed by order of the Home Secretary.

These paintings lacked what is called 'technique', but they were alive and mystical. They had a shiny surface like oleographs, caused by Lawrence sometimes smearing on the paint with his hands.

Lawrence was very pleased with his painting, which took less toll of him than writing. He said he was going to give up being an author and paint instead.

Frieda also painted occasionally. Her wonderful colour sense gave her pictures life and gaiety. One of them – of chickens at the ranch – she gave to Elsa, so I put it up on a mantelpiece at home.

'I say, I like that!' exclaimed my father. 'Who did it?'

'Oh, someone or other . . . I forget,' I replied.

At the Villa Mirenda we sang the Hebridean songs, Frieda accompanying us. Lawrence sang in a high-pitched voice. It gave the songs a weird 'other-world' sound, which suited them, although orthodox musicians would no doubt have shuddered. In fact, an elderly friend who was with me on this visit – staying disconsolately at the inn – expressed her disapproval of such amateurish singing.

'What a conceited ass she is,' remarked Lawrence's Scots friend, Miss Millicent Beveridge, who was there too.

We also sang 'Red, Red Is the Path to Glory', a tragic border song, and the 'Lay of the Imprisoned Huntsman', which Frieda liked to sing. Aunt Else told me that whenever she heard her sing it she felt sad, because there was a sound in Frieda's voice of a being also imprisoned.

One evening at Scandicci, a family of English puppet-makers named Wilkinson invited us to a party, where everyone was asked to do a 'turn'. The hostess, dressed as William Wordsworth, recited 'We Are Seven'. Lawrence, who had once seen Miss Florence Farr in London, sat down at an imaginary harp, drew his hands across it, began 'I will arise and go now' in a falsetto voice, and ended it with a 'ping-a-ling'.

This take-off of the high-faluting was over the heads of the company. On the way home Lawrence raved at Frieda for having allowed him to do it.

Lawrence was aloof. He disliked too easy intimacy, or gatherings where people 'got together'. He said once that the idea of putting his arm round a woman's waist and dancing with her appalled him.

Pretension and commonness upset him. One could sometimes see a glimpse of the working-class Midlander, but he was always remote from vulgarity.

He could be cruel, and even nagging, but never callously indifferent. He did not have the ordinary man's domineering dependence on his womenfolk, but could mend, cook and find his own possessions.

Lawrence had the clean, fresh look of so many fair people. He liked old clothes, but never looked ill-kempt.

'I don't mind a bit of vanity,' he once remarked. He would advise us about our clothes, and was interested in our dressmaking attempts. 'Sew it properly.' he would implore us. 'Things can't keep their shape unless you do.'

I remember thinking that his advice about an orange jumper I was knitting at the Mirenda must necessarily be inspired. 'The only colour that goes with yellow is pink,' he insisted. So Frieda and I finished it off with a strawberry border.

Sometimes she and I sat on one of the little balconies of the upstairs salon, among the white chestnut flowers. There one afternoon we read the MS of another feminine autobiography – an English one this time – with wicked amusement.

'Now I have two women interfering with my papers,' protested Lawrence. Things like that did not really annoy him, though.

At this time his illness made further inroads. He was more frail than he had been at Spotorno, and increasingly irritated by the people around him. When Pietro, the young Italian who did the errands with his donkey cart, came into the kitchen of the Mirenda while English friends were there, Lawrence said, 'Here he comes, thinking he will give them a chance to see the interesting young peasant.'

The two little boys of the Mirenda cottage he really did like. One had large grey eyes. 'One sees those eyes like water among the Sicilians,' he told me. I longed to see those olive-skinned people with water eyes.

'That boy has a voice like a thrush, Lorenzo,' said Frieda delightedly.

'Yes, he has,' replied Lawrence in his quick way.

Scandicci was like Paradise in the spring, the Mirenda a house of magic. I loved my big whitewashed room which Frieda had arranged with her wonderful taste. After I had gone back to England, she wrote, 'Your ghost still lingers in your room.'

The following summer (1927) I went to stay in Cologne with the old German professor who had first introduced my father to Frieda. He had a collection of photographs of her as a young woman.

At that time, Frieda and Lawrence were staying at my aunt Else's house at Irschenhausen, in Bavaria. In September I went to pay them a three-day visit.

The delightful wooden house they were staying at was a Grimm's fairy-tale place. When one walked in the forest, roebuck leapt across the path.

Frieda's younger sister, Nusch, stayed with them that summer. She was the only woman whom I ever heard Lawrence describe as 'desirable'.

She had then just married for the second time. Her choice was a bank manager. Quite a nice man, but Lawrence was afraid she had made a mistake in becoming respectable.

'She is a bit sad inside, poor Nusch,' he said. 'She belongs really to the demi-monde, and should have stayed there. She has that gift for making a man feel he counts, and *is* a man. She is a good sport, ready to fall in with people's plans, and enjoy herself.' She flirted with Lawrence, and he thought her fun.

When I read *Women in Love*, I thought that she was rather like Gudrun.

As a young woman, Nusch had visited England, where she had been disappointed to find that good manners prevented people staring at her remarkable good looks. 'When I come into the restaurant nobody *looks* at me! I might just as well be the waiter!' she had exclaimed, mortified.

When his three daughters grew up, my German grandfather expressed the hope that none of them would marry a Jew, an Englishman, or a gambler. (He had been a gambler himself.) To his disgust, these were just what they did marry.

Else, the eldest Richthofen daughter, was a very gifted woman – one of the very few people who could meet Lawrence on his own intellectual level. She translated some of his work into German.

She married Edgar Jaffé, who was finance minister for Bavaria under the Stresemann government. The strain brought on a breakdown, and he went into a nursing home.

Frieda went to see him there a little while before he died. From a neat, elegant man he had become a dishevelled wreck.

'You should not have come to see me, Frieda,' he said. 'Do you know I have not washed for three weeks?'

'Oh, Edgar, you have washed so much!' cried Frieda.

Just before I went to Germany that summer, a friend of ours had been killed in a reckless accident. Lawrence and Frieda had met the young man and some of his family in London. Frieda had really loved him.

'Poor chap,' Lawrence had written to me. 'It was what he really wanted, I suppose. That's the worst of it . . . life ought to be good enough. But he had that kind of life and sweetness the world doesn't want any more.'

'If Barby had cared about him it might have been different,' he said to Frieda.

He wrote a sympathetic letter to the mother.

I went from Alassio to stay at Scandicci the following spring, 1928, for two weeks.

Frieda told me that Lawrence had just finished a novel which would shock people very much. Pino Orioli was discussing the publication of it at that time, and he did produce the first edition in Florence of the novel which was *Lady Chatterley's Lover*.

After Lawrence's death, a Swiss film producer in Paris, Mr Siebenhaar, planned to make a film of the novel and bought the rights from Frieda. Unfortunately he was later obliged to abandon the project through lack of funds. It was in 1933 that he sent over a couple of Swiss film directors to take a look at the 'Lawrence country' and asked me to accompany them. We motored around the Midlands, and came across a country house called 'Renishaw', standing above a colliery which we were told belonged to the Sitwell family. I remembered that Lawrence had once mentioned a visit to a house belonging to Sir George Sitwell where he had seen a collection of antique beds. It was in fact the Sitwell's house in Florence which he had visited, but I jumped to the conclusion that it was this one, and thought he might possibly have used it as a model for the Chatterley home.

I sent a telegram therefore to Osbert Sitwell, who was in London. 'Discobole, Paris, propose filming Lawrence novel. May we inspect Renishaw Hall?' To this he replied, 'If you refer banned book Lady Chatterley's Lover your request gross as it is libellous.'

I was considerably taken aback by this piece of courtesy; so were the Swiss directors. After holding a mystified council, we turned our attention to one of the other stately homes of England in the neighbourhood, timidly peeping at it from the garden with the butler's consent.

That spring in Scandicci, I could not, unfortunately, do any successful paintings. But I was never bored; with Lawrence life was always absorbing, even when he was out of humour. He was brilliantly penetrating, and in assessing human relationships had an uncanny gift.

'He will leave her,' he said of a young married pair. 'Some other woman will want him, especially if she sees he has a wife and child,' This proved true. He thought that in most people the psyche was 'double', loving on one side and betraying on the other. It was our modern malady, according to him.

When my sister Elsa was going to be married, Lawrence wrote to me, 'Don't let her marry a man unless she feels his physical presence warm to her.'

'I don't need Lawrence's advice,' Elsa told me.

In this letter he also said, I think, 'Passion has dignity; affection can be a very valuable thing, and one can make a life relationship with it.'

Unfortunately these letters were all lost.

'As for Barby,' he said one evening as we sat at supper by the lamplight, 'she will never finish anything, any relationship. If she marries, she won't finish her marriage either. I tell you, Frieda,' he said, in a sharp, devastating voice, 'she won't *finish* it!'

He went on: 'I don't know what will become of her, simply I don't. If her father goes on giving her three pounds a week, she is very lucky. No one ever gave me that.'

All this was very discouraging. But Frieda stuck up for me determinedly.

After I had gone back to London, and was drifting unhappily in the way that was becoming a habit with me, Lawrence wrote quite charitably, ending, 'Don't throw yourself away; you might want yourself later on.'

One day at the Mirenda we looked through an old Italian opera brochure. There was a photograph of a woman with rich dark hair piled on top. 'I wish women looked like that now,' Lawrence remarked. Another portrait was of a full-looking man with a big moustache. 'I should like to be that man. Yes, I really would like to be just like him,' he said wistfully.

In their life together, Frieda must sometimes have suffered, and felt lonely. At first, many people had been hostile to her. Lawrence was inclined to be jealous, and would often sneer at the few friends she did have. The strain on her remarkable good humour must have been colossal. She believed in him, though. He needed her belief, and was unhappy without her.

At this time she wanted to holiday by herself. I was going back to Alassio. She came too, and then went off alone.

Lawrence said to Maria Huxley, 'Frieda has changed since she went away with Barby.'

He did not reproach my mother. One evening at the Mirenda he said to her, 'Every heart has a right to its own secrets.'

In the winter 1928–9, Lawrence and Frieda were staying at the Hotel Beau Rivage, at Bandol in the French Riviera. I spent a fortnight there just after Christmas when I was in a miserable, nervous state. Lawrence was very ill himself. It was an agonizing time.

Frieda had been in tears on Christmas Day, Lawrence told me, because she did not have a single present.

'There she was, howling like an infant,' he said contemptuously. To cheer herself up, she had put a photograph of Monty on a shelf, but Lawrence took it away, saying that to have photographs about was vulgar. A little while later he had burst out, 'Why don't your children send you presents?'

After he went to his bedroom, which led off Frieda's, we would hear his continual cough. During the day he looked exhausted and ill.

He had just finished his *Pansies* poems, and before sending them off to his

London publisher, he read them to us as we sat on Frieda's bed. These bitter poems had the effect of clearing my suffocated mind.

When Lawrence had gone to bed, I said to Frieda, 'He promised to make a new heaven and earth for your children when you went away together. Well, it's true; he has.' Frieda told me later that she had repeated this to Lawrence, and he had been pleased.

A young American from California, who was at Oxford, met us in the street at Bandol.

'Are you D. H. Lawrence?' he asked. He explained that he was looking for the 'ultimate reality'.

Lawrence invited him to come back to the hotel with us where, sitting in Frieda's bedroom, they threshed it out. Alas! The discussion was over my head.

'There *is* no ultimate reality,' said Lawrence, firmly, after a time. I doubted if this satisfied the young man. Soon after the American took me out to tea, and told me I was bad for Lawrence's genius and had better go away.

'He is mad, madder even than you are, Barby,' said Lawrence. 'He hates Oxford even more than you do your set-up. But you are both in a state of hate, and have got yourselves on the brain. . . . It's a common form of hysteria. You used to have a rather amusing temper that popped up now and then like a little devil, or Jack-in-the-box. Now it's got hold of you completely. You are cynical as well. That's dreadful.'

After a few days the news came that the *Pansies* had been seized by the police in the post. This upset Lawrence painfully. The feeling of tension increased, and there seemed a malaise in the hotel.

We had arranged to meet a friend of mine, Cynthia Kent, in Cannes, but in our distraction we went on the wrong day. As Cynthia failed to appear, Lawrence, suspecting some fresh insult, became frantically annoyed.

Lawrence was relieved when a cheerful colonial he knew wrote that he was coming to pay him a visit. 'Now don't say anything, but I think Barby might like him,' he said to Frieda. I think this was Lawrence's only attempt at match-making for me.

The young man, who was called Stephenson, proved a jolly, go-ahead sort of person. Something he had seen in a night club had given him an idea for a short story. He sat down almost as soon as he arrived and 'got it off his chest'. It was about an older woman leading a beautiful young woman astray. He read it to us as we all sat, as usual, in Frieda's bedroom.

When he had finished, Lawrence demolished it for him at once.

'It's false,' he told him. 'It wouldn't convince anybody. The emotions and situations are quite unreal. You'll have to re-write it.'

'He is *not* an artist; he is a businessman,' he told Frieda afterwards. 'Why does everyone try to write? I don't see there's so much fun in it.'

Lawrence worried about me; my depression effected him. He was rather tired now by my endless dilemmas.

'I had a dreadful dream,' he told us one morning. 'I was rescuing Barby from some disaster. She was in a fearful fix as usual.'

When I was returning to England, Frieda said, 'If you can't stand it, you can come out to us at Majorca.' That was to be their next resting-place. I believe it was from Majorca that Lawrence wrote to me: 'I think that your headaches may be due to a deep change in the psyche, and you will just have to lie low and bear the change. Don't make too many efforts, especially efforts with people, and don't try to paint at present. Later on you might be really worthwhile.'

In the winter of 1929, I had a letter from Frieda from a villa they had taken at Bandol called the 'Beau Soleil'. Lawrence was now extremely ill and spent a good deal of time in bed. People were trying to persuade him to go into a sanatorium. 'They say he must have a nurse. He says, "Can't I have Barby?"' she wrote. This pleased me, and I went out to Bandol, arriving there one winter evening.

The Beau Soleil was a little box of a villa near the sea.

Lawrence was sitting up in bed, wearing a blue cloth jacket. A ginger cat was sleeping on his bed, making him look quite homely.

After supper we sorted out some papers together. 'Don't yawn, Barby, it's boring!' he said, engrossed.

'The nights are so awful,' he told me. 'At two in the morning, if I had a pistol I would shoot myself.'

Sometimes Lawrence walked feebly into the garden, and lay on a chaise-longue. He felt Frieda could not help him any more, and this made his resentful. Covered with rugs, and lying in the garden with a grey, drawn expression on his face, he said, 'Your mother is repelled by the death in me.'

Some Americans came to see him. Lawrence said the wife was going mad because she had tried to insist on the ideal of goodness and beauty. The proprietress of the hotel came and chatted with him in her bright French way, but she, too, got on his nerves.

The person who seemed to tire him least was the cook's cracked old husband, who would come and stand at the foot of his bed, waving his peaked cap, talking inconsequently, and laughing like a noodle.

A young doctor from an English sanatorium came to see him with his consumptive wife. Lawrence liked her. 'She is like all people with chest trouble . . . gives too much life away,' he remarked.

I cooked some of Lawrence's meals, especially his breakfast, because he liked porridge. Frieda found me a little 'managing', I think, a little like Ada.

We all three decided to go to the ranch in New Mexico for which Lawrence longed, believing he could recover there. Frieda thought that I could go out first, and stay with Mabel Luhan.

Lawrence was amazed at this suggestion. 'What on earth do you think that Mabel would want with Frieda's daughter?' he demanded. 'You might just as well throw Barby into the sea!'

'But if you and your mother really could love each other,' he said to me later, 'you might make a life together.'

In early February, Lawrence had left Bandol for the Ad Astra sanatorium at Vence in the Maritime Alps. Frieda went with him; I stayed on at the Villa Beau Soleil.

A friend of mine met them at Nice, and motored them to the Sanatorium.

'Blair [Hughes-Stanton] has been as kind as an angel to me,' wrote Lawrence from there, adding, 'Here is £10 for housekeeping.' To this Frieda put a postscript. 'Be careful with the money.' This admonition impressed me so much, that when Blair and his wife came to see me, I gave them only a few rags of boiled meat from the soup for lunch, and offended them.

A little later I joined Frieda in Vence where she was staying at the Hotel Nouvel. When I went to see Lawrence at the sanatorium, I found him worse. In his balcony room, painted a dreary blue, he seemed wretchedly ill and wasted. For the first few days he had gone downstairs for lunch, but the other patients depressed him.

The superintendent was a cheerless person. 'Monsieur Lawrence is a lamp that is slowly failing,' he said to me unctiously.

Lawrence wanted to leave and go into a villa somewhere near. We had difficulty in finding this, because the French, often so reckless, seem terrified of invalids. Many whom I approached refused to let their villas on that account. At least we found the Villa Robermond on the hill just above Vence. It was a comfortable house, with a little cottage where an Italian peasant lived with his wife, who acted as concierge.

Lawrence still thought that if he could rest, and regain a little strength, he might be able to travel to New Mexico. To go there had also become my dream. In Nice I made enquiries about our passports.

Before Lawrence left the sanatorium several people visited him there. H. G. Wells, whom he did not like, came one afternoon, and told him his illness was mainly hysteria. The Aga Khan and his wife also came, and the Aga cheered Lawrence by saying he admired his paintings.

Lawrence complained to him of the way his work had been treated, and said: 'The English kill all their poets off by the time they are forty.'

Before taking Lawrence from the sanatorium, we engaged an English nurse. We also found another doctor, a Corsican, who was recommended by an American friend.

On 1 March, Lawrence drove up to the Villa Robermond with Frieda in a taxi. I saw him, in hat and overcoat, stagger up the few steps of the verandah, supported by the chauffeur. He was saying, 'I am very ill.'

After he was put to bed, the new doctor examined him. When he came out of Lawrence's room, he said, 'It is very grave. There is not much hope. Do not let him see that you know.' To our American friend Ida Eastman, he said, 'He is simply living on his spirit.'

The next morning Lawrence got up, washed, and brushed his teeth. He did not care much for the ministrations of the nurse, though she was unobtrusive enough, poor thing.

'She is so insipid,' he whispered. She was very unhappy, and sulked a good deal.

Lawrence said he thought he should rewrite the will he had once made but lost, in which he left everything to Frieda; but she feared it would tire him too much.

I cooked Lawrence's lunch, and took it in to find him sitting up in the blue jacket, tranquilly reading a book about Columbus's voyage to America.

The Huxleys came in the afternoon, and the nurse voiced her woes to Maria. Towards evening Lawrence suddenly became worse. His head began to distress him. Sitting up in agony, holding his head, Lawrence cried, 'I must have morphia.'

I put my arm round him for a few moments. I could not understand why the doctor had not come, and decided to go for him. When I left, Lawrence said to my mother, 'Put your arm round me like Barby did; it made me feel better.'

As I was leaving to go to Vence, Aldous and Maria came again from their hotel. Maria went and soothed Lawrence, holding his head in her hands. He had said she had his mother's hands.

He sat up in bed with startled brilliant eyes, looking across the room, crying, 'I see my body over there on the table!'

When I reached the Corsican doctor's house, I found that he had gone to Nice, so I hurried with a friend to the Hotel Nouvel. There the proprietor telephoned to the superintendent of the sanatorium, asking him to come and give Lawrence morphia. This was a lengthy talk, as the doctor at first refused. At last the proprietor won him round, so we called for him in a car and took him up to the villa. He complained all the way.

When we arrived there, however, his professional manner asserted itself. He greeted Lawrence kindly, and his greeting was returned. He gave him morphia, and left.

Aldous Huxley thought we had better go to Vence and try again to find the Corsican doctor, in case the effect of the injection wore off. We went to his house, but he was still away. It was about eleven at night when we walked up the hill to the villa again, talking of Lawrence and his illness. We found Frieda and Maria in the kitchen, with the peasant of the conciergerie standing by.

'We could not get the doctor,' I told them agitatedly.

'It doesn't matter,' said Frieda, gently.

Three days later, a light hearse carrying Lawrence's coffin was drawn to Vence cemetary by a small black horse, which picked its way intelligently down the rough hillside. Two wild-looking men accompanied it.

Robert Nichols, Achsah Brewster, the Huxleys, Frieda and I went to the grave. The English chaplain at Vence had sent a message, saying if he could be allowed to come and say one or two prayers, he would waive the usual burial service. This offer was refused. There was no religious rite.

The head of Lawrence's grave was against a sunny wall. One could see the Mediterranean far away below, and nearer, the dignified cypresses.

Two young Italians were commissioned to make a mosaic phoenix for the headstone. They worked it in pebbles of rose, white, and gray. Sometimes we watched these two, Domenique and Nicola, at work.

One day a tall dark woman came into the cemetary but, seeing us, went away. This was the 'Louie' of Lawrence's early days. They had been engaged for a short time, but he had broken it off, telling her, 'You see, I don't think we could make a life together.' A fortnight later he met Frieda.

Speaking once of her he said, 'She was dark, good-looking. I liked her and she attracted me very much physically. But I didn't live with her, because she would have given too much – it wouldn't have been fair. I would like to do something for Louie one day.'

After we had left the cemetary, she came back and left some flowers there. On her return to the Midlands she wrote to Ada: 'I went to Vence and saw the poor lad's grave.'

A few weeks after Lawrence's death Frieda went to London to see to her affairs. I stayed on alone at the villa. At night the peasant's dog slept on the floor by my bed for company. I never shut the door of Lawrence's room across the salon, thinking that if there should be an after-life, his spirit might like to go in and out of it.

When Frieda returned, we went to visit my German grandmother. I found that Lawrence's description of her hearty appetite was correct, and together we devoured apple cake and cream. When she said to me, though, 'You ought to speak German; your mother is German,' I was annoyed, and answered, 'My mother left me.'

It rained all the time in Germany, and I cought bronchitis. By the time we were back in Vence I was seriously ill. This lasted many months and caused Frieda more strain and worry.

Some of the memories of that time are mixed up with queer fantasies. One clear picture I have at the onset of the malady is of the tall grey-bearded Vence doctor bending over me with a benevolent look. Near him stood Madame Lilli, our staunch, queenly cook. On a chair Frieda was huddled in helpless misery.

When I was getting better, I lay in bed one bright autumn morning and Frieda came in, bringing Lawrence's early letters to her for me to read. I picked one up and began, but halfway through, feeling listless, wretched, and confused, put it down again. At that moment I clearly saw Lawrence's image bending over me. It was made up of little shimmering particles. His form was filled out, glowing, and he looked at me with a very benign expression. I blinked, startled by the vision: it vanished and, to my regret, never appeared again.

Frieda went back to Kiowa ranch and made it her home from then on.

In 1935 she had Lawrence's body disinterred and cremated, afterwards taking his ashes to the ranch, where she had built a little chapel for them on the hill above.

I had married a year before, and was with my husband in America. We went to stay with Frieda for the ceremony of placing the ashes in the chapel.

Captain Ravagli (whom Frieda later married) met us at Cimarron and motored us seventy miles to Kiowa. Beside a newer, large cabin was the small one where Frieda and Lawrence used to live. Near it their horses, Azul and Aaron, cropped the grass with two young piebald horses, 'Pintos'.

The ceremony was to be at sundown. Frieda invited some of the Taos Americans, and asked the Indians from the Pueblo to come and do their ritual dance.

A local judge she knew was to give the oration. Unfortunately some Taos busybody 'tampered' with him. The judge failed to appear, so my husband took his place.

When the casket of ashes had been put in the chapel, the sun set and the skies grew dark. A big fire was lighted on the level below, and the Indians, in feather dress, did their ceremonial dance. Trinidad, a young Indian whom Lawrence had known, led the dancers.

Afterwards a storm broke out. The horses neighed in fright. Lightning and thunder circled the ranch and the mountain.

Frieda
and Lawrence
David Garnett

Frieda was the second of the three daughters of Baron von Richthofen, a member of the Prussian nobility. Either he or his wife had Polish blood. Her cousins, of whom she had been fond as a girl were the two celebrated German air aces. Manfred, who succeeded Boelcke, developed the strategy of air fighting in what became famous as 'Richthofen's Circus' and was killed. Goering was a member of it later on. Manfred's brother, who survived, commanded the German air contingent in the Spanish Civil War which was responsible for the destruction of Guernica.

Frieda and her sisters were brought up in contact with the Imperial entourage and William II was an object of loathing from whom she would hide behind bushes in the garden when she saw him coming. Both Frieda and her elder sister escaped from their family milieu. Her elder sister's behaviour was the most shocking: she fell in love with and married Edgar Jaffé, a Jew, and though she left him, it was only to live in sin with a philosopher. Edgar, a charming little man, who was an economist, was made responsible for finance during the short-lived Communist seizure of power in Bavaria and was shot when the coup was overthrown.

After a fleeting affair with an anarchist, Frieda met an English student of languages, Ernest Weekley, who became Professor of Modern Languages at Nottingham University College. He seemed to her like an Arthurian knight out of *The Idylls of the King*, and under that impression, she married him.

Their wedding night began badly. Frieda, who had retired to their bedroom first, stripped herself naked and climbed up over the door, intending to fall into Ernest's arms. However the romantic Tennysonian figure was horrified and telling his bride to climb down and make herself decent, he left the room. Frieda's welcome had failed miserably and she regarded that first climb down as symbolic of her marriage. Although so inauspiciously begun, it lasted twelve years and Frieda had a son, Montagu, and two daughters. During this period she became disillusioned about her husband though she continued to feel proud of his work in philology, and intensely bored by Nottingham society.

Lawrence had been a pupil of Weekley's and after he had made good by rising to be a schoolmaster in Croydon, he was invited to his house by his former professor and so met Frieda for the first time. They took one look at each other – and that was that. Frieda was to visit her parents in the early summer of 1912. Her father held a position of importance in the military fortress town of Metz in Alsace. She planned that Lawrence, travelling separately, should meet her in Germany, but she had not then decided to leave Ernest and her children finally. Before her departure Lawrence brought her to see Edward Garnett at his cottage, The Cearne. Edward and she liked each other, and Lawrence and she left with his blessing.

Lawrence followed Frieda to Metz and when they were making love on what I like to imagine was one of the hornworks of the fortress, military police appeared and arrested Lawrence. While Baron von Richthofen was congratulating himself upon the capture of a British Guard's officer in disguise, Frieda had to explain that their capture was in fact her lover. Lawrence was brought in and the Baron realised that it was not possible for anyone but a German policeman to believe he was in the Brigade of Guards. I have the impression that the Baron was as much disgusted by his daughter's choice of a lover as he was disappointed by his men not having caught a British spy. Lawrence however charmed the Baroness and his warm relationship with Frieda's mother lasted until her (or his) death.

I was a science student aged twenty and was spending part of the long vacation in Munich. My father wrote suggesting I should see Lawrence who invited me to Icking where he had taken a room. Frieda was then living in the neighbouring village of Wolfratshausen in a cottage belonging either to Jaffé or her elder sister. It was a very hot day and when the little train had decanted me and a crowd of perspiring Bavarians, there was no difficulty in my recognizing Lawrence or he, me.

He was a slightly built, narrow-chested man, thin and tall with mud-coloured hair, a small moustache and a hairpin chin. He was obviously British working class. It was his eyes that charmed you and in two minutes I had fallen under their spell. They were full of gaiety, of an unspoken promise: 'We'll have fun together!' That unspoken promise was not broken. We did have fun. Lawrence was at that period – perhaps always – more alive than most human beings.

We went back to his room and he soon suggested that we walk through the woods to Wolfratshausen. We found Frieda lying in a hammock. She gave a lazy roll and a leap and was standing up greeting me. There was something in her powerful face, with its straight nose, in her gold-green eyes and her movements, which made me think of a lioness. Frieda was a noble and splendid animal. I could see at once that she was free and truthful and honest. She was not a bitch – though she did things that would have led some men to call her one. I found out that summer – Lawrence must have told me – that after they had had a row, she had gone down to the Isar and swum over to where a woodcutter was working, had made love with him and had swum back – just to show Lawrence she was free to do what she liked. I told the story to Anna Wickham who wrote a poem about it. I quote it here because I like it, not because it tells one anything about Lawrence and Frieda. I don't suppose Anna ever showed it to them after they had become friends three years later.

'Imperatrix'

> Am I pleasant?
> Tell me that, Old Wise!
> Let me look into your eyes,
> To see if you can comprehend my beauty,
> That is a lover's duty.
> I look at you to see
> If you can think of anything but me.
> Ah, you remember praise and your philosophy!
> My love shall be a sphere of silence and of light,
> Where love is all alone with love's delight.
> Here is a woodcutter who is so weak
> With love of me, he cannot speak.
> Tell me dumb man, am I pleasant, am I pleasant?
> Farewell philosopher! I love a peasant.

At that time Frieda was making a very difficult decision: whether to leave her children for Lawrence or not. Professor Weekley wrote letters almost every day in which he continually and unnecessarily pointed out that Lawrence wasn't a gentleman and that if their neighbours in Nottingham found out that she was having an affair with the son of a miner, the results would be appalling. Weekley's letters and threats had the opposite effect from what he intended – he showed himself, as jealous husbands inevitably do, as ungenerous, mean and spiteful. Moreover he was conventional, cowardly and slightly comic. But Frieda could not forget her children: she loved them passionately and Weekley told her that if she stayed with Lawrence she should never see them again. They would be brought up knowing that their foreign mother was a wicked woman whose name must not be spoken.

My first visit was followed by others and soon Lawrence was reading Ernest Weekley's letters aloud to me while Frieda stood and glared and spat out something like: 'Just imagine I have lived twelve years with that man and all he cares about is what the neighbours will think and that Lorenzo is a miner's son! He's not so very grand himself.'

We were unfair no doubt, but the world is unfair to cuckolds and partial to lovers. But only a year later Lawrence, telling me about a tumble that Frieda had had with a boy a dozen years her junior, said to me: 'He's no gentleman!' which at the time I thought one of the oddest things I had heard from him.

As his novels show, Lawrence was extremely aware of class. He was very proud of the fact that Frieda was born a Freifraulein (how splendid the German title is) and so was Frieda, who at that time had a coronet embroidered on her handkerchiefs.

Lawrence and Frieda had decided to make their way on foot to Italy and invited me to join them. I was expecting my friend Harold Hobson, coming from Moscow, to join me, and Lawrence and Frieda agreed to wait for him at Mayrhofen in the Tyrol, where I stayed with them for a few days before he turned up. During that time Lawrence got to know everyone in the little town. If he went out into the street to buy a cabbage, he would return twenty minutes later with the story of the greengrocer's wife's love-life. Everyone confided in him as soon as they met him. He had one room in which they lived: I had a bedroom across the street.

Lawrence was hard at work rewriting *Paul Morel*, as *Sons and Lovers* was then called. He also bought the food, did the cooking, and joined in the conversation if anything Frieda and I said interested him. Lawrence was more amusing and more charming then than I ever knew him afterwards. He was feeling well and he was happy: happy in creating *Sons and Lovers*, happy because Frieda had finally decided to throw in her lot with him.

Frieda gave him more than is generally supposed. I remember her telling us about Freud and his theories of the unconscious and of sex, of which scarcely any English people had heard in 1912. Frieda's sister had written about him, or talked to her about him. We were always laughing and falling into absurdities. Lawrence would mimic himself in embarrassing situations, and would mimic Ford or Ezra Pound or Yeats, and Frieda and I would roll about in our chairs helpless with laughter. All three of us were fond of miming – we laughed at each other's efforts. And my attempts to reproduce Nijinsky's leaps and bounds added to their hysteria.

Lawrence sent their two suitcases off to Italy by train and soon after Harold arrived we set off to cross the mountains on foot. Although Lawrence had, I think, only £30 in the world, he offered to lend me enough to come to Italy with them. I was foolish enough to refuse and we parted at Stertzing, after crossing the Pfitzer Joch, and Harold and I went home.

When Lawrence and Frieda revisited England they always started by staying with my parents until they had found a place of their own, or had been invited to stay by other people. And in the winter my mother went out to Italy and stayed in rooms they found for her near them at Lerici. Harold also went and stayed with them there.

My mother, Constance, like almost all women, became very fond of Lawrence, though she resented the lack of generosity he showed Frieda and was indignant about it. She did not much care for Frieda who was too sexual and too slow-witted an animal for such a blue-stocking, but her lack of interest never developed into dislike. For though we all loved Lawrence, or were fascinated by him, it was difficult not to be shocked by his jealousy of Frieda's love for her children. The more unhappy she became, the more mean and spiteful was Lawrence's behaviour to her. When she waylaid her son, Montagu, as he came out of St Paul's school, it was I, not Lawrence, who led her away sobbing and tried to comfort her. Lawrence never showed her a grain of sympathy, or of gratitude, for what she suffered on his account.

My father was, in those years, very active in promoting Lawrence's affairs. He tried with some success to sell his poems and his stories to all the weeklies and magazines and he collected the stories into a volume. At Lawrence's request, he cut *Sons and Lovers*, which has never been published in its entirety, to a length possible to be published as an ordinary novel. Incidentally this was a job which he did superlatively well as anyone can see who examines the original manuscript at Berkeley. And I, for my part, made the first selection of Lawrence's poems to be published.

But one cannot expect to rear a Phoenix in a pigeon loft and Lawrence soon outgrew Edward's usefulness. He was beginning to assume the plumage of a prophet and like all prophets he liked to be surrounded by disciples. There were many of them waiting to be picked up but Edward, Constance and I were not made of suitable material.

The last time I saw Lawrence was on Armistice Day, 11 November 1918. We were all dancing with joy but Lawrence was prophesying that the war was only just starting. He was wrong by twenty-one years and we danced on, careless of what was awaiting us – a war less terrible than the one which had just ended.

Edward's usefulness – and Constance's and my friendship – was over by then, but Lawrence was not ungrateful. He never repaid our affection by putting us into a wounding story as he did the Meynells in England, My England, or Sir Compton Mackenzie in 'The Man Who Loved Islands', though I am sure we provided excellent raw material. All he wrote, as far as I know, was the charming poem called 'At the Cearne' about making love to Frieda at the bottom of our orchard.

D. H. Lawrence
and His District
Alan Sillitoe

'I have no allocated place in the world of things, I do not belong to Beldover (Eastwood) nor to Nottingham nor to England nor to this world, but they none of them exist, I am trammelled and entangled in them, but they are all unreal. I must break out of it, like a nut from its shell which is an unreality.'

This is what Lawrence might have directly said, words he gave instead to his great heroine Ursula Brangwen at the end of *The Rainbow*. And if one may put these thoughts directly onto him, and square them with his actions, as I think one can, then he did indeed break out of Eastwood and district, going far beyond that 'dry, brittle corruption spreading over the face of the land'.

His mother died of cancer in 1910 when he was twenty-five years old:

> The sun was immense and rosy
> Must have sunk and become extinct
> The night you closed your eyes forever against me.

The road was clear for him: he jettisoned the sweetheart of his youth, Jessie Chambers, which was a painful and laborious process, and went off with Frieda the professor's wife. Eastwood was finished, rubbed away like the chalked cyphers from a schoolteacher's blackboard. Or so one might have thought. Like many English provincial writers, he did not 'like it here'. His impulse was to get away, to strike out with the only equipment readily to hand, a woman. And the woman he chose (or who was chosen for him) latched onto the only equipment readily to hand in order to get out of a deadly and failed marriage: another man. Lawrence took his first love (that is to say: his mother) from his father. He took his last love from her husband. And if, as some say, it was these two women who chose him, then one might add that he was the sort of man who had to be 'chosen'. The second vital choosing was simply a logical follow-up from the first.

D. H. LAWRENCE AND HIS DISTRICT

At any rate, Eastwood was dead – long live the world. Nottinghamshire fell into its dark and deserved oblivion – long live the sun. Who did he leave behind? A father he had been brought up to loathe, and whom he would have disliked in any case. The father was a living example of what Lawrence knew he himself might easily have become. He also saw that much of the father still existed in him, under the writer's clever and protecting skin.

Lawrence left behind his brothers and sisters, and some friends. When he went back, as he did from time to time, it was a dying landscape he visited as far as his spiritual sense was concerned, for it had little charm or reality for him after his mother had died and his youth was laid waste. One has to ruin youth in order to get rid of it effectively, and a writer does it through his novels.

From then on youth and Eastwood existed only in his writing. He screwed it out of his memory and pulled it from his soul so as to put it into his novels and stories, and to have it with him for always, but buried deep enough so that it no longer tormented him. The more he wrote about it the more its attraction died. Not only did *he* leave it, but he used the same departure theme in many of his novels as well. Alvina Houghton cleared out at the end of *The Lost Girl*, and Aaron Sisson packed it in at the beginning of *Aaron's Rod*. Even at the end of *The White Peacock* the bankrupt farmer was considering a new life in Canada. And we all know that Paul Morel can have no further truck with it after the last lines of *Sons and Lovers*.

The fact of not liking it here mattered very much to Lawrence because through it he took himself to other countries. His brittle, intelligent, hyper-sensitive, friable shell that he still had to live with accepted other landscapes more in keeping with his changing and developing ideas. And if he came back to Eastwood at all he returned not even as a tourist, but like a health-visitor wondering whether he should call in the corporation stoving-gangs either to disinfect or destroy it.

The longer he was away from Nottinghamshire the more he hated the ugliness of it. Perhaps the emphasis on ugliness increased the longer and more definitively he was away from it, as a ploy to defend himself against the charge of having so heartlessly left it and abandoned certain people there who had done so much for him. In his own estimation, Jessie Chambers might have been one of these.

At any rate his preoccupation with its ugliness grew with absence. Plain enough at the end of *The Rainbow*, it goes on through all those novels and stories in which 'The North' appears, until the final maniac rantings of Mellors the gamekeeper in *Lady Chatterley's Lover*. In this last novel he even scorns the young colliers going off to dances in Mansfield on their motorbikes, almost as if they didn't deserve such good fortune and would be much better off knitting Indian blankets under the greenwood tree.

43

Lawrence loved strong men, except his father, whom he was too close to to regard as strong. But he only ever took notice of women during his life, though nothing can be held against him for that. He was dominated by his mother, guided by Jessie, and driven by Frieda. It may well be that a man of such sensitivity and passionate talent can have few meaningful women in his life.

Another powerful factor was landscape – another sort of love. On his later travels he was infatuated with strong landscapes, grandiose and dangerous scenery. But his true love, and maybe the truest of his life, was that significant and magic circle of which Eastwood was the centre. 'That's the country of my heart,' he said in a long reminiscing letter to Rolf Gardiner, written from Florence at the end of 1926. In his various novels and stories the Eastwood locality had many made-up labels: Bestwood, Beldover, Netherthorpe, Woodhouse or Teversall. He loved the beauties of the area till he died, but what he considerd to be the ugliness he increasingly disliked, and fulminated against.

If the region was in any way responsible for some of the rage and choler in him it was perhaps because it was neither totally ugly nor completely beautiful, neither one nor the other but a jumble of ambiguities that found a ready reflex in himself.

It was the scars and still working wounds of industrialization that gave the Nottinghamshire-Derbyshire border the strength and power which was to release his descriptive genius for those parts of the world where landscape had beauty as well as power. The power of ugliness he early recognized, and maybe it acted as a catalyst for the beauty in him. The best example of this ambivalent stance comes out in his poem 'The North Country':

> The air is dark with north and sulphur, the grass is a darker green
> And people darkly invested with purple move palpable through the scene.

Much of his unreasonable hatred of the urban and industrial landscape came from the above-mentioned three women, and found fertility in himself. It was an attitude he never let go of. It also fitted in with his own sensitive nature, otherwise it couldn't have got such a grip. It might have been a literary inheritance as well, for it has always been a favourite theme with certain English writers to bewail the ruination of sweet and rural England, on the automatic assumption that towns are hell and villages paradise. It still is, for not only does tradition die hard, but so does a longing for peace and non-involvement.

Lawrence was of course always an 'involved' man, but nonetheless he fitted the isolationist person in that he saw little but deadliness in the spread of nineteenth-century industry. Such views, and the extremity with which he held them, led him to despise people more than was good for him. For this reason his early novels, ending with *The Rainbow*, are the best because he is tender and just

44

to his people, but after that work the stomach and humanity seems to go out of them.

Another factor, and one which has not perhaps yet been properly explored, is that he had to get away from England because of the suffocating class atmosphere existing in Edwardian and Georgian days – which is still with us, of course. In Italy or Germany or Mexico an Englishman was more likely to be accepted as a 'gentleman', no matter how poor he appeared to be. If his aristocratic wife washed the sheets in their Italian cottage it would be seen merely as a mark of eccentricity.

He also said early on to Jessie Chambers that people would think it silly for a collier's son to write poetry, suggesting that he could not see himself opening fully as a writer among such people and such 'ugliness'. Opening his soul to people so close to him, who were not normally able to expose themselves in this way, obviously appeared too inhibiting a factor to fight against, so sooner or later, some way or other, Lawrence had to put himself at a good distance from it.

I once wrote in an article – perhaps too hastily – that to me Lawrence was inconsistent. Before the age of thirty he was a fine writer, while after it he was something of a crank, apart from odd patches such as the first half of *The Lost Girl*, which was written mostly before he was thirty anyway, though it was not published until 1920. One might also mention the middle section of *Kangaroo*, in which he described the persecution habits of the British nation he was almost called-up to defend. To me though he never seemed much of a prophet or a philosopher, roles which I feel he was pushed into by certain people he came into contact with after he had started out on his travels.

After leaving Eastwood he created his own lyrical backwater of idealized folklore. To begin with he made his way to Catholic parts of the world, went from one to another for the rest of his life. Perhaps if there had been no Reformation in England he would have spent more time at Eastwood. But he had to go to those places where the female spirit of the Virgin Mary was in the ascendant, where mother-worship of the Latins was the norm. Either that or, as in Mexico, it was superimposed onto the Aztec spirit of the sun – a very queer mixture indeed.

By the time of *The Lost Girl*, which was published after the Great War, and *Women in Love*, published in 1921, he began to lose his grip on local topography, and in *Lady Chatterley's Lover* it was as if he were writing about a sort of black-dream country that did not seem human or real. But though he'd lost touch with his own native soil he had gained infinitely valuable contact with other areas of his soul. From leaving his own acres behind, no matter what the final motives were, he inherited the wider expanses of the earth. Many readers and erstwhile admirers may not thank him for this, but English literature is richer for it. In one sense, by not liking it here, he gained the world. In another sense he gave us the best of both worlds by leaving Nottinghamshire, even though he left the most generous part of his spirit there.

Lawrence, in fact, was born but a mile from Derbyshire. You walk down the hill of the main road going out of Eastwood until you come to the railway station on the right, which is now smashed and boarded up. Then you cross the canal and the meagre Erewash, and you are out of Byron's country. After another dozen miles you approach Matlock and get into the Pennines. The ugliness has gone. Picturesque though at times claustrophobic valleys, and wide open hill-ranges are immediately to hand. There is all the beauty in the world, or enough to satisfy a young man, only half a day's bike ride from Nottingham, and even less from Eastwood. Byron, a frequent visitor to Matlock, said that 'there are things in Derbyshire as noble as Greece or Switzerland', and the Matlocks may indeed remind one of the little valley resorts of the latter country.

After I was fourteen and bought a bicycle I took that road, sometimes alone, occasionally with others, puffing up out of Nottingham through Aspley and Cinderhill. There is a colliery at this latter place, depicted as Tinder Mill in *Sons and Lovers*. In Lawrence's time a bumpy stretch of road ran through it, over which the injured father of Paul Morel was taken on a cart to the hospital in Nottingham after a pit accident – the subject of that famous dialect poem 'The Collier's Wife'.

Beyond Eastwood, one freewheeled down to the Erewash, which was followed by a sure push-up to Codnor and Ripley, and many another walk with the bicycle before coming into Matlock. At that time, before I'd ever heard of D. H. Lawrence (I didn't 'discover' him till I was twenty-one), I'd go on Easter week-ends through Bakewell and Buxton to Chapel-en-le-Frith, and back to Notting-ham via Chesterfield and Clay Cross, sleeping in fields or barns by the roadside or under the lee of those rough stone walls marking off the fields, thinking the hills beautiful and restful, but in no way hating the small hilltop mining towns and settlements when I get back among them. In fact coming from the built-up protection of Nottingham I felt comforted by the frequent appearance of these places. And at Easter the road was often wet, and the wind could be bitter enough, but the real impulse was to wear out the body after a week in a factory, and reach as far a point from Nottingham as a bicycle could go in one long weekend.

The marathon run on a single day was to cycle the twenty-five miles to Mat-lock, climb the Heights of Abraham of several hundred feet, visit the ancient lead workings of the Rutland Cavern, row on the slate-grey Derwent for an hour and get as near as one dare to the weir without going over it or having to be rescued by an irate boatman, then cycle back to Nottingham before darkness set in – usually on a bottle of milk or lemonade and a packet of sandwiches.

The first novel I picked up by Lawrence was *The Rainbow*, and its opening paragraphs electrified me. Up to this time I had not read much anyway, but certainly nothing like this. 'Whenever one of the Brangwens in the fields lifted his head from his work, he saw the church-tower at Ilkeston in the empty sky.' I knew exactly what he was talking about, at least as far as the places were concerned. I'd walked across those fields, and seen the same church-tower. Later on in that novel Tom Brangwen rides on horseback to Matlock, and there encounters the foreigner in the hotel whom he 'loved for his exquisite graciousness, for his tact, and for his ageless, monkey-like self-surety.'

Such ambivelent remarks concerning foreigners were made by Lawrence all his life in his books and letters. Perhaps by marrying one he thought he had a right to them. It was certainly one way of combining his inbred parochial attitudes with those of the English Edwardian upper-class people he mixed with after leaving Eastwood, without such prejudices being too much noticed.

But the meeting of Brangwen and the foreigner at Matlock (in the George Hotel?) created the change of horizon that led Brangwen to propose to Anna Lensky, widow of a Polish exile who had come to work as a housekeeper at Cossethay (Cossall) vicarage.

Tom Brangwen, the grandfather of Ursula, lived at the nearby Marsh, a mile to the north, where before the Reformation there existed a Benedictine cell or chapel of St Thomas, according to Briton's topographical work (based, it seems, on Thoroton's *Antiquities*) on Nottinghamshire which I am sure Lawrence must have read, thereby showing that his first Brangwen was appropriately named.

Cossall and the Marsh are now divided from Nottingham by the M1 motorway, and a whole wood nearby has been uprooted to accommodate a service area. Tom Brangwen, in his later years, drove towards home one wet and stormy night after a drinking bout at the Angel in Nottingham. It is hard to know whether Lawrence had an actual pub in mind, because the original and notorious 'Angel' on High Pavement was pulled down in 1849, about half a century earlier.

Brangwen's horse drew him along half asleep through the dark and muddy lane winding by Bilborough and Strelley. When he got home he was drowned in the flood swirling around his farm because the Erewash Canal nearby had burst its embankment during his absence.

In thinking about the innumerable places in which an author makes his characters sort out their destinies, and from time to time act on them, it is foolish to track each one down and match it to the fictitious name and few lines of description the author gave to each. This is a game best left to literary critics, and I am too much of a writer to be one of those.

Sometimes the actual names are used, but often made-up ones, and whether an event is of vital importance or not, it is pure chance or whim which one it is. Many of these places can be traced. Nethermere Valley is the course of a stream called The Dumbles, with steep and wooded hills to the north and south, but covering a smaller area than this description suggests. The cleft of land is lush, green and wet in the late spring, when I went there recently, approaching it from Annesley. Almost hidden from the road is Strelley Mill, the Felley Mill Farm of *The White Peacock*.

It would be futile to run through the dozens of such examples. One might easily say, after much tramping and crude detective work: 'I am sitting on the exact fence that Ursula Brangwen got over in such fear and panic when the horses chased her, at the end of *The Rainbow*, – but it may not be the place at all because perhaps the writer mingled so many clues that the spot can never be found. Nor would it matter if it could. Or maybe he made it so specific, on the other hand, that it is easy to come across. We don't finally know. It isn't very important. Yet all in all, Lawrence's map of his native habitat and hunting ground was fairly accurate, especially regarding places, as one can see from a one-inch ordnance survey map. Opening it from time to time as one goes through the novels one can see that he generally tended to disguise names the closer they were to Eastwood. Further away, it did not matter so much, and he gave real names.

Eastwood was no cut-off mining village, but a thriving community. It was a well-known place in Nottingham, a sort of halfway house through which thousands of people passed to get to Matlock and the Pennines: hikers, cyclists, buses, or people out on mystery trips who might not know where they were going because they'd stopped at so many pubs already they were too sloshed to care or take notice.

There were many wealthy houses in the neighbourhood, and the area itself was by no means poor. In the nineteenth century Lord Palmerston contributed to the founding of the Mechanics Institute. Coal had already been its richness for centuries. In 1812 Britton, paraphrasing Thoroton no doubt, wrote that 'those who chuse to gossip with the sage chroniclers of the place, will be told a wonderful story of a farmer being swallowed up alive in the parlour of the village alehouse, while he was swallowing a cup of ale, to the great surprise of the host, who by this means discovered that his humble mansion was built on an exhausted coal pit.'

Set by the Erewash Valley, it was a special area which also had a southern egress to the Trent, which gave it an opening to the sea and overseas. It was under the influence of various escape routes, set between north and south, east and west. The main line from London to Manchester ran up the Erewash Valley, with a station at Pye Bridge. In *Sons and Lovers* this station is known as Sethley Bridge, and it is here that Paul Morel and his sister (Lawrence himself and Ada) went to meet their brother William coming home for a holiday from London. The train, it being Christmas Eve, was more than two hours late, and they were afraid of the meat at home getting overcooked or cold. They waited in the frost and mist until he came, so that all was forgiven when handsome but ill-fated William, carrying his Gladstone bag, went back with them and burst into the house.

In the same book Paul's mother takes him one afternoon to visit Mrs Leivers, her friend at Willey Farm (Haggs Farm) three miles away. There he meets Miriam the daughter, and his description of their long association makes *Sons and Lovers* the finest novel of adolescent love in the English language.

When he was nineteen Paul went walking with Miriam and other friends to the Hemlock Stone. It made a long day there and back. At this time he was working at Jordan's factory in Nottingham, and earned twenty shillings a week. Lawrence worked a few months in a similar factory (Heywood's, manufacturers of surgical appliances) at the age of fifteen, but his appropriate counterpart in *Sons and Lovers* stayed some three years.

The happy group crossed the railway line and went into Ilkeston, 'a town of idleness and lounging. At Stanton Gate the iron foundry blazed. At Trowel they crossed again from Derbyshire into Nottinghamshire.' Crowds of other Easter Friday trippers were at the Hemlock Stone, out for the day from Nottingham. Paul found the stone disappointing: 'a little, gnarled, twisted stump of rock, something like a decayed mushroom, standing out pathetically on the side of a field'.

Two of the party began to carve their initials on it, 'but Paul desisted, because he had read in the newspaper satirical remarks about initial carvers, who could find no other road to immortality.' The last time I was there I noticed that railings had been put around it.

In Britton's book on Nottinghamshire the Hemlock Stone is more flatteringly described, but maybe it was not so weatherbeaten a century earlier:

Between these hills, on the brow of a rising ground, is a very curious and conspicuous object, called the Hemlockstone. This is an insulated rugged mass of rock, or reddish sandstone, upwards of thirty feet high, and consisting of very thin *laminae* dipping to the west; its extreme breadth from north to south is about twelve feet at the base, but spreading at about two-thirds of its elevation; and its thickness below is about four feet. In outline, it bears some slight resemblance to a mushroom, and is evidently wearing away, from the effects of the weather.

Some say that the Hemlock Stone is a pagan relic, some that it is not. Nevertheless it is famous around Nottingham as an excursion and picnic point. The huge rock was surmounted by two broad and distinct masses of a hard-wearing green ragstone, thus giving it the mushroom appearance, called in the vernacular 'hemlock stone'. Perhaps its name derived from the colour of the plant. By some misdirection of primitive logic it was said that to run seven times around the Hemlock Stone was a sure cure for 'the rheumatics'.

On their return to Eastwood Miriam misses Paul, and goes back along the lane to look for him. He has lagged behind to mend his mother's umbrella which had got broken. The effect of the Hemlock Stone on them was said to have been insignificant, but Miriam 'always regarded that sudden coming upon him in the lane as a revelation'. It was the first sign of their relationship deepening into a love that both of them grew afraid of but thought might last for ever because they did not for a time know how to end it.

In those days the Hemlock Stone was a fair way from Nottingham city, but new houses have now crept up Stapleford Hill immediately behind, and anyone living in them who has rheumatism can run around it in their dressing-gowns before breakfast, if they believe in all that, which I imagine they don't. I often walked to it along the canal from Nottingham, or cycled down the lane from Balloon Houses, finding this route the quietest. But nowadays the lane that Lawrence took back towards Trowel and Eastwood, and where Miriam came upon Paul Morel absorbed in mending his mother's umbrella 'as a revelation' has many new houses on either side, and is no longer so isolated. It might even have been that part of the lane where it bridges the motorway.

A few days later Morel and Miriam went on another holiday excursion, to Wingfield Manor. Again with friends, they got on a train to Alfreton, and visited the church there.

The place was decorated for Easter. In the front hundreds of white narcissi seemed to be growing. The air was dim and coloured from the windows and thrilled with a subtle scent of lilies and narcissi. In that atmosphere Miriam's soul came to a glow. Paul was afraid of the things he mustn't do; and he was sensitive to the feel of the place. Miriam turned to him. He answered. They were together.

They went on, to Wingfield Manor, and 'It was past midday when they climbed the steep path. . .' to one of the finest ruins in Britain. Lawrence had the steady absorbent eye of young genius in these early novels that was never to be surpassed or even matched in later work. He not only had youth and love on his side but, what was just as important, his own land combined and wrapped up in it.

It mattered more than one thinks. It mattered perhaps more than he knew at the time. Place is everything – soil in the throat, under the feet, in the hands, the

Youth

Lawrence at 21, 'a clean-shaven, bright young prig in a
high collar like a curate'. (*Sons and Lovers*)

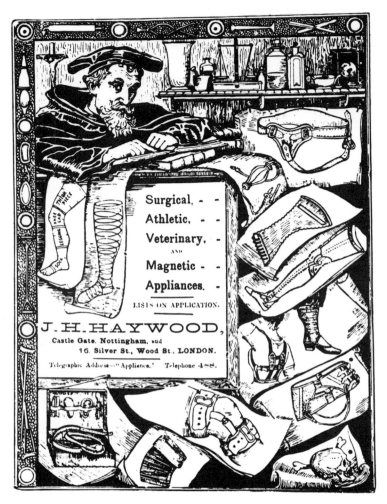

Above Haywood's Catalogue, 1902. Haywood's (the Jordan's of *Sons and Lovers*) was a firm of surgical goods at Nottingham, where Lawrence worked as a general clerk after leaving school. Among the drawings decorating the Catalogue was, curiously enough, a phoenix, *below*, which was later to become adopted as a symbol by Lawrence

The High Street at Nottingham, 'that dismal town where I went to school and college'. (*Pansies*)

One of Lawrence's optional subjects at University College was French which was taught by Professor Ernest Weekley, *above, left*, whose German wife, Frieda, was later to elope with Lawrence and eventually marry him.

above, right W. E. Hopkin, the Eastwood socialist, became a close friend of Lawrence's during the latter's years in Nottingham. 'He was a pure idealist, something of a Christ, but with an intruding touch of the goat.' (*Mr Noon*)

opposite, top University College, Nottingham: 'amorphous as it might be, there was in it a reminiscence of the wondrous, cloistral origin of education.' (*The Rainbow*)

opposite, bottom The staff and students of Lawrence's year at University College, Nottingham. Lawrence is second from the right, second row down. His supervisor described him in his report as 'well-read, scholarly and refined', but his work was found to be uneven.

right W. E. Hopkin's house in Devonshire Drive, Eastwood.

Opposite, top The Chambers family in 1901, the year that Lawrence first met Jessie Chambers (standing, third from left). 'I loved to come to you all, it was really a new life began in me there.' (Letter to David Chambers, 14 November 1928)

Opposite, bottom The Haggs, where the Chambers lived, became Willey Farm in *Sons and Lovers*. 'Whatever I forget, I shall never forget the Haggs . . . . The water-pippin by the door . . . . And stewed figs for tea in winter, and in August green stewed apples.' (Letter to David Chambers, 14 November 1928)

Right A page from Ethel Harris' Autograph Album. The entry was written by May Chambers, Jessie's sister, and illustrated by Lawrence. The dripping cat is a copy of a drawing by Louis Wain in *The Boys' Own Paper*.

Below The countryside around the Haggs inspired some of the most lyrical passages in *The White Peacock* and *Sons and Lovers*.

"Health" "Happiness" or "friendship true," This is what I wish for you.

Jog on, jog on the foot-path way
And merrily hent the stile-a;
A merry heart goes all the way
Your sad one tires in a mile-a.

When the gardener turned on the hose

Swim through the waves of time, and ne'er despair;
Lift up thine eyes, and breathe the eternal air,

May Chambers 1903

Above Jessie Chambers, the model for Miriam in *Sons and Lovers*, was, with Lawrence's mother, the dominating female influence of the decade 1900–10.

Opposite Louie Burrows, on whom Lawrence partly modelled the character of Ursula in *The Rainbow*, was also the subject of some of his most erotic early poems, such as 'Snap-Dragon', 'Kisses in the Train' and 'The Hands of the Betrothed'.

Lawrence in 1908, at the end of his training as a teacher: 'He is emphatically a teacher of upper classes,' wrote his supervisor in his final report at Nottingham.

The Davidson Road School at Croydon, where Lawrence began to teach in October 1908.
'I carry my anger sullenly 'cross these waste lands,/For tomorrow will call them all back, the
school hours I detest.' ('Evening')

Overleaf The countryside of *The White Peacock*: Felley Mill (called Strelley Mill in the novel).

Felley Mill Pond, near the Haggs. W. E. Hopkin, describing Lawrence's last visit in the region, said: 'He and I went over the old ground. When we reached Felley Dam he stood looking at the Haggs. I sat down by the pool and when I turned to look at him he had a terrible look of pain on his face.' (Letter to Harry T. Moore, 16 October 1949)

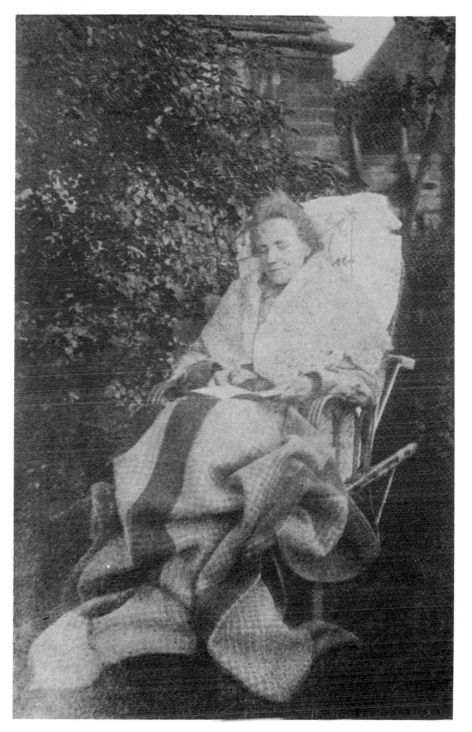

Lawrence's mother shortly before her death in 1911: '. . . my mother is a sight to see and be silent about for ever. She has had a bloody hard life, and has always been bright; but now her face has fallen like a mask of bitter cruel suffering.' (Letter to A. W. McLeod, 5 December 1910)

An Idyll, a copy by Lawrence of Maurice Greiffenhagen's picture: '. . . in love, or at least in love-making, do you think the woman is always passive, like the girl in the "Idyll". . . . I prefer a little devil – a Carmen . . .' (Letter to Blanche Jennings, 31 December 1908)

nostrils clouded with soot and pollen, the first smells and sounds of life still immediate. Cold grass bends under the frost in winter. Bracken burns in the summer. Youth is so strong that even the machinery of hope doesn't weigh into the scales in one's zest for life. Life simply *is*. Everything is in unison, tragic fate burning away, with youth coolly observing it while not being able to do much about it. But he who is going to be a writer determines early on to break up that unison in himself. He is set on leaving the place that helped him towards such intensity, because that intensity proves too much for him if he dallies and stays there, or else it dies on him.

If Lawrence hadn't been born in Nottingham he would not have been the same writer. Like all other nations perhaps, England is full of little countries, for better or worse, dozens of little class, race and geographical divisions which fortunately defy analysis or sociology. It still pertains more than is generally admitted, and only writers are properly equipped to chart a way between them to the more fundamental issues that lie beyond. In the same way I don't suppose Stendhal would have been the same writer if he hadn't been born in Grenoble, nor Balzac at Tours. But while place is everything, it is also nothing. We are all born on ships at sea as far as our souls are concerned, no matter how solid the earth into which we will fall and maybe walk as soon as we are let loose to try. We are born on all kinds of ships – spaceships, friendships, scholarships, undying relationships.

Eastwood was and is a township, and the surrounding countryside, which I know well because I have covered every lane and bridlepath, much of it on foot but also by that greatest invention of all time, the bicycle, from an early age upon my forays out of Nottingham. The nearest point to the city over five hundred feet high is Misk Hill, just beyond Hucknall Torkard church where Byron's tomb is kept. Lawrence's father used to sing in nearby Newstead Abbey choir as a boy.

From the summit of Misk Hill one can look southwest and see the church spire on the hilltop at Eastwood that Paul and Miriam looked back on from Crich Stand at the foot of the Pennines in Derbyshire when they went to Wingfield Manor. Such roaming is a constant wonder of triangulation, surveys that fix themselves in the heart and stay there.

Through Eastwood people flocked to the spas and pleasure haunts of the Peak District, but north and south of Eastwood it is half town and half country, slum and mansion, pitstock and folly, red brick and priory ruins, lime-kiln and green glen, farmhouse and ironworks. It is the mixture that makes a landscape seem so vast in small mileages, an exploring ground that baffles the mind but goes far towards opening it.

At thirteen Lawrence won a scholarship to Nottingham High School. The building always had a forbidding aspect to me when I passed it along Forest Road. It was not too far from where I lived, yet in a different sort of district. Often we threw apples over the wall to show our disapproval of it, on our way back from scrumping up Woodthorpe Grange. I sat for a scholarship examination at the school but failed to get in, so maybe this shaped my attitude, though in any case it seemed just another institution to be avoided, like the workhouse or the magistrates' court.

Lawrence's mother had once been a schoolteacher, and he was brought up by her to have no such fears and inhibitions. He liked it and, being an intelligent child, went on to become a student-teacher at Ilkeston, and then at twenty-one to do botany at Nottingham University College. The present-day university was built at High Fields near to Beeston, and Lawrence satirized it in his poem:

> In Nottingham, that dismal town
> where I went to school and college,
> they've built a new university
> for a new dispensation of knowledge.

The grounds of the university contain a boating lake and swimming baths, a good place to roam to from the hot streets of Radford during late spring and summer.

The university is the first bit of Nottingham visible from the train after coming up from London, a paleish long block on a slight hill to the northward, a bit like a slab of long cake, not too heavy from a distance, and which looks as if it can be enjoyed in various ways. Another mile or so and one sees the Castle, as ugly and menacing as ever, until one gets to the museum inside, or stands by the southern wall to look over Clifton Grove and Wilford.

In *The White Peacock* Cyril, the narrating hero of the book, went to the Castle with Meg: 'We stood on the high rock in the cool of the day, and watched the sun sloping over the great river-flats where the menial town spread out, and ended, while the river and meadows continued into the distance.' In the Castle Museum the young Paul Morel won first prize in a painting competition, and his picture was exhibited there. Lawrence himself began drawing and painting at an early age, though there is no evidence that he won any such competition.

From the Castle one can see the high wooded escarpment of Clifton beyond the Trent, and Clifton Grove which runs along the top of it, where Henry Kirk White walked and wrote his melancholy odes. The wide two-mile Grove goes along the level ridge, between elm, beech and oak trees. Paul Morel in *Sons and Lovers* took Clara there after more or less breaking with his childhood girlfriend Miriam Leivers, who in real life was Jessie Chambers. With Clara he scrambled down through the foliage to the shore of the swiftly running Trent. The bank is so steep that if it were not for the trees impeding progress one might go straight into the water.

They went on to Clifton village, and 'The old lady at whose house they had tea was roused into gaiety by them.' The cottage is still there, and I remember it well, for it was always a favourite and convenient place to have tea with your girl after a country walk and some courting up the Grove. I daresay it is even now, especially by people from the housing estate which flanks it at a rather close distance.

Those whom the gods love die young; but those whom the gods hate stay young. Lawrence, to give up his youth, had to leave Nottinghamshire, as if determined to give the gods no cause to hate him. And yet it had meant too much to him to put up with it any longer. He'd suffered a great deal and had learned enough from it to want to get out. His mother had died of cancer, and he had broken with Jessie Chambers because of her intense and possessive love. He was, she said, a man who had to have all his decisions made for him, though she had connived in this for a long time, until she sensed that maybe he wasn't her kind of man at all because of it, and that in any case there were finally some decisions over which she could not have any control.

After his time at Nottingham University College he went to London and worked as a teacher. But he was not yet free of his youth. Though there was little to hold him to it, how was he to get away from it? It was almost as if life had eaten him up already, and that he had devoured life so that it should not consume him entirely. He needed the first and final change in order to survive, that vital break which would enable him to continue writing about it.

There was little to keep him in Eastwood. He had already published *The White Peacock*, had written *The Trespasser* and was working on *Sons and Lovers*. But though he could do the fictionalized first novel while still on home ground, he could not really square with the autobiographical *Sons and Lovers* until home ground and youth was some way behind. To translate pain and love into art, one needs to be at a distance, and *Sons and Lovers* was finally finished in Northern Italy.

All that had nurtured and tormented him had to be put beyond the horizon, in every possible way. In 1912 he met Frieda Weekley, the German-born wife of a professor at Nottingham University, and the mother of three children who was some years older than Lawrence. They not only 'clicked', but went away to Germany, beginning a love-affair which led to her divorce from Weekley and marriage to Lawrence. They stayed together till his death in the south of France in 1930.

At forty-four years of age he was ready for the second great leap of his life.

The first one, in his twenties, had carried him far enough, and lifted him out of a phase that his spirit found utterly insupportable. Now, that second phase was spent, and it was time to move on to another life-era.

But life is not a series of little boxes. One cannot reckon without the cost of making the first great break, the cost of which, in Lawrence's case, robbed him of the life-force to go on into a third, final, and more fruitful phase of his life.

Though he travelled over much of the world in the last eighteen years, Nottinghamshire was still to figure in many of his novels and stories. But the local bucolic intensity that filled the first books was lacking from them, while something else took its place.

That famous last-of-England picture from *The Lost Girl* which typified Lawrence's departure from his own country after the Great War, during which four-year lunacy he had been persecuted for having a German wife, is one of the most suitable to end on:

'For there, behind all the sunshine, was England, England, beyond the water, rising with ash-grey corpse-grey cliffs, and streaks of snow on the downs above. England, like a long ash-grey coffin slowly submerging.'

It sank into Lawrence himself, and rotted in him.

D. H. Lawrence,
England and the War
Stephen Spender

D. H. Lawrence wrote to E. M. Forster in 1922: '. . . Think you did make a nearly deadly mistake glorifying those business people in *Howards End*. Business is no good.' Wilful misreading of Forster could scarcely be pushed further, one would think. However, from Lawrence's point of view, it was to damn Forster that at the end of his novel there was reconciliation between Henry Wilcox and his wife Margaret, *née* Schlegel. By 1922 Lawrence would have no patience with toleration – let alone glorification – of business people and for him toleration was glorification. What love he had left for England did not include Wilcoxes or even Schlegels. In the same year he wrote to Catherine Carswell, from New Mexico: 'In the spring I want to come to England. But I *feel* England has insulted me, and I stomach that badly. *Pero, sono sempre inglese*.' He certainly loved the country and the language – and he liked to think he liked the people.

England for Lawrence was the countryside near Nottingham which he had loved before 1914. The descriptions of this countryside and of the farm hands in *The White Peacock* have an almost unbearable poignancy, as does the opening section of *The Rainbow* which also goes back to the old pre-war England. The density of light and foliage is made the more intense by the proximity of the pits and slag-heaps gashing that countryside which he turned back to at the end in *Lady Chatterley's Lover*.

The war killed this England in Lawrence's mind. Writing to Lady Cynthia Asquith, in January 1915, he tells how at the beginning of August 1914 he had been walking in Westmorland, 'rather happy, with water-lilies twisted round my hat – big, heavy, white and gold water-lilies that we found in a pool high up – and girls who had come out on a spree and who were having tea in the upper room of an inn, shrieked with laughter'. He describes himself and three of his friends (one of them Koteliansky 'who groaned Hebrew music') crouching under a loose wall on the moors 'while the rain flew by in streams'. They shouted

71

songs, and Lawrence imitated music hall tunes. 'Then we came down to Barrow-in-Furness and saw that war was declared. And we all went mad.' For Lawrence: 'The War finished me: it was the spear through the side of all sorrows and hopes.' It made him in his own mind a bit of a persecuted Christ.

Not only was England killed for him, but there was also a sense in which the war killed him. For he was a man who died several deaths before he died. One of them was the result of the rending out of his body of his vision of an England that was both intensely of the earth and intensely of the spirit. After he had come to southern England, this became identified for him with Philip and Lady Ottoline Morrell's house in Oxfordshire, Garsington Manor, which in his letters he described in word-paintings reminiscent of a Turner landscape of the park at Petworth:

When I drive across this country, with autumn falling and rustling to pieces, I am so sad, for my country, for this great wave of civilization, 2,000 years, which is now collapsing, that it is hard to live. So much beauty and pathos of old things passing away and no new things coming: this house – it is England – my God, it breaks my soul – their England.

He writes that his life is ended so far as living in England is concerned. The beauty of England is soaked in nostalgia, it is deceptive, involving him – Lawrence – in his country's death. And nothing is clearer than that if he has to choose between England or Europe and D. H. Lawrence, he chooses Lawrence. His life style lies in that. He chose his genius.

Choosing Lawrence and Frieda meant renouncing, turning against everyone else. The hatred in his war letters is that of a man who thinks that he is the only live thing left on the world and who regards everyone and everything else as wishing to kill him and as a threat to his sanity – which had already almost gone.

At a time when other young men were offering themselves as dripping slaughtered sacrifice on an altar of England, Lawrence hated them for it, regarded their heroism as cowardice, unmanliness and lack of spunk; he even hated England for its nostalgic beauty which hypnotically demanded this of them. To him their deaths were contemptible acts of submission to an awful dupery. He hated them for being heroes and submitting. He hated the military and industrialists, and he despised the soldiers for obeying the officers. The only thing the soldiers did which raised some faint spark of sympathy in him was kill Germans. He himself would have been delighted to kill millions of Germans. He particularly hated conscientious objectors because they did not even want to kill Germans. When he thought about conscientious objectors he saw that even the despised military, by comparison, were right, and that the war had to be won. His attitude was one of utter refusal to accept any reason about anything to do with the war, either for or against it, or even refusing to participate in it. He hated everyone concerned. In the chapter called 'Nightmare' which Lawrence shoved into *Kangaroo*, his novel about Australia, the hero, Richard Somers (Lawrence's fictitious alter ego) admits that the war, with conscription, medical examinations, and so on was perhaps necessary. But – and he expletes the word 'but', which represents his 'passional instinct' against every justification of the war: 'Quite right, quite right. . . . But – And the But just explodes everything like a bomb. . . . *But* – he was full of a lava fire of rage and hate, at the bottom of his soul. . . . He felt desecrated.'

'The Nightmare' fits awkwardly into – or, rather, stands out from *Kangaroo*. This chapter is an account of the Lawrences' experiences during the war when they lived in a cottage on the Cornish coast. They were regarded with grave suspicion by the local authorities. For Frieda was a German and Lawrence did not conceal his hatred of the war and his liking for German ideas and literature. The feeling that the old England is finished is now succeeded in his writing by hatred for the new England which has taken its place. For him, the final collapse of the old England was the going under of the Asquith government in 1916 and its replacement by the coalition which Lawrence calls the *John Bull* government of Lloyd George and Horatio Bottomley (the notorious swindler and editor of that jingoist publication). When Richard Somers (Lawrence's alter ego in *Kangaroo*) learns that Lloyd George has superseded Asquith, he walks about the moors and hears a voice saying: 'It is the end of England. It is finished. England will never be England any more.'

It was indeed the end of *that* England. However, Lawrence had a revivalist temperament and he had more faith in a resurgence of England than had Forster. His opinions were Whitmanishly self-contradicting. He himself did not mind this. It was more important to express his moods than his responsibilities. He was especially unreliable about politics. He would embrace a belief which embodied his aspirations and then disclaim all responsibility for it a month later. He felt no more committed to his own violently held opinions than to the degrees of temperature his thermometer registered when he had or didn't have fever. There were the political schemes for saving England which he discussed and quarrelled about with Bertrand Russell. But his hatred boiled over Bertrand Russell to whom he wrote that he was a baby with an immense brain and no physical body and that he should commit suicide. There was the idea of emigrating and forming a community of sympathizers: Middleton Murry, Katherine Mansfield, Koteliansky, Mark Gertler, etc. But part of the attraction of this lay in the fact that on any excursion into the desert led by Lawrence – Christ with his apostles – Middleton Murry was unctuously cast in the role of Judas. Ultimately the reason for Lawrence's despair about plans for improving

England were, I think, the same as Forster's: that it was impossible to 'plan' without ruining the England. One of the deepest feelings in Lawrence – perhaps the deepest – was his intense hatred of ugliness, especially industrial ugliness. And though detesting the middle class English, he had ambivalent feelings towards the workers. *Au fond*, he thought that a proletarianized England would be an ugly and vulgar place. He suspected the workers didn't want to transform life – they wanted to become middle class.

In certain moods he felt some hope for a religious rather than a political awakening in England: for a movement based not on class or commercial interest but on the desire to fulfil the English religious character in an England which would resemble Blake's Jerusalem. In May 1915 he wrote to Lady Cynthia Asquith:

Believe me, this England, we very English people, will at length join together and say, 'We will not do these things, because in our knowledge of God we know them wrong'. . . . We shall unite in our knowledge of God – not perhaps in our expression of God – but in our *knowledge* of God: and we shall agree that we don't want to live only to write and make riches, that England does not only care to have the greatest Empire or the greatest commerce, but that she does care supremely for the pure truth of God, which she will try to fulfil.

After the war, Lawrence and Frieda went first to Italy and then to other countries, never settling down or making a permanent home anywhere, quarrelling with and being quarrelled with by the English. His feelings are conveyed by the headings in the index to his *Collected Letters* entered under 'England'.

England ('the tightness of'), ('gloom of dark moral judgement'), ('don't want to live there any more'), ('that Sunday feeling'), ('dimness in the air gives me the blues'), ('don't like E . . . . but the English are lovable people'), ('dim and woolly': of German climate 'bright and sharply defined'), ('end of my writing for'), ('collapsing'), ('a last vision of its beauty' when going to America) (hatred of) ('want to go away for ever'), etc.

The entry 'want to go away for ever' is from a letter written in 1919 saying that he wants to get out of not only England but also Europe. First the Lawrences took off for Italy, shaking the dust of England off their feet, a reaction which he describes in that extraordinary performance, *Aaron's Rod*, garrulous and a bit incoherent but perhaps of all his books the one most revealing of his psychology. It is a book split several ways down the middle. Aaron the secretary of the Miner's Union in his colliery, who suddenly walks out of his job and his house for ever and, bearing with him his flute, goes to London where he joins the orchestra of the opera, is what Blake would have called Lawrence's 'emanation', a kind of spiritual projection of him. The agonizing scene in which he steals back to his house at the mining village to witness – without his being seen – his stricken family and weeping wife complaining of him, has the mixture of cruelty and tenderness which Lawrence must have felt about leaving his own parents and family. The London scenes are of people like gibbering monkeys, almost Wyndham Lewis's 'Apes of God', but not altogether successfully satirized because Lawrence was too passionately involved for them to be completely objects of satire. In London, Lawrence the writer – called Rawdon Lilly, meets Lawrence the flautist emanation, Aaron. Aaron nearly dies of an attack of the terrible post-war influenza. Lilly, leaving his wife, nurses his emanation, Aaron, this spiritual Lawrence who would have died, had not Lilly bathed and rubbed the lower part of his body with medicated oil. As in the relationship between Birkin and Gunther in *Women in Love* there is a split between Lilly's marriage to Tanny, his wife, and his wish to escape from marriage in the *Blutbrüderschaft* relation with another man. Finally there is the war. An ex-officer called Herbertson arrives at the flat shared by Lilly and Aaron and talks compulsively about the Western Front. He piles anecdote on anecdote of horror.

When Herbertson has gone, Aaron and Lilly discuss the war. Lilly – who, being the writer in Lawrence, is really the instructor of the ex-miner-flautist – declares that the war was 'unreal'. 'And they want to hypnotise me. And I won't be hypnotised. The war was a lie and is a lie and will go on being a lie till someone busts it.' Aaron, representing those who disagree with the writer Lawrence, protests: 'It was a fact – you can't bust the fact that it happened.' Lilly replies: 'Yes you can. It never happened to me. No more than my dreams happen. My dreams don't happen. They only seem.' He goes on to argue that the war didn't happen to anyone who was 'a man, in his own self'. 'It took place in the automatic sphere, like dreams do. But the *actual man* in every man was just absent – asleep – or drugged – inert – dream-logged. That's it.'

However it was a nightmare from which Lawrence could only really wake by leaving England. The English, dream-drugged or not, suffered – those of them who had lived through the war – from post-hypnotic effects. Those who had missed the war – many of them having expected to be sent to the front when peace was declared woke up into a peace which was the war's opposite – a hysteria based on obliterating the war from memory.

In a story written in 1922, entitled 'England, My England', Lawrence depicts the death of the old England in the character of Egbert, an Englishman as instinctual as Stephen Wonham but who is filled with a profound knowledge that he is only a shadow out of the past. Egbert passes his life tinkering around, gardening but doing everything amateurishly, refusing ever to take a job. He is married to the daughter of an industrialist from the North whose real understanding is with her father. She has a sense of duty to her children and an intense physical passion for her husband, who also loves her physically, of which she is a bit ashamed. The rift in their happiness starts when Egbert's favourite child is seriously crippled, as a result of her stumbling over a scythe which he had left on the ground. After this, husband and wife drift apart. When the war breaks out Egbert enlists, not that he hates the Germans, but deep down because the war confirms his realization that the ancient England of which he is so much the shining descendant is already dead. His death in a war which he regards as meaningless and vulgar stupidity, is his private confirmation of public history.

Egbert's father-in-law, the industrialist from the North, sees the war as a conflict between German militarism and English industrialism, so he gladly supports England. But Egbert, the 'pure-blooded Englishman, perfect in his race', 'can no more be aggressive on the score of his Englishness than a rose can be aggressive on the score of its rosiness'. He refuses to decide between England and Germany. 'Egbert just refused to reckon with the world.'

Like Forster and Kipling in their deepest imagination of England, Lawrence makes Egbert's idea of the real England go back to 'the intense sensations of the primeval people of the place, whose passions seethed in the air still, from those long days before the Romans came'.

'England, My England' is Lawrence's English elegy. Not that he sympathises much with Egbert. Let the dead bury their dead, is his motto. For probably England is dead. Sometimes Lawrence thinks he is the only Englishman alive. But Egbert is nobler than the other characters in this story because, like Mrs Wilcox in *Howards End*, he lives and dies for a past which he symbolises. And like Forster's heroine he does not resist death. It is the realization in him of the fate of English consciousness.

The Novels of
D. H. Lawrence
Frank Kermode

It might seem odd to speak of Lawrence's luck, since on ordinary calculations he had very little of it; but as a novelist he had his share. He needed it, as all writers do, though 'grace' might be a better word; it is something you have to count on, something that intervenes between the willing or planning of a work and its completion. Without this grace, prayed-for but uncovenanted, destructive, when it comes, of the most carefully laid plans, all may remain inert. The praying is done by hard labour, by wrestling with the growing text. This is the angel that deforms and blesses. Meeting him is what I call luck.

Lawrence first enjoyed it when the gamekeeper Annable forced his way into *The White Peacock*. He began this novel when he was twenty, and its composition and revision dragged on for four years. Half-way through this time he was telling a correspondent that it was 'a novel of sentiment . . . all about love – and rhapsodies on Spring scattered here and there – heroines galore – no plot – ninetenths adjectives – every colour in the spectrum descanted upon – a poem or two – scraps of Latin and French – altogether a sloppy, spicy mess.' Nevertheless he carried on, lamenting the poverty, the forthcoming examinations, the schoolmastering which slowed him down. He was learning the mechanics of the job – how not to make forced conversations when two lines of telling would do the work better; how to go easy on the metaphors. More radically, he decided that regularity of construction was a chimerical requirement; that such intruders as Annable ought to be let in and welcomed.

The story of the peacock defiling the tombstone belongs to Annable, so he even gave the book its title. It would be too much to say that without him the book is nothing; Lawrence's own youthful account of it, mixing pride and diffidence, suggests some of its merits, and the experience of writing it taught him how to put a novel together, and how, without false shame, to decline to do so if he saw cause to avoid conventional wisdom on the subject. A novel has a hand in it own writing, and there are times when the author must trust it rather than external recommendations about 'form' and 'character'. Hence, in part, the importance of Annable. At this stage Lawrence was doing better with short stories than novels, and he might well have made a story out of the gamekeeper. But Annable insisted on being in the novel, a morose cultural and sexual drop-out, condemning women as peacocks, 'all vanity and screech and defilement'. He is one of those images of what Forster called 'the greenwood', tantalizing the socially secure, or those who aspire to be so, with hints of a vanishing freedom – a kind of sphinx, as Lévi-Strauss might say, reminding us of the numinous threshold between nature and culture. Nothing in this first novel is finer than the moment when the two naked men embrace and, enchanted at the contact of George's body, Cyril suddenly thinks of Annable, who despised marriage and children and met his death, like other natural creatures in the book, by a mindless brutality, under a fall of stone. Such intimations, possible harmonies, intricate nodes of sense, made it worth while going on with the task of novel writing, and put the worrying problem of 'construction' in its place.

Annable '*has* to be there', said Lawrence, and, henceforth he was always there, or thereabouts. The exercise he gave the novelist was valuable – it loosened him up for the books he was to write, encouraged him to shun the kind of contrivance he associated, perhaps unfairly, with Arnold Bennett. 'Tell Arnold Bennett that all rules of construction hold good only for novels which are copies of other novels. A book which is not a copy of other books has its own construction'. He began to understand the fluidity of the novel, its protean adaptability. It was 'incapable of the absolute', and so better suited than any other kind of writing to the business of *quickening* the reader, of penetrating the conventional crust of his thought. 'Turn truly, honourably to the novel, and see wherein you are man alive.' To be a novelist could now be named the highest of callings; it was Annable who announced this vocation.

Not that Lawrence was able to enter immediately into it. He made an understandable false start. One thinks of the confused ambitions and revelations of his Croydon days, full of new experiences and new books; the search for a model had to go on a little longer. Among the fourpence-halfpenny novels that he recommended in letters to friends, he came upon George Moore's *Evelyn Innes*. This now neglected work is the apogee of Wagnerianism in the English novel, for it is Wagnerian in theme as well as in design. The long occultation of Wagner's fame and authority had not yet begun, and it would be natural for the young writer to hear *The Ring*, acknowledge its power and its value as a model for all the arts, and read Moore with respect. An aspirant who filled his first novel with cultivated conversation and referred too often to Beardsley would not avoid these more potent influences. Lawrence must also have read some Nietzsche, some Ibsen (though he found him a bit 'skin-erupty' and *Ghosts* 'gave him the creeps'), but Wagner, above all, was indispensable to the condition of artistic seriousness. He was the poet who could have made the orchestra speak of Annable while the young men embraced. If George Moore could write a Wagnerian novel, so could Lawrence. In doing so he worked, not for the last time, from an existing story, by his friend Helen Corke – unlike him a true Wagnerian.

The Trespasser was written between 1910 and 1912 in the scant leisure of a schoolteacher. Its title contains a foreign-language pun; originally he had wanted to call it *Trespassers in Cythera*, but the less explicit title he finally chose adds to the connotation of guilty love that of death, from the French *trépas*, a sense he uses elsewhere. It fits the strange grey quality of this *Liebestod* better than the first title, *The Saga of Siegmund*. Lawrence didn't like the book, and thought seriously about suppressing it, thinking it among other things 'too erotic' – an interesting judgment from one who was later to call *Tristan and Isolde* pornographic; but he judged the critics right – Ford Madox Ford was disgusted by it, calling it 'a rotten work of genius'.

The Trespasser is not a Wagnerian success, but it has Lawrentian interest. He was at the time irritated with women who refused to acknowledge the genital character of male sexual desire, and he made Helena not only a Wagnerite but one of those women whose culture castrated their men, refined vampires in the last throes of the romantic agony, 'dreaming women whose passion exhausts itself at the mouth'. Such women, 'rejecting the animal in humanity', have grown abstract, their kindness full of cruelty; their desire is not for sexual love but for 'the flowers of the spirit' they can collect from men. They destroy the natural man. Siegmund's trespass into Cythera destroys him; he trespasses again, and kills himself.

Freud's speculation, that the women men of culture most value are precisely the kind who will inhibit their sexuality, is contemporary with this novel. Here Lawrence makes the victim an artist. Later he evolved an elaborate and explicitly non-Freudian theory to account for what he regarded as one of the root causes of the decline of the west. But he did not go very deeply into it until he wrote *Sons and Lovers*, the very title of which indicates the main source of men's troubles – the mother as mistress.

Another grace attended the writing of this novel. When he began it his mother was alive, and he had not broken with Jessie Chambers; life, precisely as he wrote and rewrote made available the material without which the book could not be finished. He was able to submit one version to the criticism of Jessie, and another to that of Frieda, with whom he eloped in 1912. All Lawrence's novels are affected by the interplay between life and story during their composition, but in none of the others is it so complex: the time of composition is also that of the great crisis of his life.

It is easy, therefore, to understand why *Sons and Lovers* has been and remains the most popular of the novels. For all its ambition it satisfies the elementary requirements of consumers. It has a story of great interest about 'real people', carefully individualized and struggling for intelligible forms of fulfilment; it has memorable scenes, in which are recorded with satisfying fullness and accuracy the life of a mining community and the culture of a provincial city. Its familial conflicts, however intense, are not unrelated to ordinary experience. One can admire the textures and identify an individual voice, yet avoid the struggle that is entailed by deliberately abrupt departures from the norms of the reader's expectations. For all its delicacy and richness and multiplicity of tone *Sons and Lovers* is a novel of fairly conventional design. What we most admire in it is a sensitive accuracy, to be found in a great variety of passages – Paul's mother, shut out and burying her face in the lily, or Paul burning the loaves, or Paul in the cherry-tree or making love to Clara.

All this may remind us of what may sometimes be forgotten: that much may be done, and in perfectly good faith, without obvious innovations. Lawrence insists on his formal freedom, he is bound only to endow the unfolding narrative with the quality he called 'quickness'. For the rest, he does as he likes, telling when telling seems more effective than showing. This randomness of technique, accompanied by a continuing willingness to 'hug the shores of the real', could not satisfy Henry James; of a book so written he could not honestly say that it was *done*, praise he reserved for novels which submitted to those constraints he found so liberating to his own imagination. So, for him, the Lawrence of *Sons and Lovers* lagged 'in the dusty rear'. Yet *Sons and Lovers* is, in another sense, 'done'. Its quickness is the gift of a mind which cared for variety of texture rather than for subtly determined structure. Having the movement of life, it enacts, at a level higher than anything Lawrence had so far attempted, the crucial struggles between women and man, between culture and nature. Paul at the end stands free of his mother; and to the end of his own life Lawrence was fascinated by the image of a man free and erect, saying always *noli me tangere*. But neither he nor Paul was an Annable, and he was so far from being free from the bitter complications of heterosexuality that the rest of his work is dedicated to them.

Nevertheless, *Sons and Lovers* enabled Lawrence to understand far better the true nature of the problem. It could not, he saw, have been the consequence of merely local cultural constraints that he was thrice a victim: of his mother's possessiveness and social aspirations, of Miriam's refined sexual timidity, of his own awkwardness and shame. He finished the book in exile, with a woman whose voluptuousness amazed him, and who was able to tell him about Freud, against whom Lawrence reacted with a vigour that was effective as submission would have been; and he was able to think about the whole matter in a new way. He could now claim that *Sons and Lovers* had a general cultural significance, calling it 'a great tragedy . . . the tragedy of thousands of young men in England'. With a real sense of power – the novel could do so much – he began work on the story that became, when he finished it after the war, *The Lost Girl*, another study in repression and redemption. But a greater project was stirring, the book that turned into *The Rainbow* and *Women in Love*. It was started before the war, though without the war it could not have developed as it did. The subject, ultimately, was that great general tragedy: for the same conditions of civilization that enforced sexual privation and distorted lives on those thousands of young men now drove them to their deaths in the trenches. The sufferings of Paul Morel led Lawrence to the study of history as repression, and the world crisis of 1914–18.

This implies that there is continuity between *Sons and Lovers* and the central masterpiece which followed it. But there is change also; *The Rainbow* and *Women in Love* are books which constantly subvert conventional expectations, and demonstrate, to a degree formerly unthinkable, the truth of the contention that the novelist is a free man, unbound by prescribed notions of form and conventional representations of scene, character and story. He may, indeed must, have a 'metaphysic', and that too will show, but it cannot take over. The development of Lawrence's 'metaphysic', and the degree to which it may be qualified by a narrative, are illustrated by the Preface he wrote for *Sons and Lovers* in January, 1913. This extraordinary document he sent to Garnett with a letter explaining that it was not to be printed. (It must be sought in Aldous Huxley's edition of the letters, for – almost incredibly – it has not been reprinted since 1932.) The theme it announces is henceforth never absent from Lawrence's fiction: for good or ill, his 'metaphysical' speculations can no longer be kept out of the novels, which at best can tame them. The Preface says that women ruin men; but it also develops a theologico-historical theory as to how they came to do so. Like most of Lawrence's subsequent expressions of this and related themes, it has a trinitarian pattern, associating women with the first person (Law and Flesh) and man with the second (Love and the Word). Historical epochs are also related to these persons. The third person, the Holy Ghost, would be manifest in a third epoch, and also in the true union of women and man. But this union has not occurred, which is why the love of women is diverted from their husbands to their sons, who are thereby themselves ruined as husbands. The story of *Sons and Lovers* is thus given metaphysical elevation, and retold in terms which, having their origin in the *Everlasting Gospel* of Joachim of

Fiora, had served occult and apocalyptic history since the thirteenth century. Ordinarily they serve as a model for crisis-historiography, and so they do in Lawrence; but he attaches to them his sexual metaphysic, for it is the peculiarity of his thought that within it sex and history are as two sides of a coin. Thus the cultural need to liberate marriage from the son-loving mother becomes part of the diagnosis of a culture which has reached the end of an age of Love and is caught in a long pause (another Joachite conception) before the entry into an age of the Holy Ghost, a utopia of which the sexual expression would be Lawrentian marriage, that 'star-equilibrium' between the isolate male and female.

This Preface is contemporary with the more celebrated expression, in a letter to Ernest Collings, of Lawrence's attack on mind-knowledge, that separation of mind and spirit from body and blood which is reflected in our distorted sexual situation; he speaks instead for 'a belief in the blood, the flesh, as wiser than the intellect', and adds that nothing can save England except a new relation between men and women, 'a making free and healthy of this sex'.

A writer who, on reflection, found so much unexpected theology in the novel he had just finished would necessarily grow aware of the possibility of doing much more; and henceforth might take a new view of the originality of his whole project. Hence perhaps, Lawrence's increasing scorn for contemporaries he had formerly admired, and his sense that even Garnett, on whom he had so far confidently depended, failed to understand what he was now doing. Garnett disliked the first version of the new book, and Lawrence at first excused this, thinking that he had abandoned an old manner without quite establishing a new. 'I have no longer the joy in creating vivid scenes, that I had in *Sons and Lovers*. I don't care much more about accumulating objects in the powerful light of emotion and making a scene of them.' But later he saw the failure as Garnett's, not his own; and in June 1914, when Garnett had again misunderstood a later version, he tried to explain to him that certain prejudiced expectations would have to be given up before this new book could be properly read. He was now, he said, dealing with something deeper than 'character'; 'that which is non-physic – non-human – in humanity, is more interesting to me than the old-fashioned human element.' He would work under the surface, find out what a woman '*is* – what she IS . . . instead of what she feels like according to the human conception'. And so he goes on, in a famous passage, to exclude from his novels 'the old stable *ego* – of the character'. In his new manner characters will not, in the old way, develop; they will 'fall into the form of some other rhythmic form as when one draws a fiddle-bow across a fine tray delicately sanded, the sand takes lines unknown'.

These meditations of 1913 and 1914, written as Lawrence struggled with the early drafts of what became his two greatest novels, are valuable traces of another wrestling with the angel, another transforming that is also a deformation. The 'metaphysic' will henceforth be much more in evidence, but it must not dominate the novel; furthermore, the humanity of the novel is now to be much more problematic, a complex of subtle interacting forces so delicate as to make old-fashioned 'character' and even conventional narrative a violation of its integrity. Lawrence continued his investigations into this new form through the succeeding versions of his new book, but he also developed the 'metaphysic' independently, in such a way that it fed back into the novel. He remained certain that the union of Law and Love, which the speculative works might discuss, could be fully figured only in the work of art, which for him must have precisely this homological relationship with the dreamed-of consummate marriage.

The 'Study of Thomas Hardy', a strange systematization of his trinitarian complaint against the perversions of the female, thus helped to shape the novel that was to be *The Rainbow*. Lawrence began it at the outbreak of a war which seemed to him to represent the Terrors which history had been moving towards since the dissociation of blood and mind at the Renaissance; for all his horror he thought of these Terrors as the prelude to his new age, the age of the Holy Ghost. The treatise goes far beyond sex, but the need to let go of the old, to rush into a new kind of life, is at the root of it. As the war went on he grew savagely pessimistic, and 'The Crown' is a version of the Hardy study which emphasises much more the bitter modern corruption, from which escape is harder than he had supposed; this is the metaphysic of *Women in Love*. But Lawrence did not forget, at this stage, that the metaphysic must not be allowed to subdue the novel, nor that if every novel needs a metaphysic, it must also contain its criticism.

The Sisters, which split into *The Rainbow* and *Women in Love*, was originally closer to the scheme of the second of these books. Lawrence started there, and worked backwards, first to Ursula's first lover Skrebensky, and then to the two earlier Brangwen generations. Thus *The Rainbow* contains three generations, three epochs – corresponding to the age of Law, which is breaking up at the outset, the age of Love, which is represented by the generation of Anna and Will, and the third, the transitional period, the pause before the third age, in which we leave Ursula at the end of the book.

The Rainbow speaks of an evil time with a note of prophetic hope that had disappeared by the time Lawrence finished the last version of *Women in Love*. He had predicted that when *The Rainbow* appeared in 1915 the war would be over; but, as he said, he set his rainbow in the sky too soon. There followed the prosecution for obscenity, and all the other sufferings and furies that make the story of his war years so harrowing; his despair was sometimes hysterical in its intensity, and it worked itself into the second novel. But *The Rainbow* lacks that modern desperation. Critics have noticed that it ends as it were between two testaments – it is a version of human history as sealed by a covenant of the Old Testament, the rainbow, and it prophesies the covenant of a New. The opening pages, describing the life of the Brangwen farmers before it was altered by the spiritual aspirations of women, have a particularly full Old Testament quality, as of Job in his plenty, or of a continuity between human and animal blood, culture and nature.

It is from these pages, perhaps, that many derive their notion of Lawrence's prose as habitually overripe, and certainly a whole book of it would be too much, but it is entirely appropriate to its unique occasion, and to the description of a life of almost mindless fulfilment, a life soon to end. For men must, since women want it, move out of this natural plenitude into a more difficult culture — more like the curate's. Brangwen takes an educated Polish wife, and with her a daughter not of his blood; and a new epoch is prepared. Not that Lawrence, recording these historical transformations, abandons his sense of how ordinary people behave. The crisis that transcends mere character must nevertheless take place in human contexts, its expression limited by human speech and gesture; one remembers the beautiful scene in which Brangwen consoles his hostile stepdaughter while her mother is in labour, and another, years later, when the girl has made love to Will Brangwen in the barn. What he no longer cared about was the mechanical registration, for the sake of authenticating an obsolete reality, of manners and speech. He was working at the level he tried to describe to Garnett, though at both levels there might be a woman in labour, cattle needing to be fed, a child to be consoled.

Far from holding one note, *The Rainbow* is distinguished for its tonal variety. Perhaps Lawrence had not entirely abandoned his Wagner; the transformation of the early stackyard scene between Will and Anna into the tense 'frictional' episode much later, when it is Ursula and Skrebensky who are together amid the moonlit corn, is as deliberate as anything in *The Ring*. Both scenes are of remarkable beauty, yet it is the difference between them that makes the larger structural point, for it tells us silently of the progression of sexual love to a point of impossibility, or anyway of decadent perversity. But for the most part Lawrence achieves his densities by other means. He is unceasingly inventive, as in the wedding sequence and the subsequent naive voluptuousness of Will and Anna, or in the Lincoln Cathedral chapter – how well it resists the temptation to be openly 'metaphysical'! Its doctrine can only be clarified by a reading of the Hardy book. Will snubbing Ursula in the garden, or making love to the girl he picked up at the music hall and plunging afterwards into a deeper sensuality with his wife – these things work at the level he was defining in the letter to

Garnett, but at more familiar levels also. And Lawrence proceeds from one to another with a deftness that is sometimes denied him. We may, remembering the book at some distance, think of the adult Ursula, in the third section of the work, as the strange sexual being of the stackyard scene and the remarkable climax on the sand dunes, or among the apocalyptic horses of the conclusion. But she is equally a daughter and a sister, a schoolteacher with hideous and difficult pupils. It is precisely this imaginative continuity that is so distinctive, and which in the end rebuffs ridicule and parody. An ordinary girl is also the representative of a great crisis in the history of women; interpreting her rainbow as a promise of 'the earth's new architecture' she speaks also for England in her crisis, in the Pause before the new age. *The Rainbow* is, if not his greatest, Lawrence's most fully characteristic achievement.

The great themes of his life and work were death and rebirth; *The Rainbow* is focussed on rebirth, *Women in Love* on death. The war was an even greater catastrophe than he had feared, and 'The Crown' adds to the 'Hardy' doctrines some desperate speculations on the proximity of the generative and the excremental, the need for total acceptance of the shamefulness of sex as a prelude to its purgation. *Women in Love* is the novel of the wartime 'Going Asunder', of the flux of corruption in which all must swim and most drown. It is so strange a book that after half a century of comment there is still no received opinion of it. Lawrence here, more than in *The Rainbow*, abandons regular narrative progress and we still have a tendency to think of the great novelists as the ones who produce, with easy force, a powerful narrative sequence. In *Women in Love* there is often little obvious causal connection between the parts; each chapter forms a whole, and may often be read out of its proper order or omitted without damage to the narrative line. We tend, unusually, to remember the book in terms of chapter titles: 'Moony', 'Rabbit', 'Excurse'; quite often each is dominated by a particular image, like Halliday's statuette, or Hermione's cat, or the chair bought in the market by Birkin and Ursula. It is all totally unlike the interactions of social notation, narrative and symbol in Forster's *Passage to India*, a work of the same period, and equally unlike another great contemporary, *Ulysses*, where the contingencies of the surface are held together by the myth on which the novel is founded. Lawrence has to trust the novel, and the action of his own imagination, to find the true and unprecedented form.

In doing so he risks charges of absurdity. 'Moony' is an example of how close he can approach, yet triumphantly avoid it; the car journey in 'Excurse', with Birken a Pharaoh at the wheel, and the ecstatic loin-stroking at the inn, may be an instance of failure. There are others, perhaps less doubtful; but the method surely justifies itself, as one wonderful novelty succeeds another: Gudrun and the lecherous workmen, or scratched by the rabbit; Gerald with the mare, or diving incessantly into the waters of the dead, or arriving from his father's deathbed, churchyard loam on his boots, to make love to Gudrun. What happens in Gudrun's bed is metaphysical, 'a terrible frictional silence of death', but the journey of Gerald is a 'real' one; he has to ask a collier the way, and in the morning must tiptoe at five out of the Brangwen house, carrying his boots. The collier is a Wagnerian touch. Throughout the work of Lawrence the colliers recur, distorted, underground, sinister, but also figures of natural power and gaiety. Gerald sometimes imitates them, embracing Gudrun in the place where they kiss their girls; yet it is he who ruins them, exacting from them a life of mechanical productiveness in return for the gift of social aspirations they were better without: a piano in every parlour, the poshed-up pubs of *Lady Chatterley's Lover*. Without the miners we should not so clearly see Gerald – for all his associations with cold Nordic corruption and death – as an emblem of the destruction that was coming to the white races.

Middleton Murry alone among the early critics saw how savage the book was, how dedicated to the idea of racial corruption. Yet *Women in Love* is more overtly 'metaphysical' than *The Rainbow*, for in Birkin Lawrence gives himself a voice in the novel. This was a dangerous move, and it caused some of the book's failures. But Lawrence remembered that if a novel must contain a metaphysic it must also contain its critique, so he ensured that Birkin's excesses are exposed, by the comments of Hermione and, more especially, Ursula. This device he used again in *Aaron's Rod*, *Kangaroo*, and *The Plumed Serpent*, in none of which does it work so well; for in none of them has the narrative the same measure of plasticity, the same endless resource. Again and again the tale saves the artist, as in the intrusion of Loerke. This figure of corruption, so attractive to Gudrun, represents the anti-Semitic side of Lawrence's evolving 'metaphysic' – the Jews, he came to think, were leading in the race to total corruption, and he gives Loerke personality and a corrupt art. But the character transcends these doctrinal constraints, just as the book does. It forces us to live with it rather than decode it; it subdues the doctrines, just as it erodes the malicious caricatures of friends and acquaintances Lawrence wrote into it. It ends without ending, on the question of the possibility of true union between Ursula and Birkin in the absence of a counterpoising male friendship, now that Gerald is dead. Who, at that moment, thinks about all the doctrinal speculation which underlies it, of Lawrence's troubled conviction that a man must have another man as well as a woman?

It seems to be a characteristic of the great works of early modernism that they can invite a kind of emperor's-clothes reaction – in certain lights they can seem vacuous or absurd. *Women in Love* is such a work. It sometimes invites exasperated sneers, a chorus led by Ursula herself; yet in its fluidity, its unpredictable tonalities, it is surely, if disconcertingly, close to the essence of the modern.

Much later in his life, Lawrence claimed to have been a liberator – he meant that after him novelists might use greater freedom and explicitness in handling the central human relationships, and so break through the old limits of character and plausibility. Formerly, as many had complained, and as Hardy discovered in his last novel, one had been asked to deal with the sexual life as if one were permitted to understand it as James's Maisie did, only in terms of its remote social effects. It is true that Lawrence contributed significantly to this liberation; but he did more, or at least he provided great opportunities, whether or no his successors wished to take them. He helped to free the novel from artificial restraints which had come to seem natural. This is not to say that the well-made novel could not survive *Women in Love*; it has obviously done so. And much of the attention due to Lawrence's novel was stolen by *Ulysses*, which is much more obviously 'experimental'. One might say that the full effect of Lawrence's greatest experiment has still not been felt.

The Rainbow and *Women in Love* are, by those who like them, usually regarded as the climax of Lawrence's career as a novelist; and this is my own view. Just as, in his life, he grew more dogmatic, less receptive to new ideas and impressions, so in his novels he became less open to the casual grace, less ready to take on that deforming wrestling-match. *The Lost Girl* is in many respects an underrated book, and it contains a number of interesting adventures, but nobody, presumably, would mention it in the same breath as the novels in which the writer is engaged in a life-and-death struggle with his text. The faults of *Aaron's Rod*, for all its qualities, are dismaying; Lawrence can jeer at his alter ego as much as he likes, allow an exasperated friend to strike him, but the book is still Lilly's, full of desperate preaching about leadership and corruption. The sense that *Aaron's Rod* does not know where it is going next – a sense quite absent from the equally unpredictable *Women in Love* – becomes oppressive. The tension is gone, and Lawrence seems to think he can take anything to hand and put it into the text; the result is not the old fascinating formal flexibility, but a complicated grumble about postwar exhaustion and postwar politics. Aaron himself is a version of Annable – he simply walks out of his marriage, though into art rather than nature; we are not sure, at the end, whether he will accept Lilly's *Fuehrerprinzip* – an issue left open, in much the same way, in *The Plumed Serpent* – but he comes close to that Lawrentian ideal, the man with no sexual obligations, the man who enjoys a kind of positive chastity: *noli me tangere*. It is out of such chastity, into a true sexual relationship, that Mellors progresses in *Lady Chatterley's Lover*, and more diagrammatically, Jesus in *The Man Who Died*. It is a death which may or may not issue in resurrection: Lou embraces it in *St Mawr*. But in *Aaron's Rod*, among so much that is merely fantasy, it cannot help seeming merely a low-powered fantasy itself.

So, too, in *Kangaroo*, a long novel written in less than two months and never subjected to the process of creative revision. Here one feels very little of the concentrated struggle with a story that so distinguishes the great novels. Lawrence calls it a 'thought-adventure', and is certainly full of his doctrines, attached, perhaps, a little perfunctorily, to a fantasy about leadership and a male comradeship which he elaborated from some hints in contemporary Australian politics. His eye did not fail him, and there are fine records of the weird Australian landscape; but at times he seems to write on and on without any real notion of what he wants to do. Not even the astringent commentary of Harriet-Frieda can quite cut the Somers-Lawrence figure down to its deserved size; there is a sort of unredeemed colonialist bad temper in his contempt for Indians and Australians, a desolating insistence on Somer's isolation and superiority in all matters of politics, friendship and marriage. Only Kangaroo himself is powerful and original; Lawrence made his failed fascist leader into an antithesis of his ideal self: a fat, loving, mother-dominated Jew who wants to be blood-brother to an Aryan hardened into male isolation, the enemy of mothers, and indeed of love. The other Australian book, *The Boy in the Bush*, is in some ways better, although, and perhaps because, it was based on a first version written by another writer. The obsessions – female submission, the ritual passage through death to life and perhaps leadership – get into the text without destroying it.

In *The Plumed Serpent* Lawrence worked much harder, but the novel retains the faults of his now perpetual exasperation, and of what had now become an arrogant overconfidence in the receptivity of the form. There is an intensified disgust for the world that resists renewal: North America, so much longed for, had not met his hopes. The white consciousness had corrupted the native, the white death was as imminent and necessary here as elsewhere, though the primitive Indian lurked somewhere as an image of what might be. *The Plumed Serpent* is fervently doctrinal; but it is saved from total aridity by Lawrence's brilliant idea of inventing a religion and a ritual to support the doctrine. The cult of Quetzalcoatl is to replace the degenerate Christianity of Mexico, and with the expulsion of whites and half breeds the old blood-consciousness may be restored. Quetzalcoatl is the Morning Star, announcing a new epoch; he reconciles Night and Day and all other opposites, including law and love, man and woman. The persistent apocalypticism of Lawrence at last finds its way back to a religion (he made a similar effort somewhat later in *Etruscan Places* and *Apocalypse*). Yet Kate, his Irish heroine, who joins the religion and accepts the role it imposes on women, is far from lacking in scepticism; she plays the role of Ursula, incapable of total acceptance or rejection. This helps the book, and qualifies both its dogmatism and its occasionally hysterical chatter about race, sex and eternity. But even Lawrence soon gave up the opinion that it was his best work; and most would say that his great American achievement is not this but the novella *St Mawr*.

The constraints of the shorter form were increasingly attractive. Lawrence wrote only one more novel, *Lady Chatterley's Lover*, and that began as little more than a novella. He wrestled with it through three versions, which, in Lawrence, is always a good sign. The ruin of England, whether you contemplate it in the blighted countryside or in the enfeeblement of the miners, was essentially the ruin of its sexuality; if that could be got right all else would be repaired. Connie Chatterley's is a typical state of privation, for she was at first spoilt by trivial sex and then married to a man made impotent by the war. Her systematic awakening into a natural condition of sexuality is an image of the longed-for and yet unlikely day when England should be restored. Her St George comes in from the greenwood; at first Lawrence was fascinated by the class difference between Connie and her lover, but in the end he gave much of that up, and saw more possibilities in making Mellors an ex-officer. And so Annable returns, though in this myth he has a more active role. Mellors stands outside class, and between nature and culture. He has dropped out of the mechanical civilization in which Chatterley leads his life-in-death. He has also given up the polite euphemisms which are used, in falsely refined society, to describe the sexual and excremental functions. When he moves out of his treasured chastity into sex it is with pain. The shock of the language – and Lawrence meant it to shock – enacts that pain; the return of the frontier between culture and nature is not an easy one. It involves, physically and lexically, the burning out of shame; it is necessary to what Lawrence, when he gave up the Leadership myth, called 'tenderness,' but it also involves a certain violence. The stripping off of the layers of dead varnish on the language is emblematical of the whole desperate process by which sex shall be restored to its original creative force.

Most of Lawrence is in *Lady Chatterley's Lover*, from Annable and the early letters to Garnett, to the sexual-apocalyptic meditations of his last years. It is an easy book to criticise or laugh at; for it has most of the faults he never corrected from the beginning, and others he picked up along his way. But it is a good book, founded on a kind of self-recognition. As the red rust crept over his England, and the postwar young increasingly disgusted him with their triviality, he remembered his blasted hopes for the novel, 'the one bright book of life'; and he remembered the greenwood and Annable. Some of the old power and flexibility came back; he could not, in the fatigue and illness of these last years, wrestle as fiercely as before, but he was right to love *Lady Chatterley* and to defend it, for in it he was, once more, fully engaged according to his strength, and the last novel stands not ignobly beside *The Rainbow* and *Women in Love*.

Women in
D. H. Lawrence's Works
Barbara Hardy

The only question to ask today, about man or woman
is: Has she chipped the shell of her own ego?
Has he chipped the shell of his own ego?
                                              'The Egoists'

It is easy to see Lawrence as the enemy. He is hard on women. He creates saints
and monsters as he sheds and fails to shed his Oedipal sicknesses, admitting,
denying, and re-admitting his mother's stranglehold, asking her to free him by
dying, then succumbing to the seductiveness of that last sacrifice. He criticises
and harangues women for coming too close, for being too personal, for wanting
to be loved, for having too much mind, for having too much cunt. He dis-
approves what he himself invents, in Miriam's intensities, in Pussum's mindlessness, in Hermione's will, in Helena's dreaming, in Gudrun's life-denying and
aggressive libertinism. He approves what he himself invents, in Ursula's life-
affirming sexual freedoms, in Kate's exalted relinquishing of her orgasm, in
Connie Chatterley's gratitude for hers, in the immolation of the Woman who
Rode Away. He yearns after touch and tenderness in male friendships but finds
Lesbianism repulsive. He allows Ursula and Harriet to criticise his *Salvator
Mundi* touch, but always gives himself the last word.

Even his appreciation of women is sometimes hard to take. Harry T. Moore
has recently published[1] two letters* written in 1913 when Lawrence and Frieda
were in Lerici, in which Lawrence says some startling things in the course of

attacking Richard Middleton, whose fears and sentimentality about women had been roused by the suffragettes:

> Frieda thinks they are stupid – Middleton's essays – particularly about women. I think myself he was stupid about women. It seems to me silly to rage against woman – as Sphinx, or Sphinx without a secret, or cunning artist in living – or in herself. It seems to me that the chief thing about a woman – who is much of a woman – is that in the long run she is not to be had. A man may bring her his laurel wreaths & songs & what not, but if that man doesn't satisfy her, in some undeniable physical fashion – then in one way or other she takes him in her mouth and shakes him like a cat a mouse, and throws him away. She is not to be caught by any of the catch-words, love, beauty, honor [sic], duty, worth, work, salvation – none of them – not in the long run. In the long run she only says 'Am I satisfied, or is there some beastly unsatisfaction gnawing and gnawing inside me.' And if there is some unsatisfaction, it is physical at least as much as psychic, sex as much as soul. So she goes for man, or men, after her own fashion, & so is called a Sphinx. . . .

He is using the figure of the woman as artist in a not altogether flattering fashion, the very comparison preserving art's province for men. Jessie Chambers and Helen Corke agreed that it was hard for him to accept mind in women, and there is plenty of crude anti-female and anti-feminist anger, spite, fear, and pity in his poems. He can be silly, as in 'These Clever Women':

> Now stop carping at me! Do you want me to hate you?
> Am I a kaleidoscope
> For you to shake and shake, and it won't come right?
> Am I doomed in a long coition of words to mate you?
> Unsatisfied! Is there no hope
> Between your thighs, far, far from your peering sight?

He can be more consciously amusing on the same subject, in 'Purple Anemones' where the idea of the anemones as 'husband-splendid, serpent heads' getting after Persephone and Ceres, 'those two enfranchised women', shows him exuberantly, cheaply and not uncharacteristically teetering on the verge of wit. There are some places where he even seems to appreciate feminism for its energy and passion, as in a series of verses in *Pansies* which shift from the rueful hope that a properly re-directed male energy might cure the 'modern Circe-dom', to a grudging recognition that women are the Lord's favourite vessels of wrath, usefully and alarmingly collecting the foreskins for Him. Occasionally he hits the right tone, amused, wary, mocking but not unappreciative:

> What has happened in the world?
> the women are like little volcanoes
> all more or less in eruption.

It is very unnerving, moving in a world of smouldering volcanoes.
It is rather agitating, sleeping with a little Vesuvius.
And exhausting, penetrating the lava-crater of a tiny Ixtaccihuatl
and never knowing when you'll provoke an earthquake.

In the other newly published letter[2] to Savage, Lawrence has this to say:
'I don't agree with you about our separation from women. The only thing that
is very separate – our bodies – is the via media for union again, if we would have
it so.' His phrases for such union in *Women in Love* are familiar: it is a 'freedom
together' and 'two single equal stars balanced in conjunction'. When Birkin
despairs of explaining his images to Ursula, he decides that talking is no good,
'it must happen beyond the sound of words. . . . This was a paradisal bird that
could never be netted, it must fly by itself to the heart.' His poetry is closer to
this soundlessness than his novels, being more sustainedly sensuous as it traces
the particulars of feeling without debate and analysis. Although it is not only
in the poetry that Lawrence denies the separation of men and women, it is
easier to begin with it. His early poems, *Look! We Have Come Through!*, and the
late collection, *More Pansies*, are not just to be negatively praised for admitting
that men and women are alike, but valued for their knowledge of sexual feeling.

Some of the poems in *More Pansies* shift from man to woman within poems
or within groups of poems. One pair of poems, 'The Gods! The Gods!' and
'Name the Gods!' balances the image of a god in a women's body and a man's,
the woman showing 'the glimmer of the presence of the gods . . . like lilies' as
she washes, the mower revealing the god not in his own body but in the 'falling
flatness' of the wheat, 'the pale-gold flesh of Priapus dropping asleep'. This
turning from man to woman or woman to man is a marked two-beat rhythm.
Many of these poems show an insistent self-consciousness about the well known
deficiency in our language, its lack of an equivalent of the German *Mensch*,
which lacks the ambiguity and condescension of *Man* and the flatness of *person*.
Particularly in the late poems, Lawrence will use 'person' as he will use 'creatures' or 'individuals' or 'people'. He often uses 'Man' all-embracingly, but
its possible condescensions are obliterated, if we read the poems as we should, as
they flow and grow into each other, by the rhythm which turns from the man
to the woman, separating in order to join in common experience: 'man or
woman', 'man and woman', most men, most women', 'no man knows, no
woman knows', 'a fellow-man or fellow-woman' 'men and women', 'when
most men die, today/when most women die', 'living women and men', 'it is no
woman, it is no man'.

In 'The Cross' he remakes that image which was ironically and aggressively
phallic in 'Last Words to Miriam', proclaiming the frailty of the sexual dis-

tinction, and merging it in that 'man' which must be more urgently distinguished from the robot:

> Behold your Cross, Christians!
> With the upright division into sex
> men on this side, women on that side
> without any division into inferiority and superiority
> only differences,
> divided in the mystic, tangible and intangible difference.
>
> And then, truth much more bitter to accept,
> the horizontal division of mankind
> into that which is below the level, and that which is above. . . .
>
> That which is truly man, and that which is robot,
> the ego-bound.

The lustrous noon in 'Andraitx-Pomegranate Flowers' reveals' a man, a woman there'. The pulsing content of 'The Heart of Man' is shut off from both sexes, 'no man knows, no woman knows'. The naked 'I' of 'Moral Clothing' approaches a 'fellow-man or a fellow-woman' who must be naked too. When Lawrence attacked and decided to give up what he called 'image-making love' it was because he had spent his life fixing and then unfixing sexual images. But certain natural and social truths forced him to see men and women as persons and not as men and women. The second letter to Savage[3] declares that 'Sex is the fountain head, where life bubbles up into the person from the unknown . . .'. The word 'person' is a vital one.

Never trust the artist, trust the tale. And since tales create certain fixities of ego and action that poetry can avoid, never trust the tale, trust the poem. Amongst the persuasive and not quite persuasive indictments of Elisco Vivas's *D. H. Lawrence*: the *failure and triumph of art* (Northwestern University Press, Evanston, 1960), is the suggestion that Lawrence's concern was with eros, and the loss of self through sex, as distinct from agape, and its loss of self in generous outgoing. Vivas is confident that Lawrence admits the reflexiveness of eros, and quotes an example from Ursula and Skrebensky's lovemaking in *The Rainbow*, which leaves each lover with the sense of maximal vitality, from which he concludes that self-knowledge is all Lawrence thought we gained from eros. There is some danger in relying on the far from beneficent relation of these lovers, who went a fair way in mutual destruction, seeming to suggest the limits and threats of pure self-possession through sex, a point which I'd have thought he was making again through Gudrun and Gerald in *Women in Love*. But it is difficult to argue briefly about the novels, and all I can do here is to suggest that Vivas could not have come to this conclusion so easily had he also been working with the poems. It is knowledge that bubbles through the unknown, in sex, and the poetry of *Look! We Have Come Through!* seems to invoke a more companionable eros than that of Ursula and Skrebensky, a loving which is a mode of other-knowledge as well as self-knowledge, while admittedly being rather less heroic than agape.

Look! We Have Come Through! has a title which announces the theme of a sexual and a moral triumph. Its 'We' is the 'We' of lovers sufficiently freed by love from anxiety, fear, and bewilderment, to make a passionate analysis of passionate love. (Lawrence shied away from the word 'love', but it seems simplest to stick to it.) One convention of love-poetry and love which he questions in these poems is the lover's praise of the beloved's beauty, and this radical questioning is made as part of his argument about liberation, for man and woman. Birkin's declared lack of interest in Ursula's good looks in *Women in Love* is of course part of the general re-definition of love argued there, but the protest against aesthetic appreciation in sex is most sensitively and lucidly found in the poems. 'She Said As Well To Me' begins with the woman's praise of the man's body, and sets against it the man's protest against her appreciation. He objects not just because aesthetic celebration is shallow (as of course it often is) but because her compliments hold sinister suggestions of instrumentality, thanks for services excellently rendered to her ego. She argues, in a way which manages to be both superficial and overpoweringly rapturous, that lovers should be free to gaze, admire, and show each other their naked beauty, but as she tries to talk him out of what she calls the typical male timidity, she does rather dwell on function. It is certainly not surprising that the man begins 'to wonder', and decides that what she says doesn't make him free but 'trammelled and hurt'. His defence is made through images of animal freedom very like those in *Birds, Beasts and Flowers*, the poems which try to do for animals what he wants her to do for him, to respect the individuality of others, and to hesitate before its strength and privacy. But such respect depends on some knowledge of the other, and is not reflexive. In all this, the *noli me tangere* felt but given up in *The Man Who Died* is not by any means shown as a matter of male feeling only. The woman in the poem generalises, matronisingly – 'Men are the shyest creatures, they never will come out of their covers' – but the images that answer and defy her are both male and female:

> Now I say to her: 'No tool, no instrument, no God!
> Don't touch and appreciate me.
> It is an infamy.
> You would think twice before you touched a weasel on a fence

94

as it lifts its straight white throat.
Your hand would not be so flig and easy.
Nor the adder we saw asleep with her head on her shoulder,
curled up in the sunshine like a princess;
when she lifted her head in delicate, startled wonder
you did not stretch forward to caress her
though she looked rarely beautiful
and a miracle as she glided delicately away, with such dignity.
And the young bull in the field, with his wrinkled, sad face,
you are afraid if he rises to his feet . . . .'

It is easy to argue that Lawrence's rejection of intimate praise and fondness comes from his Oedipal wound and produces his dangerous fascination with violence. It is easy to see the retreat from Miriam's intensities, as Jessie Chambers herself saw it, only as a fiction made in order to strengthen his mother's image. I think it is also necessary to see that such rejection of praise and appreciation beats a wise retreat from that instrumentality familiar to lovers and to artists. It was not only a response which Lawrence had to the intrusiveness of loving women, but a temptation he may have felt for himself as an artist. It was certainly one which he sometimes did and sometimes didn't resist.

The rejections and the appreciations in *The White Peacock* and *Sons and Lovers* are clearly made in the interests of defining the man; they help to show and analyse George Saxton's degeneration and Paul Morel's coming of age. Helen Corke, always unstridently alert to Lawrence's use of women, says as much in her brief essay on *The White Peacock*: 'These women are fully drawn, but Lawrence is not interested in them as individuals. He sees them only in relation to their men. "Take," he would seem to say to his reader, "a male creature! We shall now study its reactions to these various forms of feminine stimuli." '⁴ Her essay ends with the image of Erda, whose single concern is with the race, who cuts away the psyche 'so that the reproductive physical self cannot develop individually, and the woman, in motherhood, is absorbed into the lives of her children . . . sister to the servant of the One Talent'. Helen Corke seemed to Lawrence to be the defiantly dreaming and thinking woman who could resist him, and in what she calls the 'deferred conversation' in *Lawrence's Apocalypse*, she accuses him of too simply and crudely separating masculine and feminine extremities of what she saw as a spectrum of sexuality. There are occasions in both letters and fiction, when Lawrence seems to reduce the individual woman to an outline, a type, or a complex convenience, but it is essential to recognise that such reductions are not confined to his portraits of women.

There is the denigration of his father in *Sons and Lovers*, of Bertrand Russell and Middleton Murry in *Women in Love*, not to mention the reductions of Sir

Clifford Chatterley. Moreover, even where Lawrence's women present tendentious types or images, their needs and passions often turn out to derive from his own intimate experience and fantasies. Although in 'The Woman Who Rode Away' Lawrence chose a woman as an appropriate victim of *ennui*, wildness and masochistic sacrifice, there is no doubt that the feelings and values of his immolated heroine lay within his own experience. In his finest volume, 'The Ship of Death', the poems most fluidly and shiftingly create their repetitions, modulations, and permutations on the themes of death and rebirth, and we see that the crude lines of the brutal little fable have an intimate connection with Lawrence's imaginative experience of dying, dying away from deadly society, from human attachments, from a sick body. Where he seems most chauvinistic he is probably most personal. Anyone who can see 'The Woman Who Rode Away' simply as a man's sadistic immolation of woman cannot have looked properly at 'The Ship of Death', or, for that matter, compared Lawrence with de Sade.

Lawrence, like other artists, lapses into crudity when he is refusing to work with sufficient imaginative energy and thought. The allegorical modes and moments in his fiction are often reductions of human complexity which place male and female in opposition to each other instead of showing them as human beings engaged in similar struggles with class, sex, education, work, art, and mortality. But Lawrence's allegory is sometimes subtler than it appears, and we should always be very wary of accepting his characters' instant interpretations. In the 'Mino' chapter in *Women in Love*, for instance, Birkin takes Ursula through his revised syllabus of love by using the demonstration-model of male and female cats. As the female cat waits submissively, cuffed and longing, Ursula tells the cat that he is 'a bully like all males', an observation which seems especially abstract and unfair if we remember her beaked passion and hostility at the end of *The Rainbow*. (The abstraction and unfairness is of course not hers but her author's.) The Ursula of *Women in Love* has more Frieda and less Lawrence in her than the Ursula of *The Rainbow*, and so needs the lecture:

'No,' said Birkin, 'he is justified. He is not a bully. He is only insisting to the poor stray that she shall acknowledge him as a sort of fate, her own fate: because you can see she is fluffy and promiscuous as the wind. I am with him entirely. He wants superfine stability.'

'Yes, I know!' cried Ursula. 'He wants his own way – I know what your fine words work down to – bossiness, I call it, bossiness.'

The young cat again glanced at Birkin in disdain of the noisy woman.

'I quite agree with you, Miciotto,' said Birkin to the cat. 'Keep your male dignity, and your higher understanding.'

And he goes on provoking Ursula's fury about 'this assumption of male superiority'. It is worth observing, however, that Birkin, despite his ironical looks and laughs, is actually not talking about male superiority but about stability, strays, and wildness. It is equally true that Ursula's impetuous attack is created by superiority, whether it had its origin in Frieda Lawrence's jeers, as seems likely, or not. (The cat, incidentally, looks at Birkin with a look of 'pure superiority'.) Birkin insists that what the cats represent is not Gerald's bullying of the mare, the 'Wille zur Macht', but 'The desire to bring this female cat into a pure stable equilibrium, a transcendent and abiding *rapport* with the single male' because without him 'she is a mere stray, a fluffy sporadic bit of chaos'. It is essential to see the she-cat as a stray, though I wouldn't suggest that Lawrence presents the debate very ingratiatingly, especially for women readers. It suggests the need for permanence, not the need to be knocked into shape by the male.

The conjunction of stars and the fluffy bit of chaos recur in *Look! We Have Come Through!*, not surprisingly, since the early stages of Lawrence's struggles and successes with Frieda are told both in *Women in Love* and in these early unrhymed poems. The fluidity of poetry, and of this free verse in particular, has its advantage over the fixities of the prose fiction. Its dialectic is more shifting, its impersonations less hard, its moods less tethered to history and personality. In addition, irony and comedy are happily absent, for Lawrence is not at his best in either. *Women in Love* is of course a novel which refuses to be linear. It resembles poetry in its reliance on lyrical and symbolic statement, but it still has the novel's characteristic continuity. When Birkin gives up a mood or a thought in exhaustion, irony or bewilderment, it is still registered in continuous and causal patterns, whereas the poems dealing with similar ideas and feelings jump without link or explanation from one mood to another. One result of this discontinuity seems to be a greater freedom from male and female stereotypes. In the fiction, even imagery may be attached to character and therefore to gender. In the poetry, the emphasis can be placed on states of mind and passion.

Sometimes, of course, the poetry simply fills out the novel's outline. When Lawrence retreats from the woman's gratified praise of his body's fineness and function, we see precisely what he meant by that subservience to the ego of which he accuses Ursula in *Women in Love*. The poetry is fuller of feeling and is thus more lucid than the novel, with its commitments to history, debate, and character. The risen Christ's *noli me tangere* and Birkin's stoning of the reflections of Aphrodite are explained in the poems, which ruminate lengthily on the retreat into solitude, on the sense of independence and separateness, and on the conjunction of the separate persons. This poetry is about persons rather than about men and women, or man and woman. It is true to those feelings which are common to both (or all) the sexes, and proves what the novels asserted and dropped. It is the poetry, not the fiction, which really destroys the old ego of sexual difference. What the novel does is to show the attempt to break, and its difficulty.

'Song Of A Man Who Is Loved' may at a glance look like the ineffaceable mother's image, but it develops a particularity, physical and emotional, which makes it larger and newer. The lover is secured by permanence and conjunction from the surrounding space, hardness, and chaos. Here is a guarantee of rest and peace:

> So I hope I shall spend eternity
> With my face down buried between her breasts;
> With my still heart full of security,
> And my still hands full of her breasts.

The abstract concepts of security and permanence take on the definite forms of solid bone and its soft covering, both needed, bone for a lasting support, flesh for something softer than the world outside. That world's hardness and evasiveness are both present, too, in sensation and sound:

> Having known the world so long, I have never confessed
> How it impresses me, how hard and compressed
> Rocks seem, and earth, and air uneasy, and waters still ebbing west.

But the hard things are human, as well as natural, including 'Assertions! Assertions! stones, women and men!' Lawrence's unpleasant qualities, his hating and his superiority, allow him to sound aggressive about human beings as well as assertions and stones, but his more endearing need for stability links him with Ursula and the stray cat. He is not simply a provider of peace, he knows chaos too, and it is a chaos sensuously realized as it never was in the debates and arguments of the novel:

> And the chaos that bounces and rattles like shrapnel, at least
> Has for me a door into peace, warm dawn in the east
> Where her bosom softens towards me, and the turmoil has ceased.

When conjunction has happened, the gains can be demonstrated by man or woman. The knowledge cannot be simply reflexive. The man uses for himself the image of chaos and in 'One Woman To All Women' lets her use his star symbol, the 'other beauty, the way of the stars', which is also now, as Coleridge might say, attached to the reality it represents, being brought into the sensuous area of sexual rhythm, motion, and propulsion:

Love and Friendship

Frieda Weekley with her son in 1901. 'She's got a figure like a fine Rubens woman, but her face is almost Greek. If you say a word about her, I hate you.' (Letter to Edward Garnett, 2 June 1912)

Right Baron Friedrich von Richtofen, Frieda's father. 'They are a rare family – father a fierce old aristocrat – mother utterly non-moral, very kind. You should know them.' (Undated letter to Edward Garnett, *c.* May 1912)

Below Frieda with her husband, Ernest Weekley and her parents-in-law. 'To live, one must hurt people so.' (Undated letter to David Garnett, *c.* May 1912)

Long Row, Nottingham.

Katherine Mansfield, *above, left,* and her husband, John Middleton Murry, had an enduring, if violent friendship with the Lawrences. 'We are co-believers first. And in our oneness of belief lies our oneness,' Lawrence wrote to them after a quarrel on 24 February 1916.

Above, right Lady Cynthia Asquith. 'I dreamed last night, before your post card came, that I was at some party or other of yours – and that you had other people there, most desolating outsiders. I couldn't describe to you the feeling of almost sordid desolateness caused by the established presence of those other people of yours, who are outsiders.' (Letter to Lady Cynthia Asquith, 25 March 1916)

Above, left Rupert Brooke. 'He was slain by bright Phoebus's shaft – it was in keeping with his general sunniness – it was the real climax of his pose. . . . Oh God, oh God, it is all too much of a piece: it is like madness.' (Letter to Lady Ottoline Morrell, 30 April 1915)

Above right Ezra Pound admired Lawrence's poetry and published some of his poems in his magazine but Lawrence felt that 'the Hueffer-Pound faction seems inclined to lead me around a little as one of their show-dogs'. (Letter to Edward Garnett, 30 December 1913)

Left Drawing by Lawrence of David Garnett, son of his friend Edward Garnett. Lawrence was very fond of the whole family and wrote to Edward: 'You Garnetts are like the spoons in a hell-broth of tragedy – you stir and stir.' (3 March 1913)

Viola Meynell, a member of 'the formidable and poetic
Meynell family', was one of Lawrence's earliest supporters.
It was she who typed the manuscript of *The Rainbow*

'I have finished my *Rainbow*, bended it and set it firm. Now off and away to
find the pots of gold at its feet,' Lawrence wrote to Viola Meynell on 2 March 1915,
enclosing this sketch of Eastwood under the rainbow.

Above, top The school at Cossal. 'When Anna was nine years old, Brangwen sent her to the dame's school at Cossethay.' (*The Rainbow*)

Above Lambclose House, Moorgreen (Highclose in *The White Peacock* and Shortlands in *Women in Love*), 'a long, low old house, a sort of manor farm, that spread along the top of a slope just beyond the narrow little lake of Willey Water . . .' (*Women in Love*)

Above, top The cottage at Greatham, Sussex, where the Lawrences spent a few months in 1915. 'Viola Meynell has lent us this rather beautiful cottage. We are quite alone. It is at the foot of the Downs.' (Letter to Lady Cynthia Asquith, 10 January 1915)

Above The Vale of Health, Hampstead, from which Lawrence wrote in 1915: 'This is the real winter of the spirit in England.' (Letter to Harriet Monroe, 18 September 1915)

Above, left Bertrand Russell. 'What ails Russell is, in matters of life and emotion, the inexperience of youth. He is vitally, emotionally, much too inexperienced in personal contact and conflict, for a man of his caliber. Tell him he is not to write lachrymose letters to me of disillusion and disappointment and age . . .' (Letter to Lady Ottoline Morrell, 1 February 1915)

Above, right Lady Ottoline Morrell at Garsington Manor. 'I want you to form the nucleus of a new community which shall start a new life amongst us – a life in which the only riches is integrity of character.' (Letters to Lady Ottoline Morrell, 1 February 1915)

The Red Room at Garsington Manor. 'Garsington must be the retreat where we come together and knit ourselves together. Garsington is wonderful for that. It is like the Boccaccio place where they told all the Decamerone.' (Undated letter to Lady Ottoline Morrell, *c.* June 1915)

Higher Tregarthen, Cornwall, where the Lawrences lived from March 1914 to October 1917. 'I told you all about the house: the great grey granite boulders, you will love them, the rough primeval hill behind us, the sea beyond the few fields that have great boulders half submerged in the grass, and stone-grey walls.' (Undated letter to Katherine Mansfield, spring 1916)

Opposite Lady Ottoline Morrell. 'Why don't you have the pride of your own intrinsic self? . . . Primarily you belong to a special type, a special race of women: like Cassandra in Greece, and some of the great woman saints.' (Undated letter to Lady Ottoline Morrell, spring 1915)

Above, top Mountain Cottage, Middleton, where the Lawrences lived in 1918–9. 'We are here feeling very lost and queer and exiled. The place is beautiful, but one feels like Ovid in Thrace . . .' (Letter to Lady Cynthia Asquith, 7 May 1918)

Above A picnic at Mountain Cottage, Middleton, with W. E. Hopkin in the centre, and Lawrence and Frieda on the extreme left. 'It was so jolly when we were all together. And it is the human contact which means so much to one, really.' (Letter to Mrs S. A. Hopkin, 26 June 1918)

If you knew how I swerve in peace, in the equipoise
With the man, if you knew how my flesh enjoys
The swinging bliss no shattering ever destroys.

Admittedly, the last splendid line which brings the cosmos into the lovers' bed, is diminished by the refrain and title of the poem, 'You other women'. The ultimate boast and gratification can seem (immediately) rather pettily feminine and (ultimately) pettily masculine, though the poem is concerned to dismiss conventional beauty, and its rejections of cosmetic and narcissistic devices conveniently express the ego-binding of aesthetic vanities, and perhaps excuse the unattractive competitiveness.

In one of the best poems in the volume, 'New Heaven and Earth' there is a refusal to differentiate, a nervous-seeming but ultimately confident glancing from what seems a man's experience to what is felt also as a woman's. The song becomes that of a human being who is loved. Lawrence's usual way is to impersonate the woman or to speak as the man, but here he shifts from the one to the other, as he does again, momentarily, in 'Both Sides of the Medal' where he insists and shows that she has a passion for him as he has for her. 'New Heaven and Earth' is a poem which most clearly deals with the proof of sexual knowledge, with the knowledge of self, of otherness, of newness, of strangeness. It creates an exotic sexual landscape which achieves something less frequently found in Lawrence than in Donne, the sweet and violent jolt through a conceit into fresh experience, the shock given to mind through senses, here creating and re-creating the twinned delights of finding the self in finding the other human creature:

> I am thrown upon the shore.
> I am covering myself with the sand.
> I am filling my mouth with the earth.
> I am burrowing my body into the soil.
> The unknown, the new world!

This landing of the desperate castaway is followed by the sudden shock of translation. The man and his reader are grounded, in a new impact:

> It was the flank of my wife
> I touched with my hand, I clutched with my hand
> rising, new-awakened from the tomb!
> It was the flank of my wife
> whom I married years ago
> at whose side I have lain for over a thousand nights
> and all that previous while, she was I, she was I;
> I touched her, it was I who touched and I who was touched.

Lawrence does better here than in *Women in Love* with the sense of eternal *rapport*. His image of the past is in several senses more solidly persuasive than the novel's statements about the future, in a new version of the traditions of amorous pre-knowledge and eureka-feeling. The woman's flank is the strand of the new world:

> White sand and fruits unknown and perfumes that never
> can blow across the dark seas to our usual world!
> And land that beats with a pulse!
> And valleys that draw close in love!
> And strange ways where I fall into oblivion of uttermost living! –
> Also she who is the other has strange-mounded breasts and
> strange sheer slopes, and white levels.

The erotic and exotic geography works brilliantly: whiteness, curves, scents, and foreigness belonging plainly to the human body and the new world, beating pulse and closing valleys transferring an amorous life to the land, and making it more extraordinary and intense. The rapturous poem – perhaps the most Whitman-like of Lawrence's poems – delights in conjunction, separateness, and joy, with vividness which shows what the novel's debate is about.

It shows this more intricately than I have suggested, because it begins with a sense of self-nausea, itself related to the various hatefulnesses of war, the tomb, and imprisonment in self. We move to that sense of rapturous landing from an unpleasantly striking image of a man making love to himself, and of a loathsome hermaphroditic fruitfulness, 'begetting and conceiving in my own body'. The slopes are breasts, the valleys close in, the images belong to female physiology, but Lawrence can also force a sharing of the image which makes even clearer the common experience of sex, for both man and woman, as he does in 'Wedlock' which uses more obvious domestic distinctions, to make the same point about common experience. It starts with the sense of the man protecting the woman, wrapping her round, but almost immediately refuses to preserve the vital and phallic images for himself:

> Do you feel me wrap you
> Up with myself and my warmth, like a flame round the wick?
>
> And how I am not at all, except a flame that mounts off you.
> Where I touch you, I flame into being; – but is it me, or you?

The imagery of flame ceases to be phallic, passes from the obviously male candle and wick to something larger and less differentiated, 'a bonfire of oneness, my flame I flung leaping round you/You the core of the flame, crept into me'. The image is shared, like the passion. The poem stretches to take in both lovers, itself an act of love.

The outlines, actions, arguments of the novels are not only blurred but self-consciously blurred in the poetry. In 'Wedlock' Lawrence wonders what will come of their love,

> Children, acts, utterance,
> Perhaps only happiness.

and this is most precisely true, the question given poignancy by our knowledge of the final answer; only acts and utterance did come of it. The utterance comes most literally from the experience of conjunction and of discovery. Lawrence's straining and blaming in *Sons and Lovers*, his instrumental use of the women's characters in *The White Peacock*, and his re-interpretation of Helen Corke's story for *The Trespasser*, all pre-date *The Rainbow* and *Women in Love*, which argue, if less sensuously and fluidly than the poetry, the sense of freedom in the erotic break with the ego. Lawrence's eros makes no claims to generosity, let alone renunciation, but in its claim for discovery through respect for itself, and respect for other life, it seems to have some affinity with agape, after all. It is certainly a love that rejects the sacrificial nature of Christian agape. Indeed, that is what *The Man Who Died* is about, but although Christ/Osiris has to leave Isis to bear her child alone, the story of two restored and separate people is scarcely a simply erotic fable of a transient therapy. The Preface to *Look! We Have Come Through!* is argued almost entirely in sexual imagery (spasms, plasm, nudity, jetting, Aphrodite, rose) and the benefits it claims for the freedom of free verse were perhaps qualities erotically learnt, a fluidity, a momentariness, a resting in the present. This poetry is the utterance created by sexual conjunction; it is a release into the present, an ability to accept flux and resist stereotype, a respect of imaginative recognition for the other creature. Free verse most fully and warmly dramatised Lawrence's sense of union and individuality, and in so doing paid its debt to the attachment which created its pulse, flow, and motion.

Of course Lawrence did not always succeed in writing from and to the moment, and it would be peculiarly stupid to claim for him a permanent realisation of freedom, joy, and conjunction. He was not able to maintain a freedom from the sense of sexual difference. Lawrence's late phase included not only *Lady Chatterley's Lover*, where both book and title at last make room for the human couple, (though at a certain expense, in the refusal to imagine Clifford) but 'The Ship of Death', where he finds the final version of the new voyage, the new country, the new solitude, and the new discovery, not in any form of love, but in death.

Lawrence's sense of human liberation is realized when he forgets the 'he and she', in a way undreamed of by Donne. This is most fully achieved in the poems, but even in the constraints of the prose fiction there emerges some sense that women and men share the same struggle. The woman in *The Woman Who Rode Away* is, as a woman, the best equipped human being for submission and sacrifice, society having after all freely encouraged female masochism. The women at the beginning of *The Rainbow* not surprisingly resemble their sisters (and contemporaries) in the novels of George Eliot, who also look ahead into history and out into the public world. The Brangwen women look because they have windows to look through, children to plan for, the doctors and parsons to talk to, while the men of the agricultural community work with the animals in the fields behind. Ursula, like Dorothea Brooke, Isabel Archer, Little Dorrit, and Tess, is an appropriately female image of Victorian aspiration. Lawrence couldn't sympathise with the suffragettes, but he could sympathise with Ursula's attempt at liberation, permitting her to do such modern things as reject her college education for its irrelevance, choose and use the wrong lover and leave him, become pregnant and have a symbolic and convenient miscarriage.[5] Some of which things the Victorian heroines were not free to try. But Ursula, like Dorothea and Dorrit, rebels and protests against social limits which are oppressive to the woman but also oppressive to the man. Just as George Eliot moved from Maggie to Tom, from Dorothea to Lydgate, to show not only the woman's limitations but the man's, to achieve not only a feminist plea but also a human one, just as Hardy moved from Jude to Sue, so Lawrence moves from Ursula to Birkin. I would not want to exaggerate the success of his analysis. George Eliot, a woman who had to put on the indignity of a male name, for reasons both sexual and literary, and Thomas Hardy, least chauvinist of all nineteenth-century male English writers except Meredith, were capable of achieving and maintaining a balance between the plight of man and woman. But when Lawrence moved on that hinge between *The Rainbow* and *Women in Love*, his heroine became more orthodox, less introspective, forgot some of her past, changed to become more conventionally in need of an education from the man.

At the beginning of *Women in Love* Ursula and Gudrun are not making a narrowly female plea when they question marriage and the family. In the episode of the chair, both Ursula and Birkin are together, man and woman, in rejecting the furniture and fittings of family life, despite their will to permanence. Their atypical freedom has of course been observed by several critics, including Leavis and Vivas, as coming straight from Lawrence's own situation. Only in *Lady Chatterley*, did he fully admit that the problem of sexual freedom and fulfilment was bound up with property, family, households, and children. Only Connie is actually allowed the urge to conceive, perhaps as a belated reflection of Frieda's maternity. She is to have a child as well as acts and utterance, though off stage. Lawrence 'neglects' the family, perhaps because his marriage was sterile, perhaps because his attachment to his mother had been almost sterilising, perhaps because it is the man, rather than the woman, who occupies the centre of the novel. The result is that he often pays man and woman the compliment of valuing them as particular persons, not as parents and ancestors.

Lawrence set the human couple together at the end of *Lady Chatterley's Lover* in an abstract social world, almost as far removed from the average daily life as the Mexico of *The Plumed Serpent* or the Australia of *Kangaroo*. But throughout the novels there are moments when the human being can be set in her environment, to represent not only a woman's life, but something larger. In *Sons and Lovers*, where the women are subordinate to the picture of the man's development and growing-up, there is the remarkable social detail of the scene in Clara's house when Paul Morel finds her and her mother at their lace-making:

That was a little, darkish room too, but it was smothered in white lace. The mother had seated herself again by the cupboard, and was drawing thread from a vast web of lace. A clump of fluff and ravelled cotton was at her right hand, a heap of three-quarter-inch lace lay on her left, whilst in front of her was the mountain of lace web, piling the hearthrug. Threads of curly cotton, pulled out from between the lengths of lace, strewed over the fender and the fireplace. Paul dared not go forward, for fear of treading on piles of white stuff.

On the table was a jenny for carding the lace. There was a pack of brown cardboard squares, a pack of cards of lace, a little box of pins, and on the sofa lay a heap of drawn lace.

The room was all lace, and it was so dark and warm that the white, snowy stuff seemed the more distinct.

'If you're coming in you won't have to mind the work,' said Mrs. Radford. 'I know we're about blocked up. But sit you down.'

. . . .

Clara began to work. Her jenny spun with a subdued buzz; the white lace hopped from between her fingers on to the card. It was filled; she snipped off the length, and pinned the end down to the banded lace. Then she put a new card in her jenny. Paul watched her. She sat square and magnificent. Her throat and arms were bare. The blood still mantled below her ears; she bent her head in shame of her humility. Her face was set on her work.

. . . .

Clara broke in, and he told her his message. She spoke humbly to him. He had surprised her in her drudgery. To have her humble made him feel as if he were lifting his head in expectation.

'Do you like jennying?' he asked.

'What can a woman do!' she replied bitterly.

'Is it sweated?'

'More or less. Isn't *all* woman's work? That's another trick the men have played, since we force ourselves into the labour market.'

'Now then, you shut up about the men,' said her mother. 'If the women wasn't fools, the men wouldn't be bad uns, that's what I say. No man was ever that bad wi' me but what he got it back again. Not but what they're a lousy lot, there's no denying it.'

'But they're all right really, aren't they?' he asked.

'Well, they're a bit different from women,' she answered.

Clara is a suffragette, and Lawrence (and Paul) eventually pack her off again to crude old Baxter Dawes, thus settling that bit of Paul's *Bildung*. But to say that, even though it is quite true, ignores the powerful life of those scenes where full weight is given to sensuous and emotional truth, where the tale can be trusted. We see precisely why she was a feminist, perhaps also, a little, why she could go back to her bad marriage, liberated as she is into the imprisoning world of work. The white lace smothers and blocks the room. Humiliations of labour blend with humiliations of sex. It is the men who sweat the women, it is an employer and a lover who watches: 'her throat and arms were bare. . . . She bent her head in shame of her humility. . . . To have her humble made him feel as if he were lifting his head in expectation'. Here are traces of that peculiar Victorian perversion, the gentleman's excitement at the woman's hard drudgery, discussed most candidly in *Munby*[6], most romantically in Clough's *The Bothie*. But it is a moment which doesn't belong only to a problem of women, but links with the whole world of work.

Paul Morel felt the humiliation of the factory too, though Lawrence toned down some of the more brutal aspects of his own experience. The miners are smothered and blocked also. Lawrence had a clear understanding of the tedium and brutality of industrial work, for men and women, and when we think of his own domestic zest for washing up saucepans or laying tables, with care and creativity, we should remember that it was a free and chosen work that he delighted in. He is quick to seize what joy there is, even in the mines, and does so in Morel's marvellous stories, which have their part to play in casting that fatal and transient glamour over Gertrude Morel. He also realized, or at least showed, that woman had to get into the world of work, that the domestic drudgery of Miriam's mother had no zest, was all grind and service, and that Miriam was desperate to learn, to move up and move on. In her story too, for all its distortions, we see the most explicable moments of humility as she struggles to enter the desired and difficult world of learning. Her desires are Mrs Morel's for her sons, Paul's for himself. In the world of work some escape into the rare creative chance, others are imprisoned by the routines of the inhuman machine Lawrence was to indict, fight, and escape. The pressures of that world form the most striking part of Lawrence's argument against industry and science, and as he shows them in action, as he remembers and imagines, he sees the continuity of human feeling. It flows through love and labour, links men and women, calls on their energy and sometimes defeats it.

Lawrence never faced the question of the identity of man and woman's political predicament, except perhaps intuitively, but he recorded their common struggle to survive in the industrial world. Even a novel which uses women as instruments in the male artist's *Bildung* has moments which show the woman, like men, as human beings, individuals, persons.

D. H. Lawrence's
Doctrine
John Carey

'Doctrine' seems too anaemic a word for Lawrence. He professed to distrust thought, and said that ideas were the dead leaves thrown off from a living tree. They formed an insentient husk between man and the universe. 'All the best part of knowledge,' he maintained, 'is inconceivable', and consequently rational folk are unintelligent or warped. 'All scientists are liars.' Psychology he regarded as a particularly obnoxious lie, for it pretended to deal with live people but its nasty thin reasonings made the world 'a world of corpses'. It was indecent of psychologists, armed with their bare reason, to prod at other people's deepest motives. Freudian psychoanalysis showed, Lawrence felt, a 'poisoned hatred of sex', and psychological writers, at work on their characters' personalities, seemed 'to be fingering with the mind the secret places and sources of the blood'. It was irreverent, as well as false. Ibsen and Strindberg displayed this 'intolerable nastiness' at its worst, but English novelists, especially the females, were as futile if less loathsome. The parish nurse's gossip in *Lady Chatterley* is said to be 'Mrs Gaskell and George Eliot and Miss Mitford all rolled into one'. Writing clever accounts of motive and personality is a fit pastime for Clifford Chatterley in his mechanical wheelchair.

But Lawrence, if he disclaimed thought, had a set of passions and hatreds that he turned into beliefs, and his desire to impose these on others makes 'doctrine' an aptly pedagogic title. 'Blood' was the word he adopted for the departments of human activity which he approved of. 'My great religion is a belief in the blood, the flesh, as being wiser than the intellect.' Education he felt to be cold, cerebral, useless. Ursula Brangwen, in *The Rainbow*, rightly finds school lessons bewildering and trivial, except 'once when, with her blood, she heard a passage of Latin, and she knew how the blood beat in the Roman's body'. Justice, too, becomes cold if the judge uses his brain. Blood and instinct are surer guides,

Lawrence believed. Encountering at Messina an old convict whose face displeased him, he remarked:

It is a great mistake to abolish the death penalty. If I were dictator, I should order the old one to be hanged at once. I should have judges with sensitive, living hearts: not abstract intellects. And because the instinctive heart recognized a man as evil, I would have that man destroyed. Quickly.

Between men and women, in Lawrence's view, 'blood contact', not mental communion, was requisite. The opinions and personality of one's partner were utterly insignificant. A woman whose intellectual interests coincided with her husband's was 'almost sure' to be the wrong mate for him. Ideally the man should be a voiceless column of blood, having renounced 'the weary habit of talking and having feelings'. Humans should learn to make 'weird, wordless cries, like animals'. Not surprisingly, attempts to portray blood contact in words sometimes perplex. Ursula, seated beside Birkin in a car, is said to experience 'full mystic knowledge of his suave loins of darkness'. But elsewhere Lawrence can vividly convey this sense of a person's animal intensity. Cipriano, in *The Plumed Serpent* makes 'the air around him seem darker', simply by standing still; and Lydia Lensky stands in her black coat 'like a silence'. In *The Fox*, Henry talks to March 'as if he were producing his voice in her blood'.

Sight, like thought, is ultimately an irrelevance to Lawrence: a distraction from the 'vast, phallic sacred darkness' in which blood contact occurs. He stigmatized making love in the daylight as 'an evil thing'. The cinema was 'an impertinent curiosity'. If only we could be struck blind, he said in a letter, 'we should find reality in the darkness'. Maurice, in 'The Blind Man', illustrates this notion. His wife, jumpy from education and book-reviewing, hates going into the stables, but he tends the hot horses with sensual power and confidence, though he cannot see. The drugged victim in 'The Woman Who Rode Away' also comes to apprehend at a profounder level than the visual. She *hears* the womb of her pet bitch conceive, and the earth going round like 'an immense arrowstring booming'. This eclipse of sight, like Lawrence's anti-intellectualism, is traditionally Romantic. Wordsworth, similarly impatient of 'sages', had sensed the movement of the earth as he skated on Windermere, and 'felt' landscapes 'in the blood'. Hearing and touch are both 'deeper' senses than sight in Lawrence's scheme, further removed from the shallow world where people speak and think. This may seem strange in a writer who reacts to the seen so rapturously, but his apparently visual descriptions, like Keats', often escape the eye's confines. The bright orange crocuses in 'Flowering Tuscany', for instance, are heard and felt as much as seen: 'you feel the sound of their radiance'. Touch becomes almost sacramental. Mellors rubs his face over Connie's body, giving and receiving the 'warm live beauty of contact, so much deeper than the beauty of vision'. 'You Touched Me' is a strange tale about a fastidious, cultivated lady forced to marry an ex-charity-school boy simply because, when he is staying in the house, she wanders into his bedroom one night and touches his face, mistaking him for her father. Her blood, it is implied, has with a will of its own crossed the frontiers of class and education and claimed its destined spouse.

Because Lawrence venerated touch it should not be assumed that he was happy about the tactile endearments normally exchanged by lovers. These seemed to him low and undignified. He was puritanically repelled by 'cuddling and petting', and complained that nowadays 'there is plenty of pawing and laying hold, but no real touch'. Real touch, which he located among the figures in Etruscan wall paintings, was not a contact of surfaces but a 'soft flow', coming 'from the middle of the human being'. It issued from the blood, not the calculating faculty, and was not amorous in any vulgar sense. Perhaps it was to avoid the unrefined associations of touch that Lawrence developed a way of talking about 'deep' human relations which dispensed with physical collision altogether and adopted the language of electrical telegraphy. Between the abdomen of father and son, he explained, 'dark rays' pass, 'as between the Marconi stations'. These 'vibrations' make actual handling of the child needless – fortunately, for 'the true male instinct is to avoid physical contact with a baby'. Akin to this is Lawrence's 'vertebral-telegraphy', a means of transmitting messages with the spine, 'like radio-telegraphy', which in his opinion accounted for the influence exerted over mankind by great leaders like Napoleon. It also occurred, he thought, among sperm whales. Older than consciousness, this vertebral interplay was for Lawrence 'the root of our living'. It could be used destructively. Somers in *Kangaroo* sends out vibrations from his spine in an attempt (unsuccessful) to annihilate the army medical board which has offended him. But it underlies, too, all true harmony – 'the strange, dark intercommunication between man and man and man and beast, from the powerful spine'. It originated before the Flood, 'before the mental-spiritual world came into being'.

The spine, sending out its imperious tremors, must above all things reject love. Lawrence detested love and feared it. It sucked the valour and wildness out of men and glued them to their putrid routines. It was 'a vice, like drink'; 'a devilish thing'. It could lead only to 'slimy, creepy, personal intimacy'. Married couples should not be united in love – 'stuck together like two jujube lozenges' – but fiercely separate in their 'dynamic blood polarity', like copulating birds of prey, 'two eagles in mid-air, grappling, whirling'. To judge from eye-witnesses, the married life of Frieda and Lawrence resembled this quite closely at times.

Lawrence's eagles, splendidly devoid of brain, belong to a large class of exemplary wild creatures which inhabits his fiction. 'Be a good animal', counsels

Annable, the *White Peacock* gamekeeper, having turned his back on Cambridge and taken to the woods to develop his physique. It was not entirely new advice. Emily Brontë's Heathcliff taught Hareton 'to scorn everything extra-animal', and Heathcliff's Byronic rages indicate, again, the Romantic antecedents of the Lawrentian hero. From Annable on, the novels teem with characters who are recommended for their similarity to wild life and plants – men with animal eyes and girls whose wombs or mouths open 'like a flower'. Mindless and quick-eared, animals were preferable to humans, in Lawrence's view, particularly because they did not get personally involved with each other. Love was beneath them. 'I love St Mawr because he isn't intimate,' declares Lou Witt of her horse. Being a good animal, however, does not entail being rough. Lou tells her mother:

I don't consider the cave man is a real animal at all. He's a brute, a degenerate. A pure animal man would be as lovely as a deer or a leopard; burning like a flame fed straight from underneath. And he'd be part of the unseen, like a mouse is, even. And he'd never cease to wonder, he'd breathe silence and unseen wonder, as the partridges do running in the stubble. He'd be all the animals in turn.

He would also be clean in his habits, apparently, and careful not to offend civic decency. Lawrence had strict views on such matters. His surrogate in *Kangaroo*, Somers, is disgusted when a young wife displays affection in public. Her eyes glow 'like an animal's', but it is evidently an animal of the wrong kind. Likewise Lawrence called the Italian peasants 'dirty, disgusting swine' because they had 'no sanitary arrangements' and relieved themselves in the open air.

Trees have an impersonal aloofness, like animals, and are more decorous in their mating. Lawrence wished to emulate them. After being among people, 'all rattling their personalities', he was glad of the 'profound indifference of faceless trees'. Wordsworth comes to mind once more, disillusioned by the Cambridge wine-parties and communing with an ash in the college garden. The strength of trees, for Lawrence, lay in their 'aristocratic silence', and the blind surge of their sap. Man too, he felt, needed a 'blind acrid faith', like sap, to keep him going, and needed to recognize the kinship of sap and blood. Connie Chatterley, in the wood, is aware in her own body of 'the huge heave of the sap in the massive trees'. The tendency of Lawrence's people to strip and revel in the undergrowth – Connie, or Birkin, Ursula and Gudrun, or Juliet in 'Sun' – marks a reassertion of mankind's union with mindless plant life.

Besides mindlessness, the other essential in sexual relations, Lawrence considered, was male dominance. 'The old dominant male', 'the phallic wind rushing through the dark', must arise and sweep away silly modern notions of parity between men and women. The female must find her fulfilment once more in 'glorifying the blood male'. Bossiness and the desire to get jobs are among the signs of insanity in the modern woman. Properly, women should never occupy responsible posts. They have not the same fighting power as a man, and 'mental concentration' wears them out terribly. In any case, when they speak and write they 'utter not one single word that men have not taught them'. Men who defer to women are really cruel, because they place upon them the 'ghastly burden of life responsibility', which they are not fit to bear. 'Cock-sure' women are a tragedy to themselves as well as their mates, for when they have squawked and bustled their way to emancipation, all they end up with is miles of typewriting, or the vote, or years of business efficiency, which mean nothing to them. Stitching and washing her man's shirts is a meaningful occupa-tion for a woman, on the other hand, and relates somehow to blood contact. Count Dionys, in 'The Ladybird', announces that the males of his family have always had their shirts made and washed by 'a woman of our own blood'. Lady Daphne is soon stitching away. Wives should honour and obey their husbands and surrender their own wills. Even in sexual intercourse they should not attempt to gain satisfaction for themselves. The woman trying to achieve orgasm, grinding away at the man 'down there' with her 'beak', is one of Law-rence's recurrent horrors. Whereas it is imperative, for him, that marriage should be a woman's whole existence, he emphasized that a man ought to have activities outside marriage, since man's prime motivation is not sexual but creative and religious – 'the pure, disinterested craving of the human male to make something wonderful, out of his own head'. Woman, man should re-member, is for 'the camp fire', the night. His waking hours must find worthier pursuits. Quite what these should be, Lawrence leaves indefinite, but he is convinced that they should entail 'the great unison of manhood in some pas-sionate *purpose*', and from the fiction we may gather that they would entail, too, a certain amount of naked bathing and wrestling.

When Lawrence turns his attention from marriage to man in society, his deep need for hierarchy and subordination remains. Mankind is divided into natural aristocrats and natural slaves. One can easily, Lawrence insists, tell them apart, but his directions on the subject are seldom very specific. It is 'written between a man's brows' which he is. Some men have a 'star' inside them, an 'inexplic-able star which rose out of the dark sea and shone between the flood and the great sky'. These are the aristocrats, and they should be reverenced as divine beings. Other men are 'not divine at all'. They 'have only faculties', and are or should be slaves. Indeed, they will become 'vassals by choice', for it is their nature to submit. Lawrence's aristocracy is not, of course, the current social one. His natural aristocrats often occupy quite lowly positions in society. Lewis, the groom in 'St Mawr', is an aristocrat, 'but it was an aristocracy of the invisible powers, the greater influences, nothing to do with human society'. Lawrence's transcendental class distinctions, akin to the Calvinistic notion of the 'elect', reflect his religious upbringing, but they are, too, a version of something germane to the middle-class dream for well over a century. Victorian fiction swarms with gentlemen in reduced circumstances who have better blood in their veins than the wealthy upstarts. Dickens' Nicholas Nickleby and the hero of Tennyson's *Maud* epitomize the type. 'Blood' distinguishes Lawrence's aristocrats also, and though his use of the word is not primarily genealogical he was evidently seduced by the middle-class cult of 'good family'. Mrs Morel, for instance, comes of a 'good old burgher family'. Her nice tea things and tenancy of the end house elevate her to a 'kind of aristocracy' among the miners' wives. Behind such details we may detect the lower middle-class child's dream of genteel origins. When Lawrence met Frieda, he excitedly informed a correspondent 'she is ripping . . . she is the daughter of the Baron von Richthofen, of the ancient and famous house of Richthofen'. It always gave him a naive delight to be treated as upper-class. In Italy, seated in a box at the theatre, he was pleased to find the peasants regarding himself and Frieda as if they were angelic beings: 'I love to look down on the peasants'. Despite occasional protestations that people are all different, and so incomparable, he argued stoutly (and incontestably) for his own superiority to the common herd. By 'superior', he explained, he meant 'more vividly alive'. 'Life is more vivid in me than in the Mexican who drives the wagon for me'. Thus it was right that the Mexican should remain a servant, just as it was right that the horses, even less vividly alive, should go on pulling the wagon. The observant reader may object that, in view of what has been said so far, the horses should be superior to both Lawrence and his driver, on account of their animal mindlessness. That is true. But consistency was not one of Lawrence's virtues, and he never pretended that it was.

From the natural aristocrats depicted in Lawrence's stories it might seem that being vividly alive usually goes with being arrogant, sensual and selfish. Yvette, for example, in *The Virgin and the Gipsy*, shows her aristocratic nature by stealing money from the Church War Memorial Window Fund to buy herself stockings. Her father, the vicar, is morally outraged by her conduct, and this shows that he is 'base-born', a 'natural slave'. Lawrence's aristocrats believe passionately that the 'rabble', backed by police and moralists, is devoted to humiliating them. 'All their lives the Brangwens were meeting folk who tried to pull them down.' Ursula feels 'the grudging power of the mob lying in wait for her, the exception'. The mob put forward vulgar arguments about 'the common good', whereas the aristocrats know that 'the really gentlemanly thing' is to act spontaneously on one's impulses, no matter what the effect on society. Keenly aware of their exceptional abilities, the aristocrats grow angry when others fail to spot them. 'We are more intelligent than most people,' observes Ursula, 'and it ought to be admitted, simply.' The ideal would be to live luxuriously among other 'sensuous aristocrats', waited on as titled people by the commonalty.

Lawrence was aware, of course, that the commonalty would be unlikely to fit in with this scheme. He considerd them envious, self-seeking, and despicable in numerous other ways. They obeyed the laws; they polluted the earth with their teeming millions; and they worked for a living – a 'vulgar, sordid and humiliating' thing to do. They were, in short, 'smelly mongrels', without daring, beauty or passion. It followed that they should be destroyed, and the impulse to exterminate mankind is a strong one with Lawrence. 'I like', as he put it, 'to think of the world going pop!' Most people do not exist at all, Birkin avers. 'They jingle and giggle. It would be much better if they were just wiped out'. And Gudrun feels the same when a mine-worker makes a joke about her smart green stockings. 'She would have liked them all annihilated.' Meanwhile it is necessary to quell democratic murmurings, encouraged by 'Jews like Marx', which threaten to transfer power and money to the working classes. Socialism is 'an infectious disease, like syphilis'. It blinds people to the beauty of life, and fills their heads with materialism so that they 'see all mud'. Trades Unions represent 'the nastiest profiteering side of the working man'. Lawrence was always furious when workers he employed dared to haggle about their terms of employment; 'bullying', he called it. A boatman at Trapani pointed out that the normal fare exceeded Lawrence's offer, and this, to Lawrence, epitomized 'the hateful, unmanly insolence of these lords of toil, now they have their various "unions" behind them and their "rights" as working men'. People with 'passionate truth' in them should control the world's material resources, argues Somers in *Kangaroo*, and 'absolutely put possessions out of the reach of the mass of mankind'. Democratic ideas are particularly disastrous when they filter through to the coloured races. Lawrence seems to have approved of imperialism, and found that the 'gulf between the native servants and the whites' in Ceylon kept up the 'tone'. 'Those natives', he wrote to Lady Cynthia Asquith, 'are in the living sense *lower* than we are'. As for Indian nationalism, it was just an excuse for setting up native tyrants. The Indians had no real feeling for freedom. 'The niggers are the same. The real sense of liberty only goes with white blood'.

The Lawrentian aristocrat hates to see people suffering, but instead of wishing to cure them he feels that they are to blame for forcing their ugly woes on his attention. In this he shares the absolute selfishness of childhood. Ursula Brangwen, though nominally adult, hates people who have been hurt. When Hill has been caned, she feels she cannot forgive the boy for being a huddled, blubbering object. Paul Morel, in the same spirit, berates his mother, when she has cancer, for taking a long time over dying. Benevolence and pity, Lawrence despises. They are always 'maggoty', infested with the common people's lust to 'destroy the man in a man'.

Christianity, with its craven doctrines about loving one's neighbour, its 'beggar's whine' about the God of pity, naturally figures among Lawrence's detestations. Though it may once have had some use, it now serves only to enfeeble. Man must kill to live, but Christianity wants to save every lout and sponger until the world is swollen with the rottenness of man's swarming existences. The democratic leanings with which Lawrence credited Christ especially displeased him. Lawrence's Christ, who comes back to life in 'The Man Who Died', decides that he was wrong to try to uplift the peasants. They are, after all, merely 'clods of earth'. He was wrong too, he finds, to suppress his sexuality, and he copulates cheerfully with a priestess of Isis. The scene is a queer blend of primness and innocence. 'Will you not take off your things?' invites the priestess, and Christ shouts in surprise 'I am risen!' as he obtains an erection. Normal Christianity, however, thwarts man's natural impulses. It is not natural to turn the other cheek, and when Ursula Brangwen tries it she does not feel clean again until she has gone back to the girl concerned and almost shaken her head off. Christianity also eats away the fierce masculine will, 'the will to ecstasy in destruction', which survives in tigers and in soldiers, and is located above the loins 'at the base of the spinal column'.

This positioning of the masculine will relates to a psychological theory outlined by Lawrence in his two works on the unconscious, which will need some brief explanation. Lawrence assigned different impulses to what he took to be the four major nerve centres in the body. At the back of the torso he identified two spinal centres: the upper (thoracic) and lower (lumbar) ganglions. These stiffened the spine and rejected the outside world. The thoracic ganglion, squaring the shoulders, is 'spiritual'. From it flow man's creative urge and his instinct to criticize others. The lumbar ganglion (near the buttocks) is sensual and its involvement in excretion reflects its tendency to assert selfhood by repelling alien matter. At the front of the body Lawrence located the upper (thoracic) and lower (solar) plexuses, adjoining the nipples and navel respectively. Unlike the stiff-back ganglions, these are soft centres, making for human sympathy. The top one (nipples) controls breathing in, which typifies its impulse to welcome what comes along. It is 'spiritual', responsible for sight, the least sensual of Lawrentian senses, and for the Christian perversion which we call 'selfless love'. The solar plexus, on the other hand, 'the warm rosy abdomen, tender with chuckling unison', is sensual, sucks the outer world into its belly, and works feet and ears. Ideally back should balance front, and top bottom. Spiritual and sensual, rejecting and welcoming, should be in equipoise. And two individuals, sexual partners, are needed, so that the circuit between their eight poles can establish a 'dynamic' equilibrium. But centuries of Christianity, as Lawrence sees it, have ruined man's spinal centres. By consequence modern man is round-shouldered and weak-chested. He also needs spectacles, because Christianity has over-stimulated his upper-front nerve centre which connects with the eyes. Modern fathers can partially rectify matters by provoking their children's antagonism. Lawrence recommends corporal punishment ('spanking acts direct upon the spinal nerve system'), kicking the family dog, or throwing the cat out of the window.

Without reference to this anatomical theory, the novels are not fully intelligible. When, in *Aaron's Rod*, Lilly cures Aaron's constipation by rubbing his 'lower body' with camphorated oil, we are meant to realize that he is stimulating Aaron's lumbar ganglion. Aaron has become weak and over-sympathetic, letting himself be seduced by Josephine. 'Any excess in the sympathetic dynamism tends,' Lawrence notes in *Fantasia of the Unconscious*, 'to cause fever and constipation.' Lilly's treatment stiffens Aaron's backbone, expelling Josephine and other waste matter. In 'England, My England', Egbert, 'swinging away from sympathy', makes slits in his shirt so that rain and air can get to his shoulders, seat of the thoracic ganglion. On the other hand Kangaroo, corrupted by love for his fellow men, has weak eyes and a big belly. These show that his sympathetic centres predominate. But when Harriet annoys him he rolls over and sticks out his lumbar ganglion in her direction, as if to excrete her.

As we have said, then, it is Lawrence's particular grudge against Christianity that it destroys the tiger at the base of the spine. It extirpates the flesh, the senses, the self, and puts in their place science and social reform. Furthermore, because its doctrines apply equally to everyone, it is a mechanical thing. A God who works for all alike is, properly, a machine. By making this connection between Christianity and mechanized civilization, Lawrence was, of course, linking it with one of his most potent hatreds. The Lawrentian aristocrat (though ready enough, like Lawrence, to tour foreign parts in railway train and steam boat) regards machines, in theory, as debasing horrors. Even a bus-conductor's ticket-clipper sends 'a pang of dread' through Ursula Brangwen, because it is so impersonal. Man's will, forcing the sensuous animal into the grip of a machine world, is symbolized in the scene where Gerald Crich (possessor of a 'mechanical' body and 'iron men') keeps his Arab mare's head turned towards a locomotive. Railways, besides, breed envy, malice and equality. 'Bolshevists somehow seem to be born on the railway,' Lawrence remarked. Christianity's mechanical nature displays itself in figures like the crippled clergyman, Mr Massy, in 'Daughters of the Vicar', who is both 'perfect Christian' and 'cold machine', and Carlota, the unfortunate Christian spouse of Ramón in *The Plumed Serpent*, who dies making 'terrible mechanical noises'.

To replace the outworn God of Christianity Lawrence advertised new gods – or resurgent ancient gods. These would come, he speculated, from the pine forests of Germany or Mexico or Russia or Tartary, 'the destructive East, that produced Attila'. They would be dark gods of blood and human sacrifice, ousting weak Jesus, and they would enter man, as like as not, through the posterior, for it is the posterior, the lumbar ganglion, that must reconnect us with the earth. 'In the old world the centre of all power was at the depths of the earth,' Lawrence believed, 'the sun was only a moving subsidiary body.' Hence, he argued, the prominence of the snake, the earth-beast, in the rituals of Mexican Indians and in Etruscan urn paintings. Man must stop aspiring towards sun, brain and spiritual centres. The 'great God', Somers advises Kangaroo, has his advent in the 'lower self'; and portly Arnault in 'Mother and Daughter' exemplifies the power of this ancient deity by sitting 'as if his posterior were connected with the very centre of the earth'. Since the dark gods call man to blood sacrifice, they sanctify his killer instinct, providing occasion for 'the greatest man-fun', as Lawrence puts it, 'the pre-human, pine-tree fun of cutting dusky throats'. No sexual pleasure can compare, he reckons, with 'the clutching throb of gratification as the knife strikes in'. The public executions in *The Plumed Serpent* give a taste of this gratification, and recall the urge to destroy human life which has already been noted in Lawrence. 'One must be able to shoot,' he insists, 'one must kill.' It would be a mistake to regard this opinion as something Lawrence outgrew, an aberration as temporary as the obsession with power and leadership that dominates, say, *Aaron's Rod*. True, he became disillusioned with the 'great leader' cult, and meant *Lady Chatterley's Lover* to embody a new creed of 'tenderness'. But the tenderness includes shooting people whom you dislike. The tenderest thing you can do for individuals like Clifford or Bertha Coutts, Mellors maintains, is to kill them. 'Their souls are awful inside them. Death ought to be sweet to them. And I ought to be allowed to shoot them.'

Along with dark gods, Lawrence propounded a dark cosmology and a darkish afterlife. The sun, he preached, is really dark. Its apparent brightness is caused merely by refraction. Further, instead of life being drawn from the sun, the sun is an emanation from living plants and animals. It 'breathes in the effluence of all that fades and dies'. It depends for 'its heart-beat, its respiration, its pivotal motion' on the beating hearts of men and other creatures. Likewise the moon, far from being a cold, cratered world, is composed of 'some very intense element, like phosphorus or radium', and is 'born from the death of individuals'.

Man's vitality thus creates the heavenly bodies. It also ensures his immortality. Potent, vital people, the 'Lords of Life', will survive to become 'Masters of Death'. 'I shall be king in Hades when I am dead,' Count Dionys informs Daphne in 'The Ladybird'. The dead, however, who have failed to be lordly will crawl, in the words of Quetzalcoatl's hymn, 'like masterless dogs in the back streets of the air'.

As for Lawrence's ideal society on earth, it is conveyed more distinctly in negatives than positives. He speaks in a late letter of the need for 'an *enormous* revolution' to 'smash' money and possessiveness and industrialism. It should not be a materialist, Marxist revolution, merely redistributing the cash, but an assertion of life. Money and work should be as casual in human life as they are in a bird's. 'What we want is life and *trust*.' Plainly trust would be needed to an unusual degree before people gave up their possessions and lived like the birds. In a more realistic mood Lawrence himself can be found condemning trust as 'a blasphemy against life', a thing which no wild creature ever feels, and which in human transactions is rightly repaid with robbery and murder. Nevertheless the utopia which he sketches in 'A Dream of Life' contains trustful, porridge-eating natives, who combine primitivism with quiet respectability. And in *Lady Chatterley* Mellors looks forward to a similarly harmonious commonwealth, where the inhabitants will occupy themselves with folk dances and stool-carving, and wear red trousers: 'if men had fine, red legs, that alone would change them in a month'. The masses, Mellors believes, should not be taught to think; and Lawrence, too, argues that mental consciousness is 'a catastrophe' for most people. All schools should be closed at once, he advises, and no child should learn to read unless it has enough enthusiasm to teach itself. There will have to be, of course, a 'higher, responsible, conscious class', but these 'sacred few' will be such as are capable of retrieving their un-selfconsciousness, of learning again 'how *not to know*'. For the majority, minds will be starved and bodies cultivated. All boys over the age of ten will have compulsory training in primitive modes of combat. They will stay chaste, though athletic: boys and girls will be strictly segregated, and sex education (which Lawrence considers 'criminal') banned. 'The mass of mankind should *never* be acquainted with the scientific biological facts of sex.' Sex should come upon us unawares as a 'terrible thing of suffering and privilege and mystery'.

These, then, are the main currents of Lawrence's thought on epistemology, morals, religion, sociology and sex. Since he died, various ways of disparaging his ideas have been evolved. His poor physique and sexual impotence are pointed out as the explanation of his interest in dominant masculinity. His scholarship-boy class background is used to account for his rootlessness and snobbery. His pious mother, and incestuous dreams about her, are cited as the grounds, respectively, of his recoil from Christianity and his need to reject Freudian psychoanalysis. Arguments of this kind all rest, however, on the fallacy that one can discredit a body of thought by discrediting the thinker's motives. An alternative manoeuvre is to link Lawrence causally with phenomena generally agreed to be horrible, like concentration camps. Lawrence's 'mystical philosophy of "blood",' according to Bertrand Russell, 'led straight to Auschwitz.' Even granted that the beliefs of Lawrence and the Nazi killers coincided to some degree (and it would be futile to deny this), Russell's way of putting the case glosses over the plain fact that Lawrence's beliefs did not issue in mass murder but in writing novels. Unless life is to be deprived altogether (and how could it be deprived?) of violent and destructive and irrational ways of feeling, it is ludicrous not to distinguish between people who can bring these feelings to a life-enhancing end in great literature, and people who can produce only a pile of corpses. As well blame stabbings on cutlers. Besides, the Russell faction has to reckon with a third set of Lawrence's detractors who contend that a good many previous or contemporary writers – Carlyle, Nietzsche, Yeats – thought much as Lawrence did. If the responsibility for Auschwitz is to be transferred to men of letters, it will need to be thinly spread. In reply to this third charge, it has to be admitted that parallels to Lawrence's writing can be spotted all over Victorian literature. Carlyle's denunciation of materialist 'pig-philosophy' and distrust of democratic movements spring to mind, not to mention his belief that 'niggers' were natural slaves. Nietzsche's contempt for Christianity and for the weak was certainly a formative influence. By judicious selection even Matthew Arnold can be made to look rather Lawrence-like. Did he not set himself against the machine and middle-class philistinism and the tyranny of the intellect? But attempts to match Lawrence's system of thought are doomed to, at best, partial success, and their belittling intent misfires because in seeking to expose his lack of originality they merely prove that he did not write in some cranky limbo but was stirred by the same questions, and occasionally the same answers, as the rest of intellectual Europe at what we have come to think of as the end of the Christian era.

Those, however, who find Lawrence's thought disgusting, dangerous or satanic, at least do him the courtesy of treating it as real thought. Much more reprehensible are the well-meaning dilutions offered by his defenders: the pretence that really he was a decent, moderate sort of fellow, almost a Christian, and the argument that the thought cannot be separated from the 'art' in which it occurs. The aim of this gambit is to stuff Lawrence away in some cultural museum where no one asks any practical or embarrassing questions. It is true that we must constantly return to Lawrence's books, but not to shield ourselves from regarding his thought in the context of life. Rather, it is only in the books that the thought is alive. Extracted, schematized, it loses its shifting, paradoxical quality: the luminous visual and verbal power marshalled to attack the visual and verbal; the intellect deriding the intellect; the sensitivity and callousness fused together. It loses, too, its personality, its human smell – and this is a vital consideration, for it is the final paradox of Lawrence's thought that, separated from his warm, intense, wonderfully articulate being, it becomes the philosophy of any thug or moron.

D. H. Lawrence
and Homosexuality
Jeffrey Meyers

'Every man comprises male and
female in his being, the male
always struggling for predominance.'
'Study of Thomas Hardy'

Lawrence believed his intrinsic sexual nature was dual and not entirely male, and that his male and female elements were in conflict, not in balance. This mixture gave him great insight into the female being, a considerable advantage to a creative writer. But it also caused him to see sexual relationships in terms of struggle rather than harmony, and led to a fear of merging rather than a confidence in union. Lawrence's novels describe a number of cruel and mutually destructive conflicts between men and women, as well as an alternative search for satisfying relationships between men.

Lawrence's conflicting attitudes about the possibility of male love are expressed throughout his works, where his life erupts into art, and most specifically in four overt homosexual scenes: the swimming idyll in *The White Peacock* (1911), the wrestling match in *Women in Love* (1920), the nursing episode in *Aaron's Rod* (1922) and the initiation ceremony in *The Plumed Serpent* (1926). These scenes form a thematic core in the novels and share three common characteristics. First, they are modelled on the biblical friendship of David and Jonathan and not, as in works by practising and more reticent homosexuals, on the Greek ideal of male love (Lawrence has other uses for *The Symposium*). The clearest example of Lawrence's version of this male friendship appears in the play about his namesake, *David*, where the two heroes swear an almost divine covenant:

Jonathan: We have sworn a covenant, is it not between us? Wilt thou not swear with me, that our souls shall be as brothers, closer even than the blood? O David, my heart has no peace save all be well between thy soul and mine, and thy blood and mine.

David: As the Lord liveth, the soul of Jonathan is dearer to me than a brother's. – O brother, if I were but come out of this pass, and we might live before the Lord, together![1]

Secondly, in each of these scenes homosexuality is seen as an alternative to heterosexual love and invariably occurs after a frustrating humiliation with a woman. The failure of the male to achieve dominance over the female, especially the female *will*, leads directly to a triumph of the female element *within* man. Thirdly, Lawrence's inner struggle with repressed homosexual desires results in an ambiguity of presentation, for none of his heroes can commit himself completely to homosexuality although it is portrayed as a 'higher' form of sexual love. Though this ambiguity has artistic functions – it deflects attention from the physical to the symbolic aspects of the scene – it also exposes Lawrence's personal doubts about the ultimate validity of homosexual experience. Homosexual lovers like the Prussian officer, Banford in 'The Fox', Winifred Inger in *The Rainbow* and Loerke in *Women in Love* are portrayed as perverse and corrupt. Yet the homosexuality in the four scenes is described as nourishing and life-enhancing, and represents a meaningful and valuable relationship. Like T. E. Lawrence, who contrasts the clean embraces of the Bedouin with the syphilitic sodomy of the Turks, D. H. Lawrence has contradictory attitudes about inversion.[2]

In letters and conversations with friends, and in his non-fiction, especially his essays on Whitman (he destroyed his homosexual treatise, 'Goats and Compasses', in 1917), Lawrence attempts to clarify his ambiguous position. In 1913 he writes to Henry Savage:

I should like to know why nearly every man that approaches greatness tends to homosexuality, whether he admits it or not: so that he loves the *body* of a man better than the body of a woman – as I believe the Greeks did, sculptors and all, by far.... He can always get satisfaction from a man, but it is the hardest thing in life to get one's soul and body satisfied from a woman, so that one is free from oneself. And one is kept by all tradition and instinct from loving men, or a man.[3]

Lawrence, himself 'approaching greatness', characteristically uses ambiguous language ('*tends* to homosexuality'). The first sentence is similar to Oscar Wilde's defence at his trial,[4] the second affirms the superiority of male to female love, and the third places tradition *with* instinct as obstacles to male love when in his case (and in Wilde's) instinct opposes tradition.

In a letter of 1919 Lawrence seems to have found an answer in Whitman, who with his English disciple Edward Carpenter, was the greatest public apologist for homosexuality:

You are a great admirer of Whitman. So am I. But I find in his '*Calamus*' and Comrades one of the clues to a real solution – a new adjustment. I believe in what he calls 'manly love', the real implicit reliance of one man on another: as sacred a unison as marriage: only it must be deeper, more ultimate than emotion and personality, cool separateness and yet the ultimate reliance.[5]

These ideas are close to the ideas of *Women in Love*, which he had completed a few years earlier, in 1916. Lawrence values separateness and feels sexual relations with women threaten his integrity, so that male love is a 'real solution' to the struggle for dominance and conflict of wills in heterosexual love, and comradeship is justified as being as sacred as marriage. But Lawrence writes of Whitman, a practising homosexual:

He found, as all men find, that you can't really merge in a woman, though you may go a long way. You can't manage the last bit. So you have to give it up, and try elsewhere if you *insist* on merging. . . . For the great mergers, woman at last becomes inadequate. For those who love to extremes. Woman is inadequate for the last merging. So the next step is the merging of man-for-man love. And this is on the brink of death. It slides over into death. David and Jonathan. And the death of Jonathan.[6]

The paradox of Whitman's real solution is that the merging of men goes beyond women – but into a sexual dead end, into masturbation and sterility.

During his stay in New Mexico Lawrence again tried to clarify this problem:

All my life I have wanted friendship with a man – real friendship, in my sense of what I mean by that word. What is this sense? Do I want friendliness? I should like to see anybody being 'friendly' with me. Intellectual equals? Or rather equals in being non-intellectual. I see your joke. Not something homosexual, surely? Indeed, you have misunderstood me – besides this term is so imbedded in its own period. I do not belong to a world where that word has meaning. Comradeship perhaps? No, not that – too much love about it – no, not even in the Calamus sense, not comradeship – not manly love. Then what Nietzsche describes – the friend in whom the world standeth complete, a capsule of the good – the creating friend, who hath always a complete world to bestow. Well, in a way. That means in my words, choose as your friend the man who has centre.[7]

Lawrence rejects in turn intellectual equality, homosexuality in the Wildean sense (imbedded in its period) and Whitman's comradeship, for a vague and unsatisfactory definition by Nietzsche, who was betrayed by his friends and whose desperate sexual struggle ended in madness. Lawrence's homosexuality remains: 'I do believe in friendship. I believe tremendously in friendship between man and man, a pledging of men to each other inviolably. But I have never met or formed such a friendship.'[8] But his deep residue of puritanical repression and certain intellectual scruples prevent the successful culmination of this friendship.

Yet Lawrence condemned in others what he wanted for himself. 'Never bring Birrell to see me any more,' he writes to David Garnett. 'There is something nasty about him like black beetles. He is horrible and unclean. I feel I should go mad when I think of your set, Duncan Grant and Keynes and Birrell. It makes me dream of beetles. . . . It sent me mad with misery and hostility and rage.'[9] Nor would Lawrence in his extreme rage, inspired partly by the hatred of the homosexual element within himself, allow the validity of heterosexual love, at least as it was practised by middle- or upper-class Anglo-Saxons. He sees it as disguised perversion:

That is what nearly *all* English people now do. When a man takes a woman, he is merely repeating a known reaction upon himself, not seeking a new reaction, a discovery. And this is like self-abuse or masturbation. The ordinary Englishman of the educated class goes to a woman now to masturbate himself. . . . When this condition arrives, there is always Sodomy.[10]

And in a bitter poem in the aptly named *Pansies*, Lawrence completely loses his objectivity and projects his own 'instinctual' sexual fears on to the class he had come to hate:

Ronald, you know, is like most Englishmen,
by instinct, he's a sodomist
but he's frightened to know it
so he takes it out on women.

Oh come! said I. That Don Juan of a Ronald!
Exactly, she said. Don Juan was another of them, in love with himself
and taking it out on women.

Even that isn't sodomitical, said I.
But if a man is in love with himself, isn't that the nearest form of homosexuality?
    she said."[11]

Women in Love grows out of Lawrence's sexual struggles with Frieda Weekley and his attempts at male friendship, especially with Middleton Murry. Throughout his entire life Lawrence felt threatened by dominating and possessive women: his mother, Jessie Chambers, Alice Dax, Lady Ottoline Morrell, Dorothy Brett, Mabel Dodge Luhan and most important, Frieda, and from his experience with them he learned to see heterosexual love as an endless struggle of clashing wills in which man either maintains a precarious dominance or is overcome by humiliating defeat.

Though Lawrence kept up his end of the battle, as the scarifying *Look! We*

Have Come Through! testifies, he had much to fear from Frieda, whose strengths seemed to match his weaknesses. She was of noble birth, richer, older, stronger and healthier that the sickly Lawrence; she was sexually liberated and had had a number of love affairs before, during and after her marriage to Ernest Weekley and the puritanical Lorenzo. He resented his dependence on Frieda, was awed by her sexual experience and sexual demands, was fiercely jealous of the longing for her three abandoned children (they had no children of their own), hated her wilful refusal to submit to him, and was alternately enraged, depressed and resigned to her flirtations and liaisons. For Lawrence,

> The cross,
> The wheel on which our silence first is broken, [is]
> Sex, which breaks up our integrity, our single inviolability, our deep silence,
> Tearing a cry from us.[12]

It was therefore inevitable that Lawrence had sexual problems with Frieda and, as Murry writes, sought 'to escape to a man from the misery of his own failure with a woman'.[13] Several of Lawrence's other 'friends' have also attempted to diagnose his sexual difficulties. Compton Mackenzie records, in a patronizing tone, that

What worried him particularly was his inability to attain consummation simultaneously with his wife, which according to him must mean that their marriage was still imperfect in spite of all they had both gone through. I insisted that such a happy coincidence was always rare, but he became more and more depressed about what *he* insisted was the only evidence of a perfect union. 'I believe the nearest I've ever come to perfect love was with a young coal-miner when I was about sixteen,' he declared.[14]

And Cecil Gray, whom Lawrence satirized as Cyril Scott in *Aaron's Rod*, hints about an affair with Frieda[15] and categorically states: 'It might not be true to say that Lawrence was literally and absolutely impotent . . . but I am certain that he was not very far removed from it'.[16] The basis of Gray's 'certainty' is not explained, but it is clear that Lawrence was not impotent if he experienced orgasms.

Whatever the validity of these waspish accounts, Lawrence's marriage suffered two major crises: one culminating in Cornwall in 1916 during the composition of *Women in Love*, the other in Mexico in 1923 when writing *The Plumed Serpent*. In the first crisis Lawrence turned away from Frieda toward Rananim in general and Murry in particular. Knud Merrild writes:

When he spoke of his beloved idea of starting a new life and forming a colony, he never included women. He always conceived of realizing it with men alone, in the beginning at least. . . . Only at times he added, 'I suppose eventually the men shall want to take women unto themselves! . . .

There is no use blinking the fact that Lawrence included the possibility of homo-sexuality in the scheme of modern existence, that he offered it as a tentative relief for the antagonism between the sexes, a symptom of a disease that has spread over Europe.[17]

The sexually naive Murry, who agreed with Lawrence's accusation that he lacked a sensuous nature, was confused and overwhelmed by the intensity of his friend's passion: 'Lawrence was really a new experience. I was quite unprepared for such an immediacy of contact.' So he had to resort to role-playing: 'When he unconsciously sought for *me*, expecting response from me, the same uneasy bewilderment would return. The person to whom he spoke was not there. I must impersonate him.'[18] Gradually, however, Murry came to understand and accept the ambivalent and even contradictory elements in Lawrence's creed:

One was an instinctive, infra-personal sense of solidarity with men – the true, deep, gregarious experience, which Lawrence had known as a child and longed to renew, which he simultaneously desired and repudiated; the other was a curiously intense preoccupation with 'the animal of himself', which fascinated and repelled him.[19]

(as it did Murry). But Lawrence's need corresponded to Murry's, for Murry was also having serious problems in his marriage to Katherine Mansfield. In the early years of the war, writes Murry, 'By far the chief among [my desires] was the desire to live in a warm atmosphere of love. At this time it existed between Lawrence and me, and I would do anything not to break it.'[20] And he describes their perfect union in words that repeat David's lament for Jonathan: 'We did not have to, we did not want to, talk; it was good between us, better than I have ever known with a living man.'[21]

But their friendship degenerated when Katherine quite naturally resented Lawrence's assaults on her marriage and his attempt to regenerate it through his passionate attachment to her husband:

Lawrence believed, or tried to believe, that the relation between Katherine and me was false and deadly; and that the relation between Frieda and himself was real and life-giving: but that this relation with Frieda needed to be completed by a new relation between himself and me, which I evaded. . . . By virtue of this 'mystical' relation with Lawrence, I participate in this pre-elemental reality, and the 'dark sources' of my being come alive. From this changed personality, I, in turn, enter a new relation with Katherine.[22]

The emotional yet abstract language does not explain precisely why Lawrence needs completion or how the Murrys recharge themselves on Lawrence's marital battery, but it is not difficult to see how these ideas offended Katherine.

When Murry tried to placate Lawrence in Cornwall in 1916 by asking, 'If I love you, and you know I love you, isn't that enough?', Lorenzo burst out, 'I hate your love, I *hate* it. You're an obscene bug, *sucking* my life away,'[23] an insult that combined his favourite image of corruption with the suggestion of perversion. Lawrence's response to the inevitable break with Murry was his mysterious and obscure passion for the handsome Cornish farmer, William Henry Hocking, which he refers to in the 'Nightmare' chapter of *Kangaroo* (1923) and in the suppressed Prologue to *Women in Love*, which was not published until 1963.[24]

The Prologue concerns three crucial aspects of the novel: the early history of Birkin's destructive relationship with Hermione that explains her violent attempt to crush his skull with the lapis lazuli; the friendship, intimacy and attraction of Birkin and Crich that begins on an Alpine journey and clarifies Birkin's final lament, 'He should have loved me. . . . I wanted eternal union with a man too: another kind of love.' But Ursula calls this desire a perversity, for it negates Birkin's commitment to female love:

In the street it was the men who roused him by their flesh and their manly, vigorous movement, quite apart from all the individual characteristics, whilst he studied the women as *sisters*, knowing their meaning and their intents. It was the men's physique which held the passion and the mystery to him. . . . He had several friendships wherein this passion entered. . . . He loved his friend, the beauty of whose manly limbs made him tremble with pleasure. He wanted to caress him.[25]

Thirdly, the revelation of Birkin's repressed homosexual desires (which accounts for the cancellation of the Prologue, especially after the suppression of *The Rainbow* for the lesbian swimming scene) clarifies the 'Man to Man' and 'Gladiatorial' chapters:

This was the one and only secret he kept to himself, this secret of his passionate and sudden, spasmatic affinity for the men he saw. He kept this secret even from himself. . . . Gerald Crich was the one towards whom Birkin felt most strongly that immediate, roused attraction which transfigured the person of the attracter with such a glow and such a desirable beauty.[26]

Birkin's open desires and homosexual affairs with working men, in the Prologue, has a rather different emphasis from the analogous description at the end of Chapter 2 where Birkin and Crich

burned with each other, inwardly. This they would never admit. They intended to keep their relationship a casual free-and-easy friendship, they were not going to be so unmanly and unnatural as to allow any heart-burning between them. They had not the faintest belief in deep relationship between men and men, and their disbelief prevented any development of their powerful but suppressed friendliness.[27]

This passage is more covert and defensive, even ironic ('unmanly', 'heart-burning'); and Lawrence's uneasiness with this intensely personal theme is revealed as the novel thrusts toward – not away from – the development of their 'suppressed friendliness'.

Just before this passage Birkin tells Crich, 'It's the hardest thing in the world to act spontaneously on one's impulses,' and his revulsion from Hermione in the Prologue suggests what his deepest impulses really are. In the novel too Birkin is threatened not only by Hermione's bullying, clutching, powerful will, but also by Ursula's horrible, assertive 'lust for possession, a greed for self-importance in love'. The violent hostility between men and women erupts throughout the novel: in Hermione's attack, Mino's cuff, Gudrun's slap, Mr Brangwen's smack and Crich's strangulation. Even when Birkin and Ursula's love is relatively successful, Birkin fears his loss of sexual identity in submergence and 'horrible fusion':

On the whole, he hated sex, it was such a limitation. It was sex that turned a man into a broken half of a couple, the woman into the other broken half. And he wanted to be single in himself, the woman single in herself. He wanted sex to revert to the level of the other appetites, to be regarded as a functional process, not as a fulfilment. . . . Why should we consider ourselves, men and women, as broken fragments of one whole? . . . In the old age, before sex was, we were mixed, each one a mixture. The process of singling into individuality resulted in the great polarization of sex. The womanly drew to one side, the manly to the other. But the separation was imperfect even then. (pp. 223, 225)

This is Lawrence's interpretation of the Platonic theory of physical love. In *The Symposium* Aristophanes explains Love by supposing that 'the primeval man ['in the old age, before sex was'] was round and had four hands and four feet, back and sides forming a circle, one head with two faces', and was subsequently divided into two. After the divison, the two parts of man, each desiring his other half, came together, and threw their arms about one another eager to grow into one. Plato's theory is appealing because it explains the attractions of the sexes and shows that the union of masculine and feminine complements is a return to original wholeness. But in Lawrence's version the polarized broken half, frightened of merging and domination, wants to remain single and never experiences the platonic fulfilment with women. Birkin yearns for a starlike 'equilibrium, a pure balance of single beings', but Ursula immediately recognizes that what he really wants is a satellite, a woman submissive to his will. And when the woman refuses to submit, he moves away from the *pis aller* of marriage, from the *égoisme à deux*, towards the idealistic and never-to-be-achieved 'bond of pure trust and love with the other man'.

Right after his confession that he hates sex, Birkin first realizes what was apparent in the Prologue: that 'he had been loving Gerald all along, and all along denying it'. So he proposes a *Blutbrüderschaft* to Crich who, doomed and limited, denies his animal self and begs to 'leave it till I understand it better'. Just as Birkin's archaic proposal comes from dissatisfaction with Ursula so, as Murry writes in an interesting comment on this scene, Lawrence's

relation with Frieda left room, and perhaps need, for a relation with a man of something of the kind and quality of my relation with Katherine; and he wanted this relation with me. It was possible only if it left my relation with Katherine intact.

But Lawrence threatened Murry's marriage, and wanted to control his body and dominate his mind.

So at this critical moment, I began to withdraw towards Katherine. And as he felt my withdrawal, Lawrence became more urgent to bind me with him. He talked of the blood-brotherhood between us, and hinted at the need of some inviolable sacrament between us – some pre-Christian blood-rite in keeping with the primitive [Cornish] rocks about us. . . . No doubt the queer wrestling match between the two [Birkin and Crich] is more or less what he meant by the 'blood-sacrament' between us.[28]

Though there is no male blood-rite with Birkin, Gerald achieves a *Blutschwesterschaft* with Gudrun, first when he spurs his mare at the railway crossing and nearly brings Gudrun to orgasm, and then when the frenzied rabbit, Bismarck, scores their arms with blood. Bismarck symbolizes the two forms of destructive love that Gudrun experiences with Crich and with Loerke. The rabbit's racing round and round its cage 'like a furry meteorite, in a tense hard circle that seemed to bind their brains' (p. 273) represents the mindless Dionysian ecstasy ('It's like going round in a squirrel cage', (p. 283)) that Gudrun achieves with Crich. Gudrun reads Bismarck's letters in the Alps, and Bismarck's countryman, Loerke, depicts 'whirling ridiculously in roundabouts . . . a frenzy of chaotic motion' in his industrial frieze based on Mark Gertler's painting *Merry-Go-Round* (1916).

Birkin attacks this Dionysian ecstasy in the 'Moony' chapter that follows 'Rabbit', and his impossible attempt to break the image of the moon that 'shook upon the water in triumphant reassumption' symbolizes his desire to destroy Ursula's female power, to shatter her spiritual integrity. 'Like the moon, one half of [Hermione] was lost to life', but Ursula survives Birkin's attempt to violate her and leads him back toward wholeness. The following day, inspired by his love for Ursula, Birkin proposes marriage; and when this ends in a comical fiasco he turns to Crich for consolation and makes another proposal: 'let us strip, and do it properly.'

Birkin's confession that he used to wrestle with a Jap is his metaphorical revelation of homosexual experience, for Japs 'Repel and attract, both. They are very repulsive when they are cold. . . . But when they are hot and roused, there is a definite attraction.'

So the two men began to struggle together. . . . They seemed to drive their white flesh deeper and deeper against each other, as if they would break into a oneness. . . . It was as if Birkin's whole physical intelligence interpenetrated into Gerald's body, as if his fine, sublimated energy entered into the flesh of the fuller man, like some potency. . . . Now and again came a sharp gasp of breath, or a sound like a sigh, then the strange sound of flesh escaping under flesh . . . the physical junction of two bodies clinched into oneness. . . .

At length Gerald lay back inert on the carpet, his breast rising in great slow panting, whilst Birkin kneeled over him, almost unconscious. Birkin was much more exhausted. He caught little, short breaths, he could scarcely breathe any more. The earth seemed to tilt and sway, and a complete darkness was coming over his mind. . . . The world was sliding, everything was sliding off into the darkness. And he was sliding, endlessly, endlessly away. (pp. 304-5)

Birkin and Crich, by penetrating and entering the flesh and swooning into a mutual orgasm, achieve a Platonic oneness that they fail to achieve in heterosexual love. This almost religious scene alludes to Jacob wrestling with the angel of God in Genesis 32:24-30: 'And Jacob was left alone; and there a man wrestled with him until the breaking of the day. . . . And Jacob called the name of the place Peniel: for I have seen God face to face, and my life is preserved.'[29] Birkin tells Crich 'you are beautiful' and Crich confesses, 'I don't believe I've ever felt as much *love* for a woman as I have for you – not *love*.'

Though they seem completely fulfilled, one significant detail qualifies their union and links their perversity with the Bohemian set of Halliday and Minette. When they wake from sleep Crich puts on 'a gown of broad-barred, thick black-and-green silk, brilliant and striking', and this gown is similar to the colorful one Minette wears ('a loose dressing-gown of purple silk', (p. 84) just before she sleeps with Crich in Halliday's flat. When Crich wakes after sleeping with his host's pregnant mistress and puts on his 'silk wrap of a beautiful bluish colour, with an amethyst hem', he is surprised to find Halliday and Libidnikov (corruption and libido?) stark naked in front of the fire (which also burns during the wrestling match). At that moment Crich first overcomes his bodily shame and repulsion, and returns from his bath without clothes. This change prepares him for the wrestling scene.

Despite their complete satisfaction, neither Crich nor Birkin can entirely commit himself to homosexuality. Crich chooses a love with Gudrun that is doomed to frozen disaster as much as any love in Hardy;[30] and Birkin again demands Ursula's total submission while she accuses him of perverse and obscene sex with Hermione. The sexual solution, as far as the novel admits of one, comes in 'Excurse' where, like 'Gladiatorial', there are no holes barred.

The sexual transfiguration of Birkin and Ursula is again presented in biblical terms and compared to the Sons of God taking the fair daughters of men (Genesis 6:2) and to Moses smiting the rock in Horeb with his rod so 'there shall come water out of it, that the people may drink' (Exodus 17:6). At the country inn Birkin and Ursula reach the fundamental

source of the deepest life-force, the darkest, deepest, strangest life-source of the human body, at the back and base of the loins. . . . From the smitten rock of the man's body, from the strange marvellous flanks and thighs, deeper, further in mystery than the phallic source, came the floods of ineffable darkness and ineffable riches. (p. 354)

Later in the novel Ursula remembers the freedom achieved through her 'degrading, bestial and shameful' experiences with Birkin.[31] In this passage Lawrence equates anal intercourse (the back and the base of the loins, beyond the phallic source) with the deepest life-source, but he describes the heterosexuality of Gudrun and Crich as 'the terrible frictional violence of death'.

The equation of the anus with the life source is such an obscene and outrageous idea that some of the most perceptive critics have either ignored it entirely or else refused to face the full implications of Lawrence's homosexuality. Spilka believes that male friendship is 'the step beyond marriage which makes marriage possible, the break-through to a fuller life[32]. . . . Birkin must work through his "living desire" for Gerald, as well as his deathly attachment to Hermione, before he can love Ursula body and soul.'[33] But could a wife ever accept a man's claim that he would be a better husband if he practised sodomy?

Goodheart more realistically states that Birkin's 'search for transcendent states of being . . . draws him away from women, not toward them. . . . Birkin suffers from a homosexual fear of women',[34] but he does not emphasize Birkin's corresponding attraction for men. Daleski says more precisely that 'the distinct homosexual colouring of the description of the wrestling bout . . . is evidence of the pronounced feminine component in his make-up, of a latent or repressed homosexual tendency, rather than any overt homosexual intention on his part',[35] but the homosexuality in 'Gladiatorial' *is* overt. And Spilka again takes the most polyanalytic view of Birkin's buggery with Ursula: Birkin 'can even perform "responsibly" the kind of "bestial act" he might have performed with a man and perhaps did perform with Hermione – and feel liberated by it ("he was so unabashed and unrestrained") rather than degraded'.[36] These interpretations, like many of Lawrence's own pronouncements about sex, fail to reconcile the abysmal gap between sexual idealism and sexual reality.[37] For the sexual struggles in *Women in Love* (and in Lawrence's life) exemplify his disturbing statement in 'The Reality of the Peace': 'It is not of love that we are fulfilled, but of love in such intimate equipoise with hate that the transcendence takes place.'[38]

The anal intercourse in 'Excurse' is compounded of such love and hate, and it sublimates Birkin's homosexual desires by satisfying them in an alternative and perhaps even more perverse way. By denying Ursula's female integrity and her sexuality (as he did in 'Moony') and by penetrating her anus, Birkin uses Ursula as a sexual substitute for Crich and does to her what he wants to do to Gerald. Birkin's actions belie his claim that 'If he pledged himself with the man he would later be able to pledge himself with the woman: not merely in legal marriage, but in absolute, mystic marriage' (p. 398), for he never really moves beyond homosexuality. He merely substitutes anal marriage for homosexual love.[39]

Lawrence in Transit

'I am essentially a fighter – to wish me peace is bad luck – except the fighter's peace.' (Letter to Rolf Gardiner, 4 July 1924)

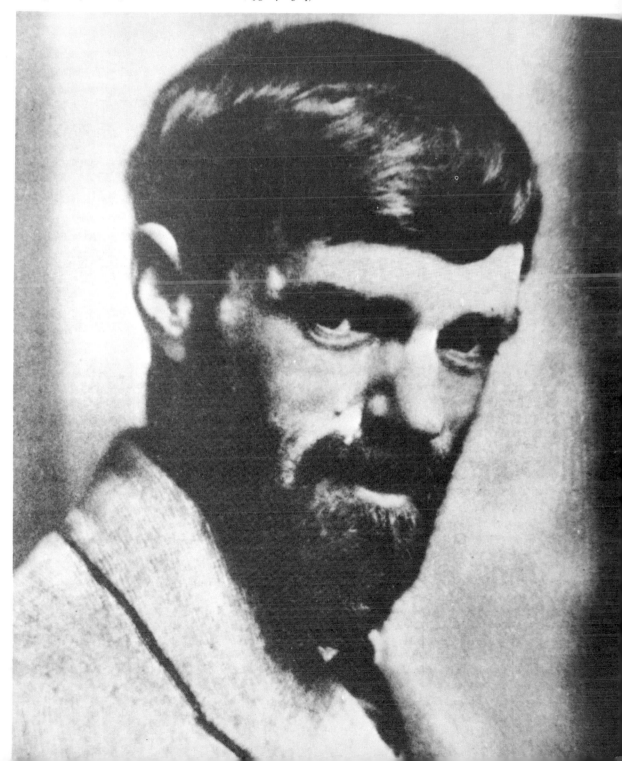

Opposite Although Lawrence grew to hate Capri, at the beginning of his stay there he was writing: 'To look down the Salernian Gulf, south-east on a blue day, and see the dim, sheer, rocky coast, the clear rock mountains, is so beautiful, so like Ulysses, that one sheds one's avatars, and recovers a lost self, Mediterranean, anterior to us.' (Letter to Lady Cynthia Asquith, 25 January 1920)

Above Italian landscape painted by Lawrence a few years later. 'The south! The south! The south! . . . Italy is still gay – does all her weeping in the press – takes her politics with her wine, and enjoys them.' (Letter to Lady Cynthia Asquith, 3 November 1919)

Right Compton Mackenzie 'has a nice villa here [Capri] and does the semi-romantic – but I like him, he's a good sort.' (Letter to W. E. and S. A. Hopkin, 9 January 1920)

Above Taormina. 'The worst of Taormina is that it is a parterre of English weeds all cultivating their egos hard, one against the other. Imagine nettle overtopping dandelion, the languors and lilies of virtue here very stiff and prickly, the roses and raptures of vice a little weedy and ill developed. Save me from my countrymen.' (Letter to Lady Cynthia Asquith, 25 March 1920)

Opposite 'Do you know what it is to be in a *dry* southern country – dry like Africa? I never knew before. But I like it. The sun is a bit overwhelming.' (Letter to Catherine Carswell, 12 May 1920)

Lake Kandy, Ceylon. The Lawrences spent two months there in the spring of 1922. 'I didn't like Ceylon – at least I liked looking at it – but not to live in. The East is not for me . . . altogether the tropics have something of the world before the flood – hot dark mud and the life inherent in it: makes me feel rather sick.' (Letter to Lady Cynthia Asquith, 30 April 1922)

Above, top The coast south of Sydney where Lawrence and Frieda had a house. 'The Pacific is just under a little cliff – almost under the doorstep: and heavens, such a noisy ocean.' (Letter to Mrs A. L. Jenkins, 28 May 1922)

Above Lawrence, Frieda and friends at Thirroul, New South Wales, 1922. 'Happy-go-lucky, don't-you-bother, we're-in-Australia. But also there seems to be no inside life of any sort: just a long lapse and drift.' (Letter to Catherine Carswell, 22 June 1922)

Opposite, top Lawrence and Frieda at Chapala. 'A man wanted me to have a banana hacienda with him here in Mexico. I suppose anyhow I'd better see England again first. And I feel, perhaps I've no business trying to bury myself in out-of-the-way places.' (Letter to John Middleton Murry, 26 May 1923)

Opposite bottom 'Mexico! The great, precipitous, dry, savage country, with a handsome church in every landscape, rising as it were out of nothing. A revolution-broken landscape . . .' (*The Plumed Serpent*)

Right Lawrence in New Mexico, 1922. 'I know now I don't want to live anywhere very long. But I belong to Europe. Though not to England.' (Letter to Catherine Carswell, 17 December 1922)

Caricature of Frieda
by Witter Bynner,
1923. Bynner was a
poet and translator
who lived in New
Mexico.

Caricature of
Lawrence by Witter
Bynner. Bynner
wrote in his memoir,
Journey With Genius:
'Lawrence's
appearance struck
me from the outset
as that of a bad
baby masquerading
as a good
Mephistopheles.'

Lawrence and Frieda at Santa Fé in 1922. '. . . it isn't *sympatisch* like Australia:
more of the will.' (Letter to W. Sibenhaar, 25 October 1922)

Portrait of
Lawrence by
Dorothy Brett,
1925.

D. H. Lawrence
in Transit
Clive James

If one were to take a wax pencil and trace Lawrence's travels on a globe of the world, the result would be an enigmatic squiggle, a squiggle that started off minutely preoccupied in Europe, was reduced still further to a fat dot formed by the cramped wartime movements within England, broke out, enlarged itself to a bold transoceanic zigzag which at one wild moment streaked right around the planet, and then subsided again into more diffident, European vagaries – still restless, but listless, tailing off. The pencil should properly come to a halt at Vence, in the Alpes-Maritimes, although if we substituted for it another pencil of a different colour we might legitimately add one last, sweeping leg of the journey, as Lawrence's mobility recovered in death and his ashes rode back mindlessly to New Mexico.

In a few minutes we could map the wanderings of nearly two decades. It wouldn't tell us much, apart from the obvious fact that he liked to move about. He was in search of something, no question of it. Headquarters, the fissure into the underworld – it had many names. But one is permitted to doubt whether it could ever have been found, the doubt being engendered less by the world's nature than by an assessment of Lawrence's insatiable hunger for meaning. There is a tendency, once Lawrence's odyssey has been identified as a spiritual quest, to suppose that Lawrence had a firm idea of his spiritual object: hence the notion that he was in revolt against twentieth-century society, or post-Renaissance Europe, or post-Columbian America, or whatever you care to name. Lawrence was in revolt all right, but the revolt encompassed almost everything he knew in the present and nearly all the past he ever came to know, and this ability to exhaust reality through intimacy shows up in his travels as much as in everything else he did.

It was not so much that familiarity bred contempt – and anyway, there were some familiarities of which he never quite tired – as that it bred unease. Never to find things important enough is the mark of a dreamer. Lawrence, thoroughly practical and businesslike in matters large and small, was no ordinary dreamer: nevertheless he could get no lasting peace from his surroundings, and as time went by felt bound to look upon them as an impoverished outwardness implying a symbolic centre – and this despite an unrivalled ability to reflect the fullness of physical reality undiminished onto the page. Lawrence is beyond the reach of any other modern writer writing about what can be seen, since whatever could be seen he saw instantaneously and without effort – which is probably why he could regard it as nothing but the periphery of the real. If he had lived longer, his novels might well have lost any touch at all with worldly objects: the sense of actuality which other men serve long apprenticeships to attain was for him a departure point. And again if he had lived longer, he might well have exhausted the earth with travel. Had he not placed such an emphasis on turning inwards to the dark, fiery centre, we could by now have been tempted to imagine him turning outwards, away from the tellurian cultures depleted by the ravenous enquiry of his imagination and towards an uncapturable infinity that actually exists: orchestrations of dark suns, unapproachable galaxies peopled by Etruscans who stayed on top, nebulae like turquoise horses, the ocean of the great desire. Quetzalcoatl's *serape*! Sun-dragon! Star-oil! Lawrence was in search of, was enraged over the loss of, a significance this world does not supply and has never supplied. For a worldling, his symbolist requirements were inordinate. As a spaceman he might have found repose. Heaven knows, he was genius enough not to be outshone by the beyond. He could have written down a supernova.

Supposing, though, that this was what his journeyings were all in aid of – home. The supposition is at least part of the truth, although by no means, I think, the largest part. If home was ever anywhere, it was at the Del Monte and Flying Heart ranches in New Mexico, whose mountains seemed to be the place he could stay at longest without feeling compelled to move on. Yet there were still times when he missed Europe, just as, in Europe, there were so many times when he missed America, and just as, on either continent, there were troubled times when he missed England. Headquarters tended to be where Lawrence was not. Places abandoned because they did not possess the secret could be fondly remembered later on – perhaps they had had the secret after all. But it never occurred to Lawrence that there *was* no secret. Out of all the thousands of pages of his incredibly productive short life, the great pathos which emerges is of this extraterrestrial unbelonging – far more frightening, in the long run, than the social challenges which by now we have absorbed, or else written off as uninformative propositions. Critical unreason often occurs in creative genius, but creative unreason rarely does: for a talent to be as big as Lawrence's and yet still be sick is a strange thing. It's easily understandable that people equipped to appreciate his magnitude as a writer should take the intellectually less taxing course, declaring Lawrence to be a paragon of prophetic sanity and the world sick instead.

Lawrence's first travels were to London, Brighton, the Isle of Wight, Bournemouth. Readers of the early letters will be rocked back on their heels to find the same descriptive power turned loose on Brighton as later reached out to seize the dawn over Sicily, the flowers in Tuscany, the desert of Sinai, the sperm-like lake in Mexico and the ranches after snow. Then, in 1912, the first run to Metz (then in Germany); Waldbröl in the Rhineland, Munich, Mayrhofen in Austria. A walk over the Tyrol. Lake Garda. Back to England in 1913, then back to Bavaria. Lerici. England again. The war confined these short European pencil strokes to a fitfully vibrating dot within England, covering Sussex, Hampstead, Cornwall; an angry return to London after being hounded from the coast and possible contact with the High Seas Fleet; Berkshire, Derbyshire.

In 1919, free to quit England, he broke straight for Italy: Turin, Lerici, Florence, Rome, Picinisco, Capri. In 1920, Taormina, in Sicily. Malta. In 1921, Sardinia. Germany, Austria, Italy. Taormina again. (Taormina is a node, like – later on – Taos, and the Villa Mirenda at Scandicci, outside Florence.)

In 1922 the emboldened pattern struck outwards to Ceylon. Australia for two months. Then America: Taos, the Del Monte ranch, the mountains. In 1923 he was in Mexico City, New York, Los Angeles, Mexico again and – England. In 1924 France, Germany, New York, Taos. The Flying Heart ranch, alias the Lobo, alias the Kiowa. Oaxaca, in Mexico.

The year 1925 ended the period of the big pattern. After a wrecking illness in New Mexico he returned to London. Then Baden-Baden. Spotorno. In 1926, Capri, Spotorno and the Villa Mirenda in Scandicci – his last real place to be. Germany, England, Scotland. Italy.

In 1927 he toured the Etruscan tombs. A score of names cropped up in his itinerary: Volterra, Orvieto, Tarquinia – short strokes all over Tuscany and Umbria, the Etruscan places. Then to Austria and Germany, and in 1928 to Switzerland, with the Villa Mirenda abandoned. Gsteig bei Gstaad, Baden-Baden (the Kurhaus Plättig) and the Ile de Port-Cros, Toulon. From low-lying sun-trap to *Höheluftkurort* the short strokes moved trembling. Bandol, in the south of France. He was in Paris in 1929, then Palma de Mallorca, Forte dei Marmi, Florence, Bandol again. In 1930 Vence, and death.

Even in Vence he wasn't too sick to use his amazing eyes. There isn't a place on the list that he didn't inhabit at a glance. And yet as we read on and on through the magnificence of his travel writings, a little voice keeps telling us that the man was never there. The man, the spaceman, never travelled except in dreams. Dreaming, while dying, of India and China and everything else that lay beyond the San Francisco gate. Dreaming of altogether elsewhere, of an England that was not England, of a Europe that was never Europe.

It was a great day, Frieda said, when they walked together from the Isartal into the Alps. Lawrence wrote it down, in a way that takes us straight there. But where was he? 'We stayed at a Gasthaus,' he wrote to Edward Garnett, 'and used to have breakfast out under the horse-chestnut trees, steep above the river weir, where the timber rafts come down. The river is green glacier water.' Compare this to one of the famous opening sentences of *A Farewell to Arms*: 'In the bed of the river there were pebbles and boulders, dry and white in the sun, and the water was clear and swiftly moving and blue in the channels', and we will find Lawrence's descriptive prose both more economical and less nostalgic, the effortless reportage of an infallibly observant visitor.

Still on the same descriptive trail, go south to Italy ('I love these people') and look at Lerici. 'And in the morning,' he wrote to Lady Cynthia Asquith, 'one wakes and sees the pines all dark and mixed up with perfect rose of dawn, and all day long the olives shimmer in the sun, and fishing boats and strange sails like Corsican ships come out of nowhere on a pale blue sea, and then at evening all the sea is milky gold and scarlet with sundown.' The fake-naive rhythms, suitable for consumption by titled ladies, can't mask the searing power of that simplicity. 'The mountains of Carrara are white, of a soft white blue eidelweiss, in a faint pearl haze – all snowy. The sun is very warm, and the sea glitters.' It still does, even though polluted with a thoroughness which even Lawrence would have hesitated to prophesy. 'The Mediterranean is quite wonderful – and when the sun sets beyond the islands of Porto Venere, and all the sea is like heaving white milk with a street of fire across it, and amethyst islands away back, it is too beautiful.' It's small wonder that Lawrence could talk about art having characteristics rather than rules, and even disparage the idea of art altogether. He had it to burn.

Reality offered Lawrence no resistance. Mysticism did, and it was into mysticism that he poured his conscious energy. Turning to *Twilight in Italy*, we can find something on every page to match the descriptions in the letters. Here is Lake Garda at dawn.

In the morning I often lie in bed and watch the sunrise. The lakes lie dim and milky, the mountains are dark blue at the back, while over them the sky gushes and glistens with light. At a certain place on the mountain ridge the light burns gold, seems to fuse a little groove on the hill's rim. It fuses and fuses at this point, till of a sudden it comes, the intense, molten, living light. The mountains melt suddenly, the light steps down, there is a glitter, a spangle, a clutch of spangles, a great unbearable sun-track flashing across the milky lake, and the light falls on my face.

But superb as this is, it isn't what this book or any other Lawrence book is about. *Twilight in Italy* is about north and south, hill and dale — it is the tentative prototype for a great sequence of increasingly confident polarities, by which Lawrence the traveller was to go on splitting the world in two until there was nothing left of it but powder. The Bavarian highlanders, it appears, 'are almost the only race with the souls of artists . . . their processions and religious festivals are profoundly impressive, solemn, and rapt.' Again, they are 'a race that moves on the poles of mystic sensual delight. Every gesture is a gesture from the blood, every expression a symbolic utterance.' Your Bavarian highlander 'accepts the fate and the mystic delight of the senses with one will, he is complete and final. His sensuous experience is supreme, a consummation of life and death at once.' Whether drinking in the Gasthaus, or 'hating steadily and cruelly', or 'walking in the strange, dark, subject-procession' to bless the fields, 'it is always the same, the dark, powerful mystic, sensuous experience is the whole of him, he is mindless and bound within the absoluteness of the issue, the unchangeability of the great icy not-being which holds good for ever, and is supreme.' Yes, it was all happening in Bavaria – or rather, it was all to happen later on in Bavaria. But the thing to grasp here is that word 'dark'. Not only (as is well known) is it the key adjective in all of Lawrence, but Lawrence's travels can usefully be summarized as an interminable search for a noun it could firmly be attached to.

No sooner is Lawrence in Italy than we discover that the Italians have dark interiors too. 'The Italian people are called "Children of the Sun". They might better be called "Children of the Shadow". Their souls are dark and nocturnal.' A feature of the dark soul is unconsciousness, as in the spinning-lady, whose mind Lawrence can apparently read.

She glanced at me again, with her wonderful, unchanging eyes, that were like the visible heavens, unthinking, or like the two flowers that are open in pure clear unconsciousness. To her I was a piece of the environment. That was all. Her world was clear and absolute, without consciousness of self. She was not self-conscious, because she was not aware that there was anything in the universe except *her* universe.

But the darkly unconscious haven't got it all their own way. Much later in the book, during the fascinating passage that deals with the local production of *Amleto*, Lawrence spies a mountain man in the audience: he is of the same race as the old spinning-woman.

He was fair, thin, and clear, abstract, of the mountains. . . . He has a fierce, abstract look, wild and untamed as a hawk, but like a hawk at its own nest, fierce with love . . . it is the fierce spirit of the Ego come out of the primal infinite, but detached, isolated, an aristocrat. He is not an Italian, dark-blooded. He is fair, keen as steel, with the blood of the mountaineer in him. He is like my old spinning woman.

To reconcile this mountain-man with the spinning-woman, we must assume she was never dark-blooded, when a good deal of what we were told about her when we were reading about her suggested that she was. And indeed, looking back, we find that she *hasn't* been given a dark soul or dark blood – she is simply 'the core and centre of the world, the sun, and the single firmament'. Lawrence hasn't at this stage entirely identified the dark soul with the earth's centre, so it's still possible to combine abstractness with being at the centre of the world, and, presumably, dark-bloodedness with not being at the centre of the world. What's difficult to reconcile, however, even when stretching the idea of poetic consistency until it snaps, is a Bavarian highlander's dark-bloodedness with a mountain man's clear abstractness: if these conditions are both different from an ordinary Italian's dark-bloodedness, are they different in different ways?

The awkward truth is that Lawrence left his Bavarian highlanders behind in his opening chapter and forgot about them while writing the bulk of the book, which even without them would still be extremely difficult to puzzle out. The confusion confesses itself in the passage about Paolo and Maria. Paolo is a native of San Gaudenzio, and therefore a hill man – fair, eyes like ice, unalterable, inaccessible. Maria is from the plain, dark-skinned, slow-souled. 'Paolo and she were the opposite sides of the universe, the light and the dark.' Nothing could be clearer. 'They were both by nature passionate, vehement. But the lines of their passion were opposite. Hers was the primitive, crude, violent flux of the blood, emotional and undiscriminating, but wanting to mix and mingle. His was the hard, clear, invulnerable passion of the bones, finely tempered and unchangeable.' As an opponent to, or complement of, the passion of the blood, the passion of the bones was evidently judged by Lawrence to be somewhat unwieldy – it never again made such an unabashed appearance. Pretty soon, the blood's passion became the only kind of authentic passion you could have.

In *Twilight in Italy*, though the destructive mechanization of the world had already clearly been perceived, Lawrence still had something to say for abstractness, intellectuality and cognate non-dark attributes. In 1915 he wrote to Lady Ottoline Morrell from Ripley, in Derbyshire:

It is a cruel thing to go back to that which one has been. . . . Altogether the life here is so dark and violent; it all happens in the senses, powerful and rather destructive: no mind or mental consciousness, unintellectual. These men, are passionate enough, sensuous, dark – God, how all my boyhood comes back – so violent, so dark, the mind always dark and without understanding, the senses violently active. It makes me sad beyond words.

It's not the first time that the word 'dark' is used like a comma, but it's one of the few times – all early – when Lawrence freely admitted the possibility that the dark soul could be as murderous on its own as intellect could. The emphasis was still on keeping a balance, on checking the word against the thing it was supposed to stand for. Lawrence's later history is the story of darkness being awarded a steadily more automatic virtue, the periodic calls for an equilibrium of forces degenerating into unfathomable proposals about establishing the correct relationship between the components of darkness itself.

Lawrence's 'dash' (his word) to Sardinia produced a book, *Sea and Sardinia*, which clearly shows his untroubled ability to uproot all the attributes he has just so triumphantly detected in a place, move them on to the next place, and then condemn the first place for either not having them in sufficient strength or never having had them. In Cagliari the men 'stood about in groups, but without the intimate Italian watchfulness that never leaves a passer-by alone'. Looks as if the Italians' dark blood wasn't dark enough, an impression confirmed by the menacing loins of the Sardinian peasants: 'a young one with a swift eye and hard cheek and hard, dangerous thighs. . . . How fascinating it is, after the soft Italians, to see these limbs in their close knee-breeches, so definite, so manly, with the old fierceness in them still. One realizes, with horror, that the race of men is almost extinct in Europe. . . .' Plainly the war period has helped sour Lawrence on Europe altogether, but even taking that convulsive time-lag into account, it's still difficult to square up *Sea and Sardinia* with *Twilight in Italy*. The real difference, it appears, is that Italy is *connu* and therefore sterile, whereas Sardinia is unknown and therefore isn't. 'There are unknown, unworked lands where the salt has not lost its savour. But one must have perfected oneself in the great past first.'

Whether in the vegetable market near the start of the book or at the peasant's procession near the end, Lawrence's colour sense is at its sumptuous best, and in general *Sea and Sardinia* is a remarkable piece of lyrical visualization. 'When we came up, the faint shape of land appeared ahead, more transparent than thin pearl. Already Sardinia. Magic are high lands seen from the sea, when they are far, far off, and ghostly translucent like icebergs.' Beautiful writing, but no lasting pledge. Lawrence was in and out of Sardinia in a hurry, and spent a good half of 1921 sitting in Taormina getting sick of Europe, which can't be said to exclude Sardinia. Just as Sardinia had it over Italy, somewhere else had it over the whole of Europe. 'I would like to break out of Europe,' he wrote to Mary Cannan. 'It has been like a bad meal of various courses . . . and one has got indigestion from every course.' He was thinking of 'something more velvety', Japan, perhaps, or Siam. The south of Europe was better than the north, but there was no denying that even the south had gone off: 'I can't get the little taste of canker out of my mouth', he told Catherine Carswell, 'The people – 'A few days later he was telling E. H. Brewster that they were *canaille, canaglia, Schwein-hunderei*, stink-pots. 'A curse, a murrain, a pox on this crawling, sniffling, spunk-less brood of humanity.'

In his mind Lawrence was already embarked for Ceylon, and in another few days Mabel Dodge by inviting him to Taos had made it possible for him to project his mental journey right around the globe. Europe was promptly pronounced to be 'a dead dog which begins to stink intolerably'. England (in the same letter, written to S. S. Koteliansky) was declared 'a dead dog that died of a love disease like syphilis'. Bad news for Koteliansky, who was living in it at the time. (This letter also featured the Lawrentian pearl about 'one of those irritating people who have generalized detestations. . . . So unoriginal.')

'I feel I can't come –' Lawrence wrote to Brewster in January 1922, 'that the East is not my destiny.' Later in the same month, destiny doubled back, and Lawrence decided to go via Ceylon after all. 'I feel it is my destiny' he wrote to Mabel Dodge 'to go east before coming west.' Destiny pulled another double-cross in Ceylon, where Lawrence found the velvety Orient inane. 'The East, the bit I've seen,' he told Mary Cannan, 'seems silly.' As he frequently did when off-balance, he thought of England, telling Robert Pratt Barlow that

the most living clue of life is in us Englishmen in England, and the great mistake we make is in not uniting together in the strength of this real living clue – religious in the most vital sense – uniting together in England and so carrying the vital spark through . . . the responsibility for England, the living England, rests on men like you and me and Cunard – probably even the Prince of Wales. . . .

The Prince of Wales was indirectly responsible for Lawrence's 'Elephant' poem, the most tangible result of the Singhalese sojourn apart from a disillusioning close-up of inscrutable platoons of dark people with dark eyes: 'the vastness of the blood stream, so dark and hot and from so far off'. As far as the East went, darkness was a dead loss. Not that the contradiction with many things he'd said before, or with nearly everything he said later, ever slowed him down. The task was to push his mystical system around the planet until it clicked; there was no obligation to explain why it kept going wrong.

Australia was a country Lawrence couldn't characterize: 'the spell of its indifference gets me'. Mystical content, zero. 'This is the most democratic place I have *ever* been in,' he wrote to Else Jaffé, 'And the more I see of democracy the more I dislike it. . . . You *never* knew anything so nothing, *nichts, nullus, niente*, as the life here,' The situations in *Kangaroo* are mainly imported, and it's doubtful if Lawrence ever gave Australia much thought after the first few days. Nevertheless the settings in *Kangaroo* have small trouble in being the most acutely observed and evocative writing about Australia that there has so far been, bearing out my point that Lawrence could reproduce reality with no effort whatsoever.

Trollope, Kipling, Conrad, Galsworthy and R. L. Stevenson all visited

Australia at one time or another, but if any of them was capable of bringing off a piece of scene-setting like the opening chapter of *Kangaroo*, he didn't feel compelled to. The moment he got to Thirroul Lawrence despatched letters announcing his longing for Europe – the dead dog lived again. The central situation in *Kangaroo* looks to be about Italian fascism; the Australian variety, which emerged much later, was very different. But *Kangaroo* is a bit more than a European play with an Australian set-designer. It has an interesting early scene in which Lawrence makes Lovat out to be a prig, reluctant to lend Jack Callcott a book of essays in case it bores him. ' "I might rise up to it, you know," said Jack laconically, "if I bring all my mental weight to bear on it." ' There is a hint here that someone might have shaken Lawrence by urging him to lay off the intensity. It's a rare moment of self-criticism, and almost *the* moment of self-deprecating humour. Lawrence was perhaps a touch less certain about the aridity of the Australian spirit than he let on.

America. Lorenzo in Taos – it was a giant step. It rapidly became clear that the most dangerous item of local fauna was Mabel Dodge Luhan, the hostess who favoured will over feeling – a priority always guaranteed to grate on Lawrence, whose will and feeling were united in Destiny. 'My heart still turns most readily to Italy,' he told Mary Cannon – a strong sign of unease – and 'I even begin to get a bit homesick for England. . . .' A certain sign. At this stage, Lawrence had decided that the Indians couldn't be copied. 'And after all, if we have to go ahead,' he wrote to Else Jaffé, 'we must ourselves go ahead. We can go back and pick up some threads – but these Indians are up against a dead wall, even more than we are: but a different wall.' And to Catherine Carswell: '*Però, son sempre Inglese*.' Even after moving to the Del Monte, putting a helpful seventeen miles between himself and the Mabel-ridden Taos, Lawrence was detecting the same *innerlich* emptiness in his surroundings as had wasted his time in Australia. Mexico, however, worked differently, and he was soon telling the much-maligned Middleton Murry that if England wanted to lead the world again she would have to pick up a lost trail, and that the end of the trail lay in – Mexico.

The Plumed Serpent is a work of uncanny poetic force which manages to keep some sort of shape despite intense distorting pressures from Lawrence's now-rampant mysticism. Kate, with her European blood and conscious understanding, is outdistanced by dark-faced silent men with their columns of dark blood and dark, fiery clouds of passionate male tenderness. In addition to the oppressive symbolic scheme, there are moments which lead you to suspect that the author might simply be cracked, as when he suggests that Bolshevists are all born near railways. Yet the fifth chapter, 'The Lake', is one of Lawrence's supreme stretches of writing. The boatman 'pulled rhythmically through the frail-rippling, sperm-like water, with a sense of peace. And for the first time Kate felt she had met the mystery of the natives, the strange and mysterious gentleness between a scylla and charibdis of violence: the small poised, perfect body of the bird that waves wings of thunder and wings of fire and night in its flight.' Frail-rippling – what a writer. The transparent purity of the book's descriptions is inseparable from its symbolic structure, which is an opposition between principles that no ordinary mortal will ever be able to clarify, since Lawrence himself could only grope towards them with incantatory phrase-making.

The book's incandescent set-pieces – the burning of the images, the execution of the traitors, and so on – are spaced apart by impenetrable thickets of unmeaning. 'But within his own heavy, dark range he had a curious power.' Kate learns of Cipriano. 'Almost she could *see* the black fume of power which he emitted, the dark, heavy vibration of his blood . . . she could feel the curious tingling heat of his blood, and the heavy power of the *will* that lay unemerged in his blood.' What the Bavarian highlanders and plains Italians had lost, the sons of Quetzalcoatl had gained.

Lawrence learned about Indians during the hiatus between writing the tenth and the eleventh chapter of *The Plumed Serpent*. His mystical conclusions are distributed between the later part of that novel (e.g. the snake in the fire at the heart of the world) and *Mornings in Mexico*, a travel book of unusual difficulty, even for Lawrence. Certainly he no longer pleads for a balance between the disparate consciousnesses of the white man and the dark man. You can't, it appears, have it both ways. The most you can hope for is to harbour a little ghost who sees in both directions. Yet ghost or no ghost, Lawrence seems to be trying hard to belong to the Indian way, to the 'abdomen where the great blood-stream surges in the dark, and surges in its own generic experiences'. What we seek in sleep, Lawrence says, the Indians perhaps seek actively, 'the dark blood falling back from the mind, from sight and speech and knowing, back to the great central source where is rest and unspeakable renewal'. Relieved by some of his most brilliant descriptive passages, the rhetoric is short of totally suffocating, but still fearsomely turgid. It takes the letters to remind us that he could write in an unfevered way during this period. 'Here the grass is only just moving green out of the sere earth,' he wrote to Zelia Nuttall, 'and the hairy, pale mauve anemones that the Indians call owl flowers stand strange and alone among the dead pine needles, under the wintry trees. Extraordinary how the place seems *seared* with winter: almost cauterized. And so winter-cleaned, from under three feet of snow.' A cold towel for the reader's forehead. Green glacier water.

Back in Europe to stay, Lawrence unpacked his mystical machine and set about applying it to the Etruscans. At the same time, and without any disabling sense of contradicting himself, he started rehabilitating Europe, even the long-forsaken north. 'I am very much inclined to agree,' he wrote to Rolf Gardiner in July 1926, 'that one must look for real guts and self-responsibility to the Northern peoples. After a winter in Italy – and a while in France – I am a bit bored by the Latins, there is a sort of inner helplessness and lack of courage in them. . . .' Writing from Lincolnshire to E. H. Brewster, he claimed to have rediscovered 'a queer, odd sort of potentiality in the people, especially the common people. . . .' The common English people, back in the running at long last! Whether or not the Prince of Wales qualified wasn't stated.

As a traveller through ordinary space, Lawrence got back on slanging terms with his repudiated Europe. Baden-Baden, for example, was a *Totentanz* out of Holbein, 'old, old people tottering their cautious dance of triumph: *wir sind noch hier*. . . .' As a traveller through time and thought, he moved on a grander scale. *Etruscan Places* is a gentle book, endearingly characteristic in its handy division between Etruscan and Roman and disarmingly uncharacteristic in its emphasis on delicacy and humour: it's the book of a strong man dying. 'We have lost the art of living;' he writes, 'and in the most important science of all, the science of daily life, the science of behaviour, we are complete ignoramuses.' The Etruscans weren't like that. Their art had the 'natural beauty of proportion of the phallic consciousness, contrasted with the more studied or ecstatic proportion of the mental and spiritual Consciousness we are accustomed to.' The contrast, as always, is asserted with a degree of confidence which is bound to draw forth a preliminary nod of assent. It remains a fact, however, that this kind of argument has practically nothing to do with post-Renaissance art or pre-Renaissance art or any kind of art, since art is more likely to depend on these two sorts of proportion being in tension than on one getting rid of the other. Lawrence's binomial schemes were useless for thinking about art, as those of his disciples who tried to employ them went on to prove. Without them, though, we wouldn't have had *his* art.

In January 1928, Lawrence told Dorothy Brett that he still intended coming back to the ranch. 'It's very lovely,' he wrote to Lady Glenavy, 'and I'd be well there.' But his seven-league boots were worn through, and he was never to get out of Europe alive. We have only to read 'Reflections on the Death of a Porcupine' or the last part of *St Mawr* to realize that his ashes ended up on the right spot. The mountains were a cherished place. They weren't home, though. Home was at the Source, and the Source – he said it himself – is past comprehension.

D. H. Lawrence
and America
Tony Tanner

Lawrence arrived in America on 11 September 1922, his thirty-seventh birth-day. He entered through San Francisco, having come from Australia. He finally left America on 22 September 1925, sailing from New York to Europe where he moved around for the next five years until his death. During his time on the American continent he spent part of the summer of 1923 in Mexico, returning to New York where Frieda left him to return to England while Lawrence went to Los Angeles to stay with two Danish artists the Lawrences had befriended in New Mexico. With one of them, Kai Gótzsche, he went back to Mexico whence he finally left for England in September of 1923. He returned to New Mexico in March 1924, again went down to Mexico, this time for the winter months, before returning to America for six months before his final departure. When he left there is no doubt that he was a sick man, if not actually a dying one, and whereas it would be completely misleading to suggest that America had 'killed' him, it does seem as though he went through some sort of mental crisis during his American stay, which at times took on the appearance of madness to friends who were with him. How much was due to provocations and tensions he ex-perienced in America, and how much it was a culmination of the strains of a volatile and violent marriage, an inability to resolve his feelings about relation-ships with men, and perhaps as well the gradual undermining effects of the first stages of the dreaded tuberculosis (which he would never mention), it is im-possible to estimate. But we do have some records of his behaviour in America, apart from his own comments in letters and essays, and it is worth briefly con-sulting two of these reports, by Mabel Dodge Luhan and Knud Merrild.

Mabel Dodge Luhan gave her account of Lawrence's American stay in her book *Lorenzo in Taos*. She was the woman who not only invited Lawrence to Taos, but 'willed' him to come. She had read Lawrence's work and had decided that he was the man who was needed to describe the Taos country and the

Indians, and for Mabel Dodge Luhan such a decision became tantamount to an order. 'I'd had the idea of having *him* come to *Taos*, and I'd sit there and draw him until he came. I'd go down inside myself and call that man until he would have to come.' Her account often reverts to the refrain '*My* will be done', and it is perhaps small wonder that she became for Lawrence the most fearful incarnation of the white American woman, living by the pre-emptive and possessive will. Nevertheless he and Frieda accepted her hospitality in Taos until they could not stand the pressures any more and went to live in a dilapidated rented ranch up in the hills, called Del Monte. They persuaded two Danish artists to stay the winter with them, which hardly soothed the angry, thwarted Mabel Dodge Luhan. Later she gave the Lawrences a ranch where they lived for a time. A large, rich, powerful woman, she was used to having her own way, and she wanted Lawrence near her, on her own terms, and if possible nearly all to herself. Such a presence could hardly have induced Whitmanesque sentiments in Lawrence at this stage in his life, and some of his verbal and literary violence during this period may be traced to his determination to fight back for his independence with the only weapon he could really wield – the word.

However, Mabel Dodge Luhan's account is not entirely devoid of perception and self-knowledge, and some of her comments are worth introducing here. She noted, for instance, that Lawrence was compulsively restless (as did the Danish artist, Knud Merrild) that he was always fussing around the house; that he, who praised an achieved stillness as a most important form of action, had no gift for leisure. He was obviously very unsure of himself and to this end could not bear to have his word questioned in anything, even subjects in which he had no expertise (Merrild records the same impression). That there were bitter rows between Lawrence and Frieda, both Mabel Luhan and Knud Merrild record; indeed Mabel Luhan states that when they all went to bathe in the Hot Springs she often saw Frieda's body and that it was not uncommon for there to be 'great black and blue bruises on her blond flesh', the result of blows inflicted by Lawrence.

Mabel Luhan is of course a far from reliable witness; she was too emotionally involved, too bent on her own form of emotional appropriation, to be able to see how her role appeared at the time. When she is washing some dishes with Lawrence and their fingers happen to touch in the soapsuds, for her there is a 'clamour of magnetic bells'. Whether Lawrence also heard them is open to question. However, we may believe her when she attested to the sort of joy and vitality which Lawrence's presence could bring to simple tasks, or a picnic, or playing charades (not dancing which he seems to have hated). Some of Mabel Luhan's anecdotes are informative: for instance, it seems that she took Lawrence to visit an ancient ceremonial cave above the village of Arroyo Seco. The cave appears in 'The Woman Who Rode Away' but for reasons of his own Lawrence has shifted the locale to Mexico, perhaps to give a more cruel, 'Aztec', feeling to the story. But so much of her account concerns her emotional states at the time, that it is hardly worth recapitulating many details here. We may well believe her when she says that when Brett came with the Lawrences on their second visit to Taos, thus bringing the number of jealous women around him to a total of three, there was plenty of tension in the air: 'we all tried to drag at him and wrestle with him and prevent him from having his way'. It is perhaps not surprising that Lawrence felt the need to get away. But given the number of times he vilified Taos after he had left ('Spit on Taos for me' he wrote in a letter to Knud Merrild), it is rather touching to find that having kept up a correspondence with Mabel Luhan during the years after he left America, on 21 January 1930 Lawrence wrote to her: 'If we can manage it, and I can come to New Mexico, then we can begin a new life, with real tenderness in it.' Just over a month later he died.

The other memoirist of Lawrence's American period, Knud Merrild, is inevitably more impartial. With fellow Danish artist Kai Gótzsche, he made his way to Taos when Lawrence happened to be there. They did not impose themselves on the Lawrences, were quite independent, and were not seeking anything from Lawrence himself. In the circumstances it is perhaps not surprising that Lawrence turned to the two Danes for relief and it seems that both Frieda and he urged them to spend the winter with them at the Del Monte ranch. Inevitably, Lawrence vented a lot of his fury at Mabel Luhan in front of the two Danes, and their account of Mabel Luhan suggests that she could indeed be overbearing and manipulative to a degree. However, although Merrild obviously admired Lawrence greatly and stresses that they never had a 'truer friend', he was too much his own man to capitulate totally to Lawrence's influence and not to notice the stranger aspects of his behaviour. Thus there is a dispassionate account of an 'hysterical outbreak' on Lawrence's part against Frieda, though he says that this was singular. There is also a rather unpleasant account of Lawrence losing his temper with a dog he had at the time, Pips, who was not so undivided in her loyalties as Lawrence apparently would have liked. The usually temperate Merrild describes Lawrence as 'completely out of his mind' and he goes on to tell how Lawrence threw the dog around, kicked it, swore at it, until finally Merrild interposed himself and Lawrence backed away.

Much of the account is in a happier vein, as it does seem as if Lawrence was more at peace up at the ranch than down in Taos nearer Mabel Luhan. He fussed, meddled, attempted jobs he was too weak to manage, indulged in his 'everlasting teaching,' cooked, cut their hair, and was, it would seem, a remarkable person to be near. But even Merrild, who is determined to be loyal, cannot avoid giving the impression that Lawrence was entering into a very black period of his life. He would apparently speak passionately about the 'lust of killing' and seems to have imagined himself doing it. He is quoted as speaking of cutting Mabel Luhan's throat. (Apparently he always carried round with him a copy he had made of the *Death of Procris*, the painting by Piero di Cosimo in the National Gallery. He said he loved the blood and killing in the picture. Is it entirely a coincidence that Procris was a jealous wife who was unintentionally speared down by her husband while spying on him?) And towards the end of their period together Lawrence 'saw darkness and death everywhere': 'one often felt so utterly hopeless about Lawrence and his ideas. All this devastation, destruction, and death—death—he breathed death, spake and saw death everywhere, and only darkness, the darkness of death.' In addition Merrild corroborates the feeling one has that Lawrence in all his talk about the need for authority really envisaged himself as the new necessary leader: 'he wanted to be a leader'. But 'none of us believed in Lawrence as a leader of men . . . how could he be a leader of men? He contradicted himself at almost every turn.'

Lawrence himself wrote no specific travelogue of America as he had done for other countries: one reason for this may be that so much of modern urban America simply meant nothing to him. He visited San Francisco, Los Angeles, New York, New Orleans and Chicago, to name just the more major cities, but you would hardly guess it from his writings. At a time when so many things induced a disproportionate rage or irritation in him, the great urban conglomerates of America left him curiously unmoved, unvituperative – simply with nothing to say. And indeed, if we turn to his letters written while he was in America, just such a mood of non-response seems to have been a dominant one. 'One forms not the slightest attachment, especially here in America. . . . It is all inwardly a hard stone and nothingness. Only the desert has a fascination – to ride alone – in the sun in the forever unpossessed country. . . .' (29 September 1922). From the Del Monte ranch: 'Altogether it is ideal, according to one's ideas. But *innerlich*, there is nothing. It seems to me, in America, for the inside life, there is just nothing. All this outside life – and marvellous country – and it all means so little to one.' (17 December 1922). 'America exhausts the springs of one's soul.' (24 September 1923). The American ideal of 'freedom' meant for Lawrence a deprivation, a loss of attachment or connectedness with any power or energy or rhythm which could give life a more than materialistic meaning. He keeps coming back to the same complaints – that Americans live by will, that they cannot trust life until they control it, that he feels out of place. Ultimately it seems America induced in Lawrence a sense of unreality. 'America makes me feel I haven't a word to say about anything. Not that I dislike it so badly – but it seems unreal and makes me feel more remote.' (15 August 1923).

Characteristically, after a return visit to Europe, he reacted as always to the stimulus of contrast and temporarily saw Taos in a new light. 'I must say I am glad to be out here in the Southwest of America – there is the pristine some-thing, unbroken, unbreakable, and not to be got under even by us awful whites with our machines – for which I thank whatever gods there be.' (8 April 1924). But that unbreakable 'something' offered no possibilities of rapport, or contact, or new harmonies, such as the younger Lawrence had dreamed of, and his final reaction to being in America is, perhaps, one of exhaustion. 'One needs a *rest* after America: the hardness, the *resistance* of all things to all things, inwardly, tires one.' (9 December 1924). It is debatable whether Lawrence ever fully recovered from that profound inner tiredness during the remaining years of his life.

'In some curious way, it is the Indians still who are American. This great welter of whites is not yet a nation, not yet a people.' 'Certain Americans and an Englishman', *Phoenix* II
'But I stand on the far edge of their firelight, and am neither denied nor accepted. My way is my own, old red father; I can't cluster at the drum any more.' 'Indians and an Englishman', *Phoenix*

Mabel Luhan records one aspect of Lawrence's talk which has an authentic ring, namely a constant oscillation between a contemptuous empiricism and an incantatory mysticism, particularly in relation to the significance of the Indian and the land.

When he was in temporary harmony with Frieda, he would, in brilliant vituperative talk, sling mud at the whole inner cosmos, and at Taos, the Indians, the mystic life of the mountain, and the invisible, potent powers of the embodied spirit or at every-thing, in fact, not apparent, scheduled, and concrete. Then, sometimes, he would go back on the limited scale of obvious, materialistic living and, forgetting Frieda's presence or defying it, would talk just wonderfully, with far-reaching implications, of the power of consciousness, the growth of the soul, its dominion and its triumphs.

How much of such alterations of mood were related to his current relationships with Frieda is, for us, an imponderable consideration. But the sort of ambiva-lent, shifting perspective that is implied in this account is in line with Lawrence's writings about his reactions to New Mexico. Sometimes he felt drawn into its Indianness and his writing then reaches out for forgotten religious intimations and vibrations; at other times it threw him back on his Englishness and his tone becomes commonsensical, no-nonsense, colloquial, sceptical, derisory, or antic. Thus, within a few lines of each other in one essay, we find these two statements: 'We have to feel our way by the dark thread of the old vision. . . . Before the pueblos disappear, let there be just one moment of reconciliation between the

The Last Years

The Feast of the Radishes, painted by Lawrence in Mexico.

Above The ruins at Mitla. 'Mitla
under its hills in the parched valley
where a wind blows the dust and the
dead souls of the vanished race in
terrible gusts. The carved courts of
Mitla, with a hard, sharp-angled,
intricate fascination, but the
fascination of fear and repellence.'
(*The Plumed Serpent*).

Right Quetzalcoatl. '''I am
Quetzalcoatl, lord of both ways,
star between day and the dark.'''
(*The Plumed Serpent*)

'The country gave her a strange feeling of hopelessness and of dauntlessness. Unbroken, eternally resistant, it was a people that lived without hope, and without care.' (*The Plumed Serpent*)

Overleaf Mexican landscape near Oaxaca. 'It was a place with a strange atmosphere: stony, hard, broken, with round cruel hills and the many-fluted bunches of the organ-cactus . . .' (*The Plumed Serpent*)

Lawrence and Frieda at Villa Mirenda, 1926. 'We live very quietly, picnic by the stream sometimes.' (Letter to the Hon. D. Brett, 23 June 1926)

Left Painting by Lawrence of Villa Mirenda. 'It's sunny weather, full summer . . . We have come to the lying in the garden stage, and I go off into the woods to work, where the nightingales have a very gay time singing at me.' (Letter to Martin Secker, 29 April 1927)

Opposite Dancing man, detail from the Tomb of the Triclinium, Tarquinia. '. . . they really do rather puzzle me, the Etruscans.' (Letter to Catherine Carswell, 25 October 1921)

Below Lawrence and Aldous Huxley. 'Well, I feel there's not much of me left,' wrote Lawrence to Huxley in 1928. 'What little there is gives you the Easter Kiss and hopes we'll crow in the chorus once more, one day, like risen Easter eggs.' (Letter to A. Huxley 31 July 1928)

Above Lawrence and his sister Emily at Gstaad, 1928. 'How I loathe ordinariness! How from my soul I abhor nice simple people, with their eternal price-list.' (Undated letter to A. Huxley, *c*. August 1928)

Opposite Lawrence and his sister Ada at Marblethorp, Lincolnshire, 1926. 'I still feel queer and foreign here, but look on with wonder instead of exasperation this time. It's like being inside an aquarium, the people all fishes swimming on end.' (Letter to J. M. M. 6 October 1925)

Opposite A small square at Vence, where Lawrence was to die on 2 March 1930. 'I am rather miserable here.' (Letter to L. E. Pollinger, 20 February 1930)

Right, top Lawrence's grave at Vence.

Right The Lawrence Memorial Chapel at Taos, New Mexico, where Lawrence's ashes were taken in 1935. Frieda is buried outside the chapel.

white spirit and the dark.' 'And then, again, what business is it of mine, foreigner and newcomer?' ('Certain Americans and an Englishman'.) At times, getting close to 'the Indian vibration' stirred in him strange atavistic feelings; at other times it made him feel sick, 'like breathing chlorine'. ('Taos') One essay in particular reveals this dualism of attitude, 'Indians and an Englishman' (and note the assertion of *national* identity in the title). Lawrence describes a visit to an Apache reservation, his first contact with red men. It was a shock: 'something in my soul broke down, letting in a bitterer dark, a pungent awakening to the lost past, old darkness, new terror, new root-griefs, old root-richnesses'. But listening to an old Indian preaching or reciting, he feels, not an ancient connectedness being re-established, but an enhanced sense of his separation and difference from the Indian.

The voice out of the far-off time was not for my ears. Its language was unknown to me. And I did not wish to know. . . . Our darkest tissues are twisted in this old tribal experience. . . . But me, the conscious me, I have gone a long road since then . . . there is no going back. Always onward, still further. The great devious onward-flowing stream of conscious human blood.

And so he concludes the essay with a picture of himself standing apart from the tribal circle round the fire, wrapped up in his blanket, his individualized identity – his white consciousness. Which did not mean that he felt a deeper allegiance with white America after this sense of extrusion and recoil from the Indian tribal experience. On the contrary, the white people in the southwest seemed to him to be playing out a 'comic opera' existence with misplaced solemnity. Lawrence in fact effectively defines himself as an outsider, and he can adjust his rhetoric to suit his mood and to maintain his sense of uncommittedness.

However, if he could not dance to the tribal drum any more, Lawrence was drawn to the Indians as in some way incorporating the secret essence and mystery of the ancient American continent. If his imagination was not aroused by New York and San Francisco, it was deeply stirred by the pueblo, the desert, the mountains, the Indian. His most important essays and works of fiction relating to America are all concerned in some way with the Indian and the New Mexican landscape.

It was good to be alone and responsible. But also it is very *hard* living up against these savage Rockies. The savage things are a bit gruesome, and they try to down one. – But far better they than the white disintegration. – I did a long novelette . . . about 2 women and a horse – 'St Mawr'. . . . And two shorter novelettes . . . 'The Woman Who Rode Away' and 'The Princess'. 'St Mawr' ends here. They are all about this country more or less. . . . They are all sad. After all, they're true to what is. (Letter to Catherine Carswell, 8 October 1924)

Opposite Lawrence's grave in the chapel at Taos.

'Here' was the Del Monte ranch which, as a place to live was as far as Lawrence advanced into the American wilds. And it was here that he wrote his most important fictions based on his American experience (I exclude a few relatively unimportant short stories, and also the novel *The Plumed Serpent* which he completed in Mexico and which is too complex a phenomenon, relating to Lawrence's whole development, to be considered in this essay). In each of the three stories an independent strong-minded white woman in one way or another abandons the society which gives her her position, her mentality, her security, and submits to (or at least experiences) the unsocialized savagery of the American landscape such as Lawrence could see from his ranch; in each case the transition between the two worlds is associated with Indian figures acting as servile or brutal initiators. The three pieces imagine three different conclusions to the experience: an imminent death, a return to white society, and a kind of stasis of waiting in the wild landscape, the old life sloughed off, the new life not yet begun. The society of white civilization is in each case portrayed as being unreal, insubstantial, mechanical, somnambulistic, a noisy realm in which things and words alike rattle meaninglessly, a world in which men have lost whatever they might once have had of nobility, authority, virility. It is a world which cannot satisfy the awakened woman unless, like the Princess, she prefers to return to her charmed 'sleep' again. In it thwarted or distorted passions hide behind manners and empty social routines or childish games, and find expression in ugly battles of opposed wills, flashes of temper, or self-sealing fantasies. Out of touch with the source of life, people live by their nerves and fuss with the trivial appurtenances of the surface of life. It is civilization experienced as non-being. The savage American landscape is by no means unequivocal in its effect on the woman awake. Whatever else it is, it is *real*, but such unmediated reality has its terrors. It can be awesome, beautiful, sumptuous, holy, particularly when experienced as 'distance' or background. However, as 'nearness' or foreground, it can be verminous, destructive, malign, cruel, a malicious underminer of man's efforts, a downward-pulling energy reducing life to its lower forms. Sitting in the Del Monte ranch, with Europe in his memory, and the American landscape filling his eyes, Lawrence was in a unique position to explore his feelings about the relationships between the two realms: 'white disintegration' and 'the savage things' that 'try to down one'. The result was three remarkable and disturbing works of fiction.

In *St Mawr* it is the American woman Lou Witt who finds white society like a dream full of nonenties, in which her own life is like 'a dot of shadow in a most of nothingness'. For her, it is a cardboard world inhabited by 'pancake' people, and Lawrence's summary, abrupt description of it seems to catch her feeling that it is simply too unimportant to spend much time evoking it; why waste words on unrealities, particularly when words themselves are among the unrealities? For this, too, is the world of language, in which 'clever' men knit endless little word patterns; and Lou longs for the 'absolute silence of America' which 'in the empty spaces of America was still unutterable, almost cruel'. Even the English stillnesses seem to her full of murmuring voices, the very air too much lived-in, used up. One great attraction of the American desert is that it is still 'virgin of idea, its word unspoken'. It would seem that at this time Lawrence felt that mind, consciousness, actively contaminated natural spaces and places, and that language, to use one of his own similes, moved through the silent growths of nature 'like a bad wind'. The paradox of his having to convey this vision through a word pattern which he was busily knitting together on the edge of the silent American wilderness will not have escaped him. Part of his anguish during this period, and indeed his stylistic inconsistencies, could be due to his realization that it is difficult, if not impossible, to use language to free oneself from language, to employ consciousness in the process of its own negation. And an important part of Lawrence, the part which was a creative writer, cannot have wanted finally to abandon words and mind. For they were the basis of that identity which he felt he could assert even against the annihilating presence of the great mountains. He, after all, returned to Europe. It was his fictional characters who died or lingered on in the American vastnesses.

Lou's feeling that there must be another world, another dimension to reality, is of course awakened by the horse St Mawr; he is 'a living background' into which she feels she wants to retreat from the meaningless routines of the foreground world. This foreground world increasingly makes her feel numb, weary, indifferent, disillusioned, futile, not-alive. What the story explores is what is the nature of that 'background world' and what steps a person may take towards entering it. Somewhere between Lou Witt and her mother and this background world stand the grooms, the Indian Phoenix and the Welshman Lewis. What they have in common is that they come from outside the society that the Witts know. They are distinctly non-Christian; what religious feelings they do have come down from pre-historic modes of existence. They are now the servants of white people, for Christian civilization has superseded the old religions; but in their responses to nature and animals they seem to preserve vestiges of the old modes – Aztec, Druidic. Neither of the two American women has sexual relations with either of these representatives of primitivism-within-the-gates. In different ways they go beyond them, or leave them behind. Mrs Witt, as the name suggests, has her power very much in the mind, but it is a mind gone sour and turned against the civilization that nurtured it. One of her pastimes is watching funerals, wondering whether, since people seem hardly to live, one can actually speak of them as dying. Failing to find anything or anyone who could truly master her, Mrs Witt has rejected life as an illusion; she returns to America but finds it no better than Europe; by the end she is in something approaching a catatonic trance – 'crystallized into neutrality'. Lou, her daughter, turns away from mind toward mindlessness, from intimacy to isolation, from an illusory fullness of life to a scouring emptiness. But she also turns, and it is an important difference in her quest, from 'wit' to 'wonder'. ' "Ah, no, mother, I want the wonder back again, or I shall die. I don't want to be like you, just criticising and annihilating these dreary people".' To what extent she gets the wonder back is not established; instead we see her making herself ready for it, when it should come. For Lou the quest is a stripping, a denudation, moving towards an achieved and waiting nakedness.

The horse St Mawr plays an important part in her quest. But we should not assume that because of the glowing, flaming dangerous life and awesome otherness she senses in him, that the horse is simply a brute phallic positive to show up the emasculated puppets of human society. For there is something wrong with the horse too. For one thing, he was meant to be a stud but he doesn't care for mares. Then, he is too highly-strung, nervous, given to freakish fits of violence, in which respect he is *like* Rico, Lou's husband. Of course one could infer from this that man has affected the animal realm with his own impotence and neurasthenia, but even then St Mawr remains something far more ambiguous than a symbol of maimed phallic energies. When he rears up and throws Rico in the central episode in the story, much blame indeed attaches to the man who no longer knows how to ride or control the animals he has mastered; civilized man was very much out of the saddle as far as Lawrence was concerned. But the terrific picture of the horse on its back, kicking its legs in panic and terror, precipitates a vision, not of man's enfeebled state, but of an evil welling up from the core of things. 'Now, like an ocean to whose surface she had risen, she saw the dark-grey waves of evil rearing in a great tide. . . . There was no relief. The whole world was enveloped in one great flood.' An important aspect of the picture is that the horse is 'reversed', inverted, suggesting a fearsome convulsion of values, such as, perhaps, Lawrence felt Europe had been through in the Great War.

No matter whether man has thrown the horse or the horse has thrown the man; the picture is one of vital energies in dreadful disarray, a flailing mess where there should be a noble concourse and the ensuing vision is of an oceanic evil emanating, not from man with his mental ineptitudes, but from the very centre of nature. The vision comes to Lou, but the prose at this point detaches itself from her consciousness and it is clear that we are reading a crucial meditation on the part of Lawrence himself; and her conclusion reads very like a decision Lawrence himself had come to. 'What's to be done? Generally speaking, nothing. . . . The individual can but depart from the mass, and try to cleanse himself.' It is with this intention to 'cleanse' herself that Lou goes to America and finally to the mountain ranch. Human life in America is quite as unreal as in Europe, it strikes her as being like life in a mirror, or like a film. 'What was real? What under heaven was real?' The question she puts to herself is perhaps the key to her whole quest, and explains why she finally gives herself to the mountain and the desert.

But Lawrence's sense of an evil at work in nature operates powerfully in his account of the New Mexican landscape. He writes of 'a curious disintegration working all the time, a sort of malevolent breath, like a stupefying, irritant gas coming out of the unfathomed mountains'; the ubiquitous rats are 'symbols of the curious debasing malevolence that was in the spirit of the place'. The previous owner had found it initially awesomely beautiful, but the landscape 'attacked' her and she found herself deprived of any language, her mind like an empty cupboard. She realized that there was no God of mercy, but just life, a fierce ruthless battle, and ultimately an entropic battle in which the higher forms succumb to the lower forms which are constantly 'seething the soul away'. The experience finally broke her, yet it is to this landscape that Lou wishes to give herself as a sort of perverse preference to the unreal social contacts and sexual intimacies offered in the social realm. Her imagination transforms the landscape – all 'rats and hopelessness' in her mother's eyes – into the lover that she wants, not tender and considerate, but big, dominating and ruthless. ' "There's something else even that loves me and wants me. I can't tell you what it is. It's a spirit. And it's here, on this ranch. It's here, in this landscape. It's something wild, that will hurt me sometimes and will wear me down sometimes. I know it. . . . I am here, right deep in America, where there's a wild spirit wants me, a wild spirit more than men. And it doesn't want to save me either. It needs me. It craves for me. . . . It saves me from cheapness, mother." '

The story concludes with one of her mother's characteristic belittling ironies and it is an important part of the book that the rhetoric of wonder should have to co-exist with the rhetoric of wit; Lawrence is not asking us to accept without qualification Lou's somewhat masochistic romanticization of the landscape. But he does convey how a person who wakes up to the sustained inauthenticity of civilized life may set about systematically desocializing herself, a process involving the Welshman, the Indian, the horse, until even these are left behind and Lou just waits to be alone and to give herself to 'the unseen presences'. The geographical equivalent of the process is the move from London to New Mexico. But Lawrence does not pretend that we can be sure that Lou's terminal situation can be extended into a way of life which will finally satisfy her. And we note that she is, oddly, with her mother, who is very much a 'seen' presence and whose mordent and sceptical comments about rats and hopelessness, and general maternal chiding, may well prevent Lou from sustaining her devotional attitude to the spirit of the place. On that, and on the savage things that try to down one, there could be more than one perspective as Lawrence himself had felt. It is part of the brilliance of the story that the multiplicity of perspective on the various realms is for the most part sustained. The ending is bare, dissonant, inconclusive – a pause. It seems exactly appropriate to this stage in Lawrence's life.

'The Woman Who Rode Away' imagines a greater state of abandonment of white consciousness, a literal sacrifice of the white woman to an extremely alien Indian tribe which worships the sun. The setting is notionally Mexico but in fact it is once again the landscape of New Mexico as apprehended by Lawrence. Much more than Lou Witt, the nameless woman of the story feels dead from the start, inhabiting not just an unreal world but a dead one. In the 'thrice-dead' little town near where she lives, she sees a dead dog, 'Deadness within deadness'. The Indians will only enact what the landscape has effectively done already. Hearing one evening of some savage Indian tribe living in the remote mountains which is rumoured to indulge in human sacrifice, she turns her imagination to that realm. 'She was overcome by a foolish romanticism more unreal than a girl's. She felt it was her destiny to wander into the secret haunts of these timeless, mysterious, marvellous Indians of the mountains.' In narrative terms, she simply rides into the mountains until she is taken up in the Indian tribe, the Chilchuis, who, after various ritual preparations, take her to a ceremonial cave where she is to be sacrificed to the sun. The story ends with the sacrificial knife poised to strike. But what the story really dramatizes is a progressive dissolution of consciousness. The woman starts out feeling dead, as though she is living a sort of posthumous existence, and the feelings of weariness, remoteness and unreality only increase on her journey towards her actual death. She has no volition, once she has set out, and she seems to exist in a state of unconsciousness and trance. Her 'unspeakable fatigue' is often referred to, as is the sensation she has of having already died. The Indians are inhuman, remote, fierce, inaccessible, they look at her as a thing without any sexual feeling whatever. It seems this is what she wants, as though she finds it preferable to be reified into an object rather than bear any longer the strain of white consciousness and individuation.

Her trance state is heightened, or deepened, by hallucinogenic drugs which the Indians give her. She feels a great langour, that she is 'bleeding out into the higher beauty and harmony of things'; 'she had gone into that other state of passional cosmic consciousness like one who is drugged'. She is literally stripped naked by the Indians (again the theme is one of denudation), and all vestiges of her white mind and identity are eradicated. She experiences 'diffusion', a dissolving of self which is at once a blissful and a terrifying experience. She knows that she is going to be a victim, but 'She wanted it'. It is hardly necessary to point out the extreme masochism of her mood, her mindless drifting towards a death in death. Lawrence himself had strong religious feelings about the sun, and he felt that white men had trivialized it and so lost their connection with the cosmos (see *Apocalypse*). So some of the reasons which the Indians give for the need to sacrifice a white woman to the sun may be meant seriously by him. But they can scarcely be taken seriously by us. What is arresting in the extraordinary trance-like atmosphere which Lawrence establishes and then intensifies, is simply the fascinated move on the part of the woman towards a desired and dreaded annihilation at the hands of men who are conspicuous for their hardness, cruelty and fierce indifference. They are 'primitively male' and that is their deeply ambiguous attraction, for her, and for Lawrence too, no doubt. The idea of being 'sacrificed' by ferocious silent men, whose 'power' is emphasized as their cardinal quality, seems to hold a terrifying attraction for both the author and his character. The last sentence, rather ominously, reads: 'The mastery that man must hold, and that passes from race to race.' And the story ends with the knife poised to strike – what? Mabel Dodge Luhan, the generic American female, white consciousness itself – or perhaps a tormented and ambiguous part of Lawrence's own psyche? One cannot finally say; but the story is sufficiently disturbing to make one sense that Lawrence himself must have been in a very disturbed state when he wrote it. It would seem as though, for him, at this time, Nature had withdrawn all her beneficences, leaving only a hard residue of destructive ruthlessness.

'The Princess', Dollie Urquhart, is the third woman that Lawrence sends into the most savage parts of the American landscape. She is very much a sleeping beauty, the daughter of a mad father who brought her up in a fantasy world in which he and she were the only royalty and all the rest are to be regarded as vulgar and unimportant: all this was a great secret. Asleep in this fantasy, she is as 'impervious as crystal' with no notion at all of establishing relationships with other people. After her father's death she goes to a ranch in New Mexico to do some riding in the mountains. The only person who interests her at all is one of the guides, Romero, a descendant of one of the economically depressed Mexican families. Lawrence depicts these Mexicans as being in some way degenerate, and one of his comments on them perhaps tells us something about his own mood at the time. 'They had found their *raison d'être* in self-torture and death-worship. Unable to wrest a *positive* significance for themselves from the vast, beautiful, but vindictive landscape they were born into, they turned on their own selves, and worshipped death through self-torture.' In any case neither Dollie and Romero are from the stable centres of their respective races; they both seem to exist in some peripheral state of consciousness, isolated and cut off. Dolly is attracted to Romero and asks him to act as her guide into the mountains because she has a slightly mad passion to look into 'their secret heart', into 'the inner chaos of the Rockies'. She, we remember, has her great secret. It seems as if she wants to find out whether Nature has one too.

The climb, described at length and with the sort of mounting atmosphere of anticipation and dread to be found in the previous story, has few pleasures. Nature's secrets are hardly elevating. Dollie senses 'decay and despair' in the virgin forests. The mountains look beautiful from the distance – 'a fence of angels' – but once into them the angelic qualities disappear and they become heavy and cruel and dead. 'In front now was nothing but mountains, ponderous, massive, down-sitting mountains, in a huge and intricate knot, empty of life or soul. . . . It frightened the Princess, it was *so* inhuman. She had not thought it could be so inhuman, so, as it were, anti-life.' Her secret is that she is empty and anti-life. She discovers that this is the secret of the mountains too. She continues with the climb, but she feels 'the dread and repulsiveness of the wild'. In the intense cold of the night on the mountains she invites Romero into her bed, though the idea of physical contact is repellent to her. Having willed herself to give herself to the man, she immediately sets about re-establishing possession of her self. If this was the degenerate kiss which awakened the mad princess – the tale has become more than a little warped in Lawrence's retelling of it – then the princess immediately longs to return to her sleep, her untouchable apartness. Challenged by this insult to his manhood Romero keeps her up in the mountains forcibly and attempts to break her, but though he takes her physically he cannot conquer her. Finally she undermines him, and he succumbs to her powers of negation. In the desolate winter landscape they lie together like corpses. 'They were two people who had died.' It is a veritable wasteland, devoid of emotion, belief, hope, contact, warmth, and meaning – a solstice of the spirit.

The conclusion is brief, peremptory. Romero is shot by men who come to rescue the Princess. She herself goes 'slightly crazy' and, in the last sentence of the book, 'she married an elderly man, and seemed pleased'. She is safely back with a second father, and need not wake up again. What is disturbing in the story, apart from the general air of mental instability, is the implication that if society is an empty fantasy, nature, at heart, is an empty nightmare. It would seem that, at this period, whichever way Lawrence looked he could see only the possibility of madness, not of renewal. Lawrence had brought three fictional women to the American desert and mountains; the first dedicates herself to the spirit of the place, the second submits to a ritual sacrifice, the third allows herself to be sexually violated. All of them, in one way or another, leave an old way of life and meaningless relationships and come up against the harsh ferocity, the cruel power of the landscape and of its ancient inhabitants the Indians. But there is no sense of a 'new life' being made possible by these more or less brutal initiations, no hint of the new relationships and new connections coming into being which were the possibilities that Lawrence had initially attached to America. Nature's secret heart seems to be anti-life, sex is repugnant, intimacies are meaningless and to be avoided, love is an illusion and a nauseous one at that, white society is disintegrating, but the savage life has its squalors and negations: in the void of all values, only power has meaning.

At one point in 'The Woman Who Rode Away' we read this account of her state of mind. 'She was not sure that she had not heard, during the night, a great crash at the centre of herself, which was the crash of her own death. Or else it was a crash at the centre of the earth, and meant something big and mysterious.' It would seem as if, during Lawrence's short American stay, he heard a crash which, at times, he thought was at the centre of society or of the earth; and in due course there were enough of such crashes to be heard. However, it does seem as though, whatever other crashes he heard, one of them was at the centre of himself.

'I think New Mexico was the greatest experience from the outside world that I have ever had. It certainly changed me for ever.' 'New Mexico', *Phoenix*

Looking back on America some four years later, Lawrence wrote an essay in which he outlined what his American experience had meant to him: for him America was essentially New Mexico, and New Mexico meant the Indian.

Curious as it may sound, it was New Mexico that liberated me from the present era of civilization, the great era of material and mechanical development. Months spent in holy Kandy, in Ceylon, the holy of holies of southern Buddhism, had not touched the great psyche of materialism and idealism which dominated me. . . . But the moment I saw the brilliant, proud morning shine high up over the deserts of Santa Fé, something stood still in my soul and I started to attend. . . . In the magnificent fierce morning of New Mexico one sprang awake, a new part of the soul woke up suddenly and the old world gave way to a new . . . for *greatness* of beauty I have never experienced anything like New Mexico. . . . It had a splendid silent terror, and vast far-and-wide magnificence which made it way beyond mere aesthetic appreciation . . . it is curious that the land which has produced modern political democracy at its highest pitch should give one the greatest sense of overweening, terrible proudness and mercilessness: but so beautiful, God! so beautiful!

The second revelation the land afforded him was an authentic feeling of religion:

I had no permanent feeling of religion till I came to New Mexico and penetrated into the old human race experience there. It is curious that it should be in America, of all places, that a European should really experience religion, after touching the old Mediterranean and the East. It is curious that one should get a sense of living religion from the Red Indians, having failed to get it from Hindus or Sicilian Catholics or Singalese.

For Lawrence, the Indian was 'a remnant of the most deeply religious race still living' and it was this America which moved him, not the America which epitomized modern white society, with its machinery and cities and democratic mobs. There were, then, two Americas for Lawrence: the dominant one an ephemeral illusion; the ancient one, awesomely real, and partaking of eternity.

But there it is: the newest democracy ousting the oldest religion. And once the oldest religion is ousted, one feels the democracy and all its paraphernalia will collapse, and the oldest religion, which comes down to us from man's prewar days, will start again. The skyscraper will scatter on the winds like thistledown, and the genuine America, the America of New Mexico, will start on its course again. This is an interregnum.

It seems that Lawrence has by this time forgotten the exhaustion and feelings of alienation that contemporary America had induced in him. Its hard, menacing, modern actuality is dismissed in a dream of effortless demolition, and in imagination it becomes, once again, the continent of the richest of things past, the rarest of things to come.[1]

'Till the Fight Is Finished':
D. H. Lawrence in his letters
Denis Donoghue

One of the risks incurred by a reader who takes an interest in Lawrence is that such an interest is likely to become omnivorous. It is hardly possible to place *The Rainbow* and *Women in Love* in the centre of that interest without engrossing, as one moves toward the circumference, pretty nearly everything else in the canon. In theory, it is possible to discount Lawrence's metaphysic, and to assume that his recourse to the idiom of Father, Son, and Holy Ghost is merely vulgar, a minor essay in blasphemy. Some readers consider themselves free, when Lawrence's poems are offered, to take them or leave them. As for the argumentative Lawrence, T. S. Eliot was not alone in concluding that Lawrence had no talent for sustained thought: a glazed look descends upon such readers when he stops describing things and takes to the high horse of doctrine. There is always an implication in such readers that Lawrence wrote the major novels by default, and that if he had acted more characteristically he would have made a mess of them. According to these reservations, he was an untutored genius who developed, by sheer determination, a late and wilfully declared vocation for thought. The simplicity of this argument has a certain charm, it is pleasant to dispose of a writer by saying that he did not know enough and that he was ill-advised to go to the trouble of knowing anything. But it will not do. If you want to get rid of Lawrence you must do so with a certain majesty by ignoring him, or by setting up as the co-ordinates of modern literature those lines of force which exclude him; as Hugh Kenner did in *The Pound Era*, taking possession of the early twentieth century on behalf of Pound, Eliot, Wyndham Lewis, Joyce and Yeats, with James in the shadows nodding assent. But if you admit Lawrence at all, you are likely to make the admission complete, retaining everthing merely because he wrote it. I have no fault to find with this attitude, I do not think idolatry a necessary consequence. If Lawrence is received as a major presence in modern literature, we ought to have his rough with his smooth. So I am not daunted to hear that hefty batches of letters are turning up day by day, and that the big edition now being prepared will run to several volumes. When James received a selection from Hawthorne's French and Italian note-books, he raised the question of the proper limits of curiosity, while recognising that its actual limits would be fixed only by a total exhaustion of matter. But James had particularly in mind his sense of Hawthorne's retiring nature, and he thought the collection of his jottings made excessively liberal excisions 'from the privacy of so reserved and shade-seeking a genius'. Hawthorne was someone to whom James felt a particular obligation to be tender. It is unnecessary to feel such an obligation to Lawrence. He did not seek the shade, he thrust himself forward into the life of his time as into the life of his fiction and poetry; one feels no obligation to cherish him, or to protect him from the heat of the sun. So our attitude to the accumulation of letters must be: the more, the better.

This is not to confess to an appetite merely gross. Lawrence's letters are objects of independent interest, they are not mere messages delivered to make up for the absence of a telephone. The interest they incur is consistent with a still greater interest in the art of his fiction: the letters are continuous with the fiction, they punctuate a life which is embodied in the novels and stories. It is hardly too much to say that they are more intimately related to his art than to the daily events upon which they appear to feed. If you want to know what Lawrence was doing on Friday, 5 May 1916, you will find one part of the answer in a letter, the following Thursday, from Katherine Mansfield to S. S. Koteliansky: i.e. Lawrence was engaged in an appalling row with Frieda, which started from a remark of Frieda's about Shelley's 'To a Skylark'. Lawrence screamed at her and, according to Katherine Mansfield, ended up beating her and pulling her hair. Another part of the answer is that Lawrence was meditating on the Easter Rising, Yeats's theme and Ireland's blood-sacrifice, the War, the end of democracy: he was reading Kitty O'Shea's *Life of Parnell*: he was at work on 'my novel', evidently the first draft of *Women in Love*. The row with Frieda does not appear, so far as I know, in Lawrence's letters. Katherine Mansfield's version is confirmed, as we would expect, in Middleton Murry's *Between Two Worlds*, but the most concentrated reading between the lines of Lawrence's correspondence does not yield as much information as one would expect about the imperfection of the life, set off against a possible perfection of the work. Six months later, the violence of 5 May has been assimilated. 'Frieda and I have finished the long and bloody fight at last, and are at one,' he wrote to Murry on October 11. So the *Collected Letters* does not make an autobiography, any more than an autobiogrpaphy makes a life: in both cases, we have to reckon with the diverse interventions of evasion, silence, form, and art. Reading the letters is a strenuous exercise because the reader cannot take them at face value, he must understand them as subject to many of the same forces which are at work in the fiction; he must interpret them, even when they appear to be merely offering themselves as vehicles of information. On 15 April 1908, Lawrence wrote to Blanche Jennings: 'and to be sure I am very young – though twenty two; I have never left my mother, you see.' What Blanche saw is of little account: what the reader sees is what he makes of the sentence, how he disposes its several notes, *naïf*, *faux-naïf*, ingenuous, disingenuous, coy, and so forth. It is never enough if the reader merely takes the correspondence as a neutral context for the fiction, with an assumption that the correspondence is simple even when the fiction is complex. The simplicity is merely ostensible, as anyone can see who compares *Sons and Lovers* with Lawrence's several accounts of it in letters to Edward Garnett. The reader has to enter into a relation with the letters comparable, for tension and interrogation, with his relation to 'The Crown', the 'Study of Thomas Hardy', and the novels themselves. He cannot take the letters as they appear to come, straight from the shoulder or the heart: their origin is more obscure than that. They are to be read, like Keats's letters, with a sense of their belonging to the creative work, even if there is a sense, too, that at a certain point a distinction between them and that work must be made. In both enterprises, the same forces are engaged; feeling, imagination, rhetoric, style, the symbolic act of language. What distinguishes the fiction from the correspondence is the more imperious vocation of form to which the fiction responds; what the correspondence responds to, in respect of form, is a relatively minor demand.

It is generally agreed, however, that Lawrence's letters are among the most achieved letters in English literature: that they are regularly compared with Keats's letters is sufficient testimony. But there is at least a marginal case to be made against them, at least in normal terms, and it is well to consider it sooner rather than later. Bluntly, it amounts to this; that too many of the letters are essays in self-pity, that some of them disclose a mean spirit, even though 'many a true work is spoken in spite', that they are good for nothing but intensity. Some of the harm can be taken out of these charges by reducing them to such a formula as the following, from Kenneth Burke's novel *Towards a Better Life*: 'When people are both discerning and unhappy, they tend to believe that their unhappiness is derived from their discernment.' Generally, and especially in the early adult years, the declared form of Lawrence's unhappiness was poverty. He was poor because he insisted on living by his pen, he would not go back to teaching. But Frieda had some money, friends were generous with their houses, gradually the novels began making a good deal of money, and after 1920 the Lawrences were reasonably comfortable, with Mabel Luhan as their chief benefactress. Lawrence protested his poverty too much. The latitude of his spite is a more serious matter. Of Gordon Campbell: 'He lies in the mud and murmurs about his dream-soul, and says that *action* is irrelevant. Meanwhile he earns diligently in munitions.' Of Hugh Walpole: 'Is he anybody? Could I wring three ha'porth of help out of his bloody neck?' Heinemann was regularly described as 'his Jewship', Murry as a stench, 'a little muck-spout'. Katherine Mansfield, demonstrably ill, was on the Riviera 'doing the last-gasp touch, in order to impose on people'. Philip Heseltine and his wife were 'such abject shits it is a pity they can't be flushed down a sewer'. Perhaps we should call it spleen rather than spite, a momentary rage rather than a settled habit. In rage, Lawrence seized the first available object to attack, mostly a friend: sometimes the spleen was exhausted by its expression. But he was niggardly in praise of other artists, unless they were dead. He was generous to Mark Gertler on the strength of his *Merry-Go-Round*, but generally he defined himself in relation to his contemporaries by denouncing them. He was often right, as in denouncing Bertrand Russell's Cambridge.

These and other charges can be documented from the letters. Some parts of the correspondence are so obnoxious, at least on first appearance, that one is astonished to find them issuing from a writer so zealous in defence of his reputation. Surely, we say, he must have known that these things would be brought to public light one day, and that they would not easily be forgiven. A writer who determined, as James said of Emerson, 'to limit and define the ground of his appeal to fame' would have schooled himself to hold his tongue, or would at least have withheld the most ferocious letters from the mail-box until his wrath had subsided. A cannier man would have done so. But the fascination of Lawrence's letters consists precisely in the relation between the rough and the smooth: we respond to their authenticity, warts and all. But there is another reason which makes forgiveness easy once it makes it possible. 'Of course I say all sorts of things—you yourself know perfectly well the things I say about people—but they aren't malicious and *méchant* things, just momentary. People who *repeat* things are really wicked—because they *always* pour in vitriol of their own.' This was offered to Juliette Huxley on 26 April 1928 when Lawrence had got himself into a tangle because of something he was reported as saying about Catherine Carswell. Another version of the same defence was given to Mabel Luhan, on 17 October 1923: 'As for reviling you, when I am angry, I say what I feel. I hope you do the same.' I find the defence acceptable. Lawrence could forgive anything, so long as it came as a manifestation of energy: a momentary explosion of rage or resentment was true to its occasion, it was a form of energy, so it was not a sin. But he did not always consult this criterion. When Aldous Huxley sent him a copy of *Proper Studies*, Lawrence thanked him with a rigmarole of teasing comment (? 14 November 1927) ending in praise: 'very sane and sound and good.' But his true opinion was reserved for Koteliansky, a week later: 'Huxley's *Proper Studies* is a bore!' I concede that such duplicity is exceptional. Generally, Lawrence told the truth even when it would have been easier to tell a white lie; when he refused to write for Murry's *Adelphi*, or when he told Aldington to stop presenting himself as a pillar of society: 'I never knew a man who seemed more to me to be living from a character not his own, than you. What is it that you are afraid of?—*ultimately?*—is it death? or pain? or just fear of the negative infinite of all things? What ails thee, lad?' (24 May 1927). But he could also be wonderfully tactful and generous. He wrote to Rachel Annand Taylor, a minor poet, (? 15 November 1910): 'All I meant was that some of the poems in *Rose and Vine* seemed made to fit experiences which you have hidden in yourself and then dreamed different, so that the verses seemed fingered by art into a grace the experience does not warrant.' Shortly after meeting Katherine Mansfield and Middleton Murry in 1913, Lawrence trounced Murry for refusing to take Katherine's money: 'Make her certain – don't pander to her – stick to *yourself* – do what you *want* to do – don't *consider* her – she hates and loathes being considered. You insult her in saying you wouldn't take her money.' Lawrence was right, as Murry eventually acknowledged. He was right again when he told Murry, after the dreadful months together in Cornwall: 'Till the fight is finished, it is only honourable to fight,' while adding: 'But, oh dear, it is very horrible and agonizing.' (11 October 1916). And I love Lawrence for the strong tenderness with which he wrote to poor Caresse Crosby, after her husband had killed himself and his mistress: 'I hope time is passing not too heavily for you – time is the best healer, when it isn't a killer' (14 February 1930).

I have said that Lawrence was niggardly in praise. That is true; but he could praise, when his temper allowed him. Or, better still, he could rise to an occasion and genuinely enter into a relation with other writers. With Wells, for instance, whose strength he admired; or Whitman, Synge, Swinburne, Shelley, Melville, Balzac, Hardy. He made inordinate demands upon literature, as upon life; a writer touched by Lawrence's attention was never the same again, for better or worse. Who, before Lawrence, could have read Fenimore Cooper as Lawrence read him: who can read him now without feeling Lawrence's presence in the reading? It was the same with Lawrence's friendships. Lady Glenavy has a passage in *To-day We Will Only Gossip* in which she reflects somewhat harshly upon Lawrence's talent for friendship, comparing him unfavourably with Koteliansky in that respect. Koteliansky was, by normal standards, a more amiable man than Lawrence, and a more reliable friend, but on the other hand he approached friendship in a much less demanding spirit.

Prepare a list of Lawrence's major friendships, beginning with Frieda in 1912, Katherine Mansfield and Middleton Murry in 1913, Koteliansky, Hilda Doolittle, Aldington, and Gertler in 1914, Lady Ottoline Morrell, Aldous Huxley, Heseltine, and Bertrand Russell in 1915. Some of these people lived to curse the day they met Lawrence, but not one of them passed through the relationship without bearing an indelible mark. The evidence is in Lawrence's letters, and in their own testaments. What Lawrence demanded of friendship was tension, energy, desire. 'God in me is my desire.' The nature of a friendship is the flow of feeling, going both ways, and energy is the sign of value. In love, 'I go to a woman to know myself, and knowing myself, to go further, to explore into the unknown, which is the woman, venture in upon the coasts of the unknown, and open my discovery to all humanity.' (2 February 1915.)

This is only another way of describing Lawrence's sensibility, by recourse to his congenial idiom. A frail man, he loved strength, he loved to invoke the source of vitality and power. 'I want to write live things, if crude and half formed, rather than beautiful dying decadent things with sad odours' (20 January 1909). This is not the whole story, but it marks its direction. 'Writing should come from a strong root of life: like a battle song after a battle' (22 December 1913). So he hated the mere ego or the mere will as a malignant force setting itself against 'the real genuine sacred life'. The famous letter (5 June 1914) in which Lawrence warned Garnett that he must not look in *The Rainbow* for 'the old stable *ego* – of the character' is not as clear to me as it is, apparently, to other readers. 'There is another *ego*, according to whose action the individual is unrecognizable, and passes through, as it were, allotropic states which it needs a deeper sense than any we've been used to exercise, to discover are states of the same single radically unchanged element.' He then talks of diamonds, coal, and carbon. Now the dictionary says that allotropy means the variation of physical properties, without change of substance, to which certain elementary bodies are liable. Presumably the substance, in Lawrence's sentence, is human feeling, it can hardly be anything else, but it may be supposed, under his persuasion, to change its properties, changing especially the tendency to gather its energies together in a tight, self-protective form: in that form we insist on becoming 'independent little gods, referred nowhere and to nothing, little mortal Absolutes, secure from question' (16 August 1915). Against this, Lawrence urged another attitude: 'Let us be easy and impersonal, not for ever fingering over our own souls, and the souls of our acquaintances, but trying to create a new life, a new common life, a new complete tree of life from the roots that are within us. I am weary to death of these dead, dry leaves of personalities which flap in every wind' (12 December 1915). This is about as much as I can make of Lawrence's argument, and I find it difficult to see how he can speak of the happier condition as that of 'another *ego*'. He told us to take life easy, not to insist upon our separateness, but to see ourselves as parts of 'the whole'. I am not sure that the argument amounts to much more than that. Still, it is clear enough to explain why Lawrence, immediately after *Sons and Lovers*, moved away from the conventional idea of a novel as an arrangement of characters and scenes. He is not now interested in characters as statuesque figures cut out from their backgrounds: after 1914 we do not find him praising writers, as he praised Garnett in 1912, for getting characters to 'stand off from one another so distinctly'. 'I don't care much more about accumulating objects in the powerful light of emotion, and making a scene of them', he explains to Garnett (29 January 1914). He calls his new procedure 'the exhaustive method', as distinct from that of 'pure object and story', and he warns Garnett that the new style 'may not be sufficiently incorporated to please you'. That means, I suppose, sufficient to the development of separate characters in action. 'I prefer the permeating beauty', he says. It is hard to say how much of this argument is merely an attempt to answer the War with a corresponding gesture of distaste for individual people; and how much is genuinely achieved vision. 'I find people ultimately boring: and you can't have fiction without people. So fiction does not, at the bottom, interest me any more. I am weary of humanity and human things. One is happy in the thoughts only that transcend humanity.' (23 May 1917). The War, the suppression of *The Rainbow*, the lapse of friends: only a brave reader would presume to disentangle these threads of outrage from the fabric of Lawrence's aesthetic or his metaphysic. Francis Fergusson gives Lawrence's attitude in a somewhat milder version when he says that Lawrence's characters interest their author far less than the emotional states they share. Suppose a number of congenial people were to come together in a common purpose, holding their separate personalities in abeyance or sinking them in a good cause. Presumably this is the kind of thing Lawrence had in mind. There is a crucial letter to Gordon Campbell in which he attacks those writers who 'see only the symbol as a subjective expression'. Lawrence thought Yeats guilty in this respect, so that even when he invoked the ancient symbols his invocation was sickly, merely an expression of himself. True symbolism, in Lawrence's terms, 'avoids the I and puts aside the egotist': it is that whole in which, if we are in the right spirit, we can take 'our decent place' (? 19 December 1914). 'That was how man built the cathedrals. He didn't say 'out of my breast springs this cathedral!' But 'in this vast whole I am a small part, I move and live and have my being'.

I am still in doubt about the theory. Perhaps it only means that people are no good by themselves: by themselves, they are nothing but self-delighting, self-devouring egos. They are good only when they are stirred to share a common life. Ursula is no good by herself. Birkin, by himself, is a menace. Together, they are as good as the vitality they engender, the energy of their relation. Readers of *Women in Love* are likely to say that Fergusson is right, Lawrence is less interested in Ursula and Birkin than in the magnetic field between them, and the nature of the feeling transacted there. This feeling is compatible with Lawrence's reverance for pre-cognitive states of being, presumably allotropic states before the mind has broken the substance, once for all, into separate elements. In theory, transcendence has a similar advantage, except that it must be understood as coming after the human event, not before: it has every merit, except a future. So it begins to appear that Lawrence is outraged by society, by the governing institutions, by his discovery that feeling is humiliated in the public forms offered for its reception. Perhaps this explains why he always speaks of institutions as if they were bad minds, evil forms of mentality which have already imposed themselves upon human feeling. In a good relationship, according to this argument, a space is cleared and the domination of institutions is broken. In such spaces, there you feel free.

When Lawrence dreamed of a new society, a colony for a common purpose, he called it Rananim, taking the name from one of Koteliansky's Jewish hymns. When he formed a friendship, he sprang to the conviction that now at last it would be possible to make a new Eden, inhabited by aristocrats of feeling. At one time or another he issued invitations to W. E. Hopkin, Lady Ottoline, Murry of course, Gordon and Beatrice Campbell, Lady Cynthia Asquith, the Huxleys: they must set off together to Florida, or New Mexico, or wherever, 'California or the South Seas', and 'we can be a little community, a monastery, a school – a little Hesperides of the soul and body' (8 January 1917). To Lady Ottoline he explained his plan:

I want you to form the nucleus of a new community which shall start a new life amongst us – a life in which the only riches is integrity of character. . . . I hold this the most sacred duty – the gathering together of a number of people who shall so agree to live by the *best* they know, that they shall be *free* to live by the best they know. The ideal, the religion, must now be *lived, practised.* . . . Curse the Strachey who asks for a new religion – the greedy dog. He wants another juicy bone for his soul, does he? Let him start to fulfil what religion we have.

The gospel of this Rananim would not be 'Follow me', but rather 'Behold' (1 February 1915). Some of Lawrence's most touching letters are draft Constitutions for his dream: they cannot be set aside as merely the latest version of pastoral, Lawrence's Brook Farm with a better climate. Of course it never came to anything: the nominated members shied away from an Eden already occupied by Lawrence and Frieda. With that beginning, there was no need of a serpent. But Lawrence kept coming back to the theme, even after the War when things began to look up a little of their own accord. His friends, those few who had survived the initiation ceremonies, constituted the Remnant: 'we must still be the chosen few', he told Cecil Gray, 'who smear our doorposts with hyssop and blood' (Summer 1917). Sometimes the chosen few were to live as if in *Under the Greenwood Tree* or *The Deserted Village*, their only obligation a matter of getting the Morris dances right. Sometimes the new life must take an Indian or Etruscan form, compounded of ancestral intuition and snake-dances. In Autumn 1917 Lawrence came to the apocalyptic stage, longing for another Deluge and a Noah's Ark suitably small, just big enough for the remnant, the few, the best. Life must begin again; history must be abolished, since it is merely a heap of broken promises, the only sanctioned tenses are present and future.

On these scores, Lawrence was never entirely free of misgiving. Denouncing ego and will, he was still required to find a place for individual feeling. Society was a miserable affair, but he was still left with 'my primeval societal instinct', which he thought 'much deeper than sex instinct' (13 July 1927). The correspondence with Trigant Burrow brought Lawrence yet again to this acknowledgment, though he insisted that the present moment, August 1927, was like 'the time between Good Friday and Easter' (3 August 1927). 'One has no real human relations – that is so devastating'. Humanity is still the bad egg it was in 1917.

It is indisputable that Lawrence, in the last years, turned away from people and looked to the earth itself for the only genuine values. In fiction after *The Plumed Serpent*, and in the corresponding letters, there is a new recognition of the plentitude of the natural world, with a new distrust, deeper than ever, of man's interventions. 'Inhuman' becomes a term of praise. Mexico 'is so lovely, the sky is perfect, blue and hot every day, and flowers rapidly following flowers. They are cutting the sugar cane, and hauling it in in the old ox-wagons, slowly. But the grass-slopes are already dry and fawn-coloured, the unventured hills are already like an illusion, standing round inhuman'. (15 November 1924.) Lawrence was ready to argue that the relation between men and the earth was more profound, because more fundamental, than their relation to others of their kind. 'There is a *principle* in the universe, towards which man turns religiously – a *life* of the universe itself' (31 July 1927). In May 1929 he wrote to the Huxleys, describing a trip to Chopin's Valdemosa. The description registers the beauty and splendour of the place with an art which corresponds to the fiction in its sense of the 'quickness' of life; then the atmosphere, the 'queer stillness where the Moors have been, like ghosts'. Everything is strong and vivid, except the people: 'the people seem to me rather dead, and they are ugly, and they have those non-existent bodies that English people often have, which I thought was impossible on the Mediterranean.' Before the letter is finished, the ugly Major-cans have become humanity itself, everybody is ugly. Conclusion: 'the world is lovely if one avoids man – so why not avoid him! Why not! Why not! I am tired of humanity.' He stayed tired till the end. 'When the morning comes, and the sea runs silvery and the distant islands are delicate and clear, then I feel again, only man is vile.' (4 October 1929.) It is the idiom of *St Mawr*, with Lou Witt heading for the freedom of the desert.

So Lawrence, too, ran from one place to another. Usually there was a prag-matic reason for packing up and moving on: the climate was hard on his health, someone offered him the loan of a house, a disciple wrote from afar to say that the grass was green, the sea incredibly blue, the welcome so warm that it must not be refused. 'One's *ambiente* matters awfully,' Lawrence told Earl Brewster. It mattered so much because of the demands Lawrence placed upon it: it must make up for the gruesomeness of the time, the people, the War, his health. It is my impression that Lawrence wanted the earth to do for him what his friends had failed to do, and that he moved from one place to the next partly because the first place, like a friend, had let him down, and partly because he craved diversity in places as in friends. When he was pleased with Majorca, he loved the 'stretches of wild coast, and little uninhabited bays on this island, really lovely, like the first day of time' (17 May 1929). That was the note he wanted; the earth to begin again, the first day, and now the entrance qualifications would be more stringent than in the historical world. The place of good hope was always the South. Reading the letters, one is struck by Lawrence's deter-mination to keep going South, when it came to a change, not only for the warmth, but because he associated the South with the place of ancestral wisdom, home of the old gods. 'I prefer the pagan many gods, and the animistic vision,' he told Rolf Gardiner (4 July 1924). On those mornings in Mexico it was easy to fill the open spaces with gods of one's own devising, and to ascribe to them the grandeur of one's passion: easy, and better for Lawrence's purposes than the 'Pale-face and Hebraic monotheistic insistence'. Let the dark gods thrive, propitiated by the dancing Indians. Lawrence needed the gods for several reasons, but mostly to certify his belief in 'blood-consciousness', the great dark half of life, denied by the other half, the mind, the nerves.

I hope I have not given the impression that Lawrence made himself a 'citizen of the world', as if in preference to the complex fate of being an Englishman. He was hardly a citizen at all, at least in the sense of acknowledging social and moral obligations to his nation. But he was always an Englishman at heart, if not on principle. England irritated him beyond endurance, but it also made him what he was. Lawrence acknowledged his fate: 'I am English, and my Englishness is my very vision' (21 October 1915). We might be listening to

Blake. 'If England goes,' Lawrence said during the War, 'then Europe goes.' His sense of the decay of old England is often like Forster's in *Howards End*. 'So much beauty and pathos of old things passing away,' Lawrence was not ashamed to find himself saying of the view from Lady Ottoline's Garsington. As late as December 1926, writing to Gardiner, he went back in his mind's eye to Hucknall Torkard and Newstead Abbey, Annesley and Felley Mill: 'that's the country of my heart.' Even when he felt himself insulted by England, it was an English form of insult he registered: when he persuaded himself that America was the only hope, it was because he thought America had already gone all the way in corruption, with England lagging behind, and that the new seed must spring from total decay.

Finally, of course, he trusted nothing but his genius. As early as 1913, when evidence was still thin on the ground, he told Garnett 'I *know* I can write bigger stuff than any man in England.' He never doubted it: indeed there is a sense of impersonal truth in his certainty. Perhaps this gives us a clue to that 'other ego', which still troubles me as a working theory. Genius is at once personal and impersonal; the writer's own nature, and yet the god he serves. If he claims genius, he claims nothing for himself, it is a gift, his ego has not demanded it. Genius is therefore 'the whole' in which the mere man, the mere ego, finds his decent place. So Lawrence made every experience grist for his mill. Even when he detested a new experience, in another sense he welcomed it, and held it forever in his memory. He detested Ceylon: 'not wild horses would drag me back.' But wild horses could not have dislodged the memory, the images, sights, sounds, and smells, which he retained for their force, while hating them for other qualities. Everything was a blessing, however dreadfully disguised; a blessing to the artist, if a misery to the man. The artist hid every experience in himself, and then dreamed it different. It comes back to the question of energy. Lawrence always thought of himself as a fighter. 'I am essentially a fighter – to wish me peace is bad luck – except the fighter's peace' (4 July 1924). 'All truth – and real living is the only truth – has in it the elements of battle and repudiation' (30 August 1926). This explains why he distrusted Gordon Campbell's cult of ecstasy, in which conflicts are transcended. 'All vital truth contains the memory of all that for which it is not true' (? 19 December 1914), an aphorism endlessly responsive to meditation. Even his rows with Frieda: Katherine Mansfield thought them merely appalling and obscene, but it is probable that Lawrence engaged in them in a warrior's spirit. He had Keats's feeling, that a quarrel may be a fine thing, if genuine energies are engaged. What Lawrence could not bear was what he called friction, 'the sort of mental and nervous friction and destructiveness' which he ascribed to the Huxleys. Hating the War, he insisted that it was merely friction on a grotesque scale.

It was not heroic; or at least it did not answer to Lawrence's sense of the heroic. It was mechanical, obsolete, and therefore hideous. 'I know that, for me, the war is wrong. I know that if the Germans wanted my little house, I would rather give it them than fight for it: because my little house is not important enough to me. To fight for possessions, goods, is what my soul *will not* do. Therefore it will not fight for the neighbour who fights for his own goods. One is too raw, one fights too hard already, for the real integrity of one's being' (9 July 1916). It is hard to know what to say about this. If someone were to accuse Lawrence of being a coward, of hiding his cowardice in the safety of words while better men were shot to hell at the Somme, I would not be able to produce a ready answer. He hated the War; so did everyone. What more is there to say? I do not agree that his attitude was cowardly, or that a debate on it would necessarily use the idiom of Quakers or conscientious objectors who turn the other cheek. Lawrence was not indifferent: his letters in the years of war are desolate. But I think he judged the War by reference not to the fate of Europe or even the fate of the world but by reference to the laws of his own sensibility, his own genius. He could not live by any other criterion. His genius, propelled by intimations of life as energy, purpose, 'blood-consciousness', was outraged by the mechanical perversions which traded under their names from 1914 to 1918. There is nothing as galling to the propounder of a personal text than the public apocrypha which usurp its place. So I have no difficulty in finding Lawrence's wartime letters poignant, because beneath every cry of rage there is a cry of pity, present even when least audible. We are too ready to assume that words mean what they say, and only that. When reading Lawrence's letters, I often recall that passage in Machado's *Juan de Mairena* where Mairena, the greatest of teachers, tells Martinez, a student, to go to the blackboard and write: 'The olden blades of a glorious day . . .' Martinez complies. Then Mairena asks him: 'To what day do you think the poet is alluding?' Martinez, finest of pupils, answers: 'The day in which the blades no longer were olden.' Martinez would be the best reader of Lawrence's letters, because he would listen to the silence between the words, and sense the pity which surrounds the rage. When Rupert Brooke was killed, Lawrence wrote to Lady Ottoline: 'The death of Rupert Brooke fills me more and more with the sense of the fatuity of it all. He was slain by bright Phoebus's shaft – it was in keeping with his general sunniness – it was the real climax of his pose. I first heard of him as a Greek god under a Japanese sunshade, reading poetry in his pyjamas, at Grantchester, – at Grantchester upon the lawns where the river goes. Bright Phoebus smote him down. It is all in the saga. O God, O God, it is all too much of a piece: it is like madness' (30 April 1915). I find it remarkable that Lawrence's sense of the pity of it all has survived, in that passage, the apparent severity of 'pose'. That Lawrence's assessment of Brooke as an artist would be a limiting critique, there is every reason to believe; but there is also, competing with that severity, a sense of Brooke's beauty which includes the charm as well as the Narcissism of that pose. It is all in the saga, but only if Brooke is felt as bright Phoebus himself, as well as the appropriate victim of his shaft; his death in some measure a case of suicide. Even in letters of a less elegiac note, there is often the equivalent of this tact, the gentleness. Often in a most hostile and bitter letter, when the venom has expelled itself, Lawrence ends with a paragraph not of apology but of recognition; as if to say that beneath the flow of violence and rage there is another flow, of consanguinity and peace.

It is beautiful, especially toward the end. Readers of the letters probably agree with Lady Glenavy who spoke of Lawrence as overwhelmed by Frieda: Frieda 'whose over-vital and noisy presence usually reduced him to a gentle, bearded shadow'. Lawrence saw the fun of that, too, as well as its figurative truth. When he and Frieda combined in a letter, he said that Frieda's hand sprawled so large over the page that he had to squeeze himself small, and he added: 'I am very contractible' (? 18 April 1913). Frieda's 'God Almightiness' was always to be taken into account: she was a German *hausfrau*, and she wanted a *haus*, not Lawrence's next Paradise. She stayed large: Lawrence, consumed with illness, wasted away, he weighed six stones at the end. A few days before he died he had visits from Wells, a disappointment; from the Aga Khan, in whose fat face he discerned 'a bit of real religion': from the Huxleys, their play running its last week. He died on 2 March 1930, in Vence.

Lawrence's Poetry:
The Single State of Man
A. Alvarez

Art itself doesn't interest me, only the spiritual content.
D. H. Lawrence, Letter to Eunice Tietjens, 1917

The only native English poet of any importance to survive the First World War was D. H. Lawrence.[1] Yet his verse is very little read. As a minor adjunct to the novels it has come in, on occasions, for a little offhand comment. More often it is used as a go-between, joining the prose to the biography. Anthologists have printed a few poems grudgingly, out of piety, and even the critic who introduced the best English selection, in *The Penguin Poets*, seemed to feel that the poems succeed despite themselves, because they were written by Lawrence.

I had better state my position straight away: I think the poems very fine indeed, with a fineness of perception and development that was always Lawrence's, and an originality that makes them as important as any poetry of our time. For their excellence comes from something that is rare at best, and now, in the 1950s[2], well-nigh lost: a complete truth to feeling. Lawrence is the foremost emotional realist of the century. He wrote too much verse, like Hardy and Whitman, the two poets who influenced him most. But even his badness is the badness of genius; and there are quite enough good poems to make up for it. As for the influences and the styles he brushed with, Georgian and Imagist, I will have nothing to say of them here. They have no part in his best work.

Lawrence's poetry is usually hustled out of court by way of its 'carelessness'. I believe it was Eliot who first said that Lawrence wrote only sketches for poems, nothing ever quite finished. In one way there is some truth to this: he was not interested in surface polish; his verse is informal in the conventional sense. Indeed, the tighter the form the more the poet struggles:

> Many roses in the wind
> Are tapping at the window-sash.
> A hawk is in the sky; his wings
> Slowly begin to plash.   ('Love Storm')

It is the last word that jars. I see what he means, but the need to rhyme is like a wedge driven between the object and the word. The thing is forced and uneasy, even a little journalistic. Again and again, when Lawrence uses strict metrical forms, the poetry fails because of them, or succeeds despite them. At times he can manage complicated stanzas, but only because they allow him to get away from close correspondence of rhyme; they give him space to move around. The fainter the chime, the more remote the echo, the more convinced the poetry seems; close and perfect rhyme is invariably a constriction to him. For an essential part of Lawrence's genius was his fluency; and I mean something more literal than the ease with which he wrote: rather, the sense of direction in all the flowing change and variation in his work. This fluency has its own forms without its own conventions. It is not plottable: ear-count, finger-count and what might be called the logic of received form have nothing to do with it. What matters is the disturbance. 'It doesn't depend on the ear, particularly,' he once wrote, 'but on the sensitive soul.' It is something that can never be laid out into a system, for it comes instead from the poet's rigorous but open alertness. And so there is care, even discipline, but no formal perfection and finish. In an introductory note to *Fire and Other Poems* Frieda Lawrence wrote: 'He just wrote down his verse as it came to him. But later, when he thought of putting them into a book to be printed, he would work them over with great care and infinite patience.' And she has remarked that in a way he worked harder at his poetry than at the novels. When the prose would not go right he threw it away and began afresh. But the poems he worked over again and again. As proof there are the early drafts of 'Bavarian Gentians' and 'The Ship of Death', which are now printed as an appendix to the *Collected Poems*. Still, his diligence had nothing to do with mere technical efficiency. Lawrence's controlling standard was delicacy: a constant, fluid awareness, nearer the checks of intimate talk than those of regular prosody. His poetry is not the outcome of rules and formal craftsmanship, but of a purer, more native and immediate artistic sensibility. It is poetry because it could not be otherwise.

He was well aware of what he was about. He put his case in the introduction to *New Poems*:

To break the lovely form of metrical verse, and dish up the fragments as a new substance, called *vers libre*, this is what most of the free-versifiers accomplish. They do not know that free verse has its own *nature*, that it is neither star nor pearl, but instantaneous like plasm. . . . It has no finish. It has no satisfying stability, satisfying for those who like the immutable. None of this. It is the instant; the quick.

If Lawrence is trying to get the weight of formalism off his back, it is not for laziness. 'The instant; the quick' is as difficult to catch, to fix in exact language, as the most measured and stable formulations of experience. For this sort of impulse is in opposition to poetic conventions. The writer can never rely on a code of poetic manners to do part of the work for him. At the same time, of course, Lawrence knew his own powers and limitations well enough to realize that 'art' in some way deflected him from the real poetry. 'Art for my sake,' he said. Perhaps this is what he meant in the introduction to the *Collected Poems*:

The first poems I ever wrote, if poems they were, was when I was nineteen: now twenty-three years ago. I remember perfectly the Sunday afternoon when I perpetrated those first two pieces: 'To Guelder Roses' and 'To Campions'; in springtime, of course, and as I say, in my twentieth year. Any young lady might have written them and been pleased with them; as I was pleased with them. But it was after that, when I was twenty, that my real demon would now and then get hold of me and shake more real poems out of me, making me uneasy. I never 'liked' my real poems as I liked 'To Guelder Roses'. . . . Some of the earliest poems are a good deal rewritten. They were struggling to say something which it takes a man twenty years to be able to say. . . . A young man is afraid of his demon and puts his hand over the demon's mouth sometimes and speaks for him. And the things the young man says are very rarely poetry. So I have tried to let the demon say his say, and to remove the passages where the young man intruded. So that, in the first volume, many poems are changed, some entirely rewritten, recast. But usually this is only because the poem started out to be something which it didn't quite achieve, because the young man interfered with his demon.

This is at the opposite pole to Eliot's defence of Pound's hard work. For Eliot, the continued business of versifying was a way of keeping the bed aired until such time as the Muse should decide to visit. Lawrence's work was in coming to terms with his demon, so that the utterance would be unhindered. For it was the utterance, what he had to say, which was poetic; not the analysable form and technique. So for all his trouble, he never innovated in Pound's or Eliot's way. His discoveries were a matter of personal judgment and response. In the poems the speed and stress varies with the immediate, inward pressure. This is why the words 'loose' and 'careless' so clearly do not describe Lawrence's verse.

To have an example down on the page, there is 'End of Another Home Holiday'. To my mind, it is the best of the early *Rhyming Poems*. The demon has his say without awkwardness, but there is just enough of the earlier contrivance to show what Lawrence had left behind:

> When shall I see the half-moon sink again
> Behind the black sycamore at the end of the garden?
> When will the scent of the dim white phlox
> Creep up the wall to me, and in at my open window?

Why is it, the long, slow stroke of the midnight bell
    (Will it never finish the twelve?)
Falls again and again on my heart with a heavy reproach?

The moon-mist is over the village, out of the mist speaks the bell,
And all the little roofs of the village bow low, pitiful,
    beseeching, resigned.
– Speak, you my home! what is it I don't do well?

Ah home, suddenly I love you
As I hear the sharp clean trot of a pony down the road,
Succeeding sharp little sounds dropping into silence
Clear upon the long-drawn hoarseness of a train across the valley.

The light has gone out from under my mother's door.
    That she should love me so! –
    She, so lonely, greying now!
    And I leaving her,
    Bent on my pursuits!

        Love is the great Asker.
        The sun and the rain do not ask the secret
        Of the time when the grain struggles down in the dark.
        The moon walks her lonely way without anguish,
        Because no-one grieves over her departure.

Forever, ever by my shoulder pitiful love will linger,
Crouching as the little houses crouch under the mist when I turn.
Forever, out of the mist, the church lifts up a reproachful finger,
Pointing my eyes in wretched defiance where love hides her face to mourn.

        Oh! but the rain creeps down to wet the grain
        That struggles alone in the dark,
        And asking nothing, patiently steals back again!
        The moon sets forth o' nights
        To walk the lonely, dusky heights
        Serenely, with steps unswerving;
        Pursued by no sigh of bereavement,
        No tears of love unnerving
        Her constant tread:
        While ever at my side,
        Frail and sad, with grey, bowed head,
        The beggar-woman, the yearning-eyed
        Inexorable love goes lagging.

The wild young heifer, glancing distraught,
With a strange new knocking of life at her side
   Runs seeking a loneliness.
The little grain draws down the earth, to hide.
Nay, even the slumberous egg, as it labours under the shell
   Patiently to divide and self-divide,
Asks to be hidden, and wishes nothing to tell.

But when I draw the scanty cloak of silence over my eyes
Piteous love comes peering under the hood;
Touches the clasp with trembling fingers, and tries
To put her ear to the painful sob of my blood;
While her tears soak through to my breast,
   Where they burn and cauterise.

The moon lies back and reddens.
In the valley a corncrake calls
   Monotonously,
With a plaintive, unalterable voice, that deadens
   My confident activity;

With a hoarse, insistent request that falls
   Unweariedly, unweariedly,
Asking something more of me,
   Yet more of me.

I have put the poem there in full because, like all of Lawrence's verse, it needs its whole length to express its complexity. It seems to me a difficult poem. Yet there is nothing immediately incomprehensible about it, none of those tough intellectual obstacles that stop you short in Eliot's work. There is a curious intermixing of people and scene and nature. But beyond that the difficulty is in the state of mind: the pull between love and guilt, the tension between man and child.

It is all in the first four lines. They have a kind of awakened rhythm which cuts below the expectations of formality to the 'sensitive soul'. As Lawrence said of a line by Whitman, 'It makes me prick my innermost ear.' Only in the first ten-syllabled line will finger-count pay. After that the poem moves off on its own way. There is more in question than nostalgia: the speed of the lines varies with the flexibility of the talking voice. Part troubled, part meditative, the nostalgia is quickened instead of being expanded into a mood. If my comments are vague and assertive, I can only add another assertion: they have to be.

Everything depends on the reader's direct response to the rhythm. In that is all the disturbance which the rest of the poem defines.

Perhaps 'define' is the wrong word; 'draw out' might be closer. For what follows is done without a hint of abstraction. What is there to be defined is a complex of feelings, nothing that can be tidily separated out into formulae. All that is possible, and all the poet attempts, is to reach through intelligence some balance in the conflict.

> Why is it, the long, slow stroke of the midnight bell
> (Will it never finish the twelve?)
> Falls again and again on my heart with a heavy reproach?

There are three forces: the young man, literary and fond of word-painting; then, undercutting him, uneasy impatience; and finally, guilt. Mercifully, there is no need to go through the poem line by line to show how these two feelings take over all the details of the scene, so that it becomes a disturbing living presence for the poet to face. The result is that he can move from his village to his mother, from natural to artistic creation, without the least strain.

The poet is peculiarly unembarrassed and open about his feelings. He values his independence, but he doesn't assert it: the hint of self-absorption in 'Bent on my pursuits' has the same touch of irony about it as, for example,

> But when I draw the scanty cloak of silence over my eyes
> Piteous love comes peering under the hood;

And his central theme, 'Love is the great Asker', is both acknowledgement *and* criticism: the demands of love touch the vital part of him, 'Where they burn and cauterize'; yet even while they expose what is shallow and selfish in him, they expose themselves by their own nagging insistence.

The theme is love, but there is nothing in the poem of a 'Definition of Love', with all that implies of dapper logic and clear-cut distinctions. Lawrence's logic is more intimate. It is carried forward by a rigorous worrying, probing down to the quick of the feelings. Although the personal conflict is set off by the cycle of nature, no parallels are drawn. The forces work in harmony rather than in contradistinction. Despite all the talk of the sun and the moon, the grain and the heifer, and even that 'slumberous egg', the focus stays personal. In phrases like

> No tears of love *unnerving*
> Her constant tread

you see how the same difficult, intimate preoccupation runs under the whole thing. So without any of Marvell's syllogizing there is still a completeness to the

215

poem; in the end, something has been settled. It is done by what Eliot called a 'logic of sensibility' (though, in fact, he probably meant something quite different). The toughness, instead of being in the logic, is in the truth to feeling, the constant exertion of the poet's intelligence to get close to what he really feels, not to accept on the way any easy formulation or avoidance.

This is why a set metre would have been impossible – as it was impossible in Coleridge's 'Dejection'. Each line has its own force and rhythm, and they flow together, varying with the shifts in feeling. This is true of almost all Lawrence's poems: the inner pressure and disturbance gives to every one its own inherent form. Each starts afresh and appeals directly to the attention of 'the sensitive soul'. The controlling factor is in the intelligence. His poems are not effusions; they don't run off with him. Instead, the intelligence works away at the emotions, giving to each poem a finished quality, an economy in all the repetitions. It is a matter of the fullness with which the subject is presented.

This intellectual honesty and pertinacity of Lawrence's verse has had very little attention. The poems which have come in for most notice, the *Birds, Beasts and Flowers*, are usually thought of as little more than vivid little pieces of description, like the so-called 'lyric' passages in his novels. In fact, the nature poems are quite as personal as any of his others. In them he doesn't merely describe, nor does he go at his subjects with a preconceived idea and try to twist them into meanings they would not naturally take. They are neither all subject nor all poet. It is a matter of a vital and complex relationship between the two, difficult, fluent, inward and wholly unabstract. He even avoids the final abstraction of formal perfection. For that gives to experience a kind of ghostly Platonic idealness: in the end, everything is so perfectly accounted for that the poetic world is complete and isolated. In the relationship Lawrence tries to catch, everything is in flux; it is a flow between two creatures, with nothing fixed. The artist has constantly to improvise at the full pitch of his intelligence. And according to Lawrence, who judged intelligence by its delicacy and awareness, not by its command of rationalization, the greater the intelligence the nearer the result came to poetry:

It has always seemed to me that a real thought, a single thought, not an argument, can only exist easily in verse, or in some poetic form. There is a didactic element about prose thoughts which makes them repellent, slightly bullying.

Foreword to *Pansies*

The same sort of intelligence is at work in the novels, but the actual method is rather different. Again, the didactic sections hardly matter – though in some of the later novels they take up more space than they are worth. The whole method is to set the characters in motion, so there is a curious fusion of feeling and action, each dependent on the other, deepening the other, and yet resisting any single interpretation. Hence the word 'symbolism' that is often tacked on to his method; I prefer Dr Leavis's term, 'dramatic poem'. Of course, Lawrence himself is there in all his novels; but at the remove of fiction. There is no need to make an exact identification, for the author has given himself enough room to dramatize and judge with a free hand. The poems are more intimate, and their personal statements are outright. He said of the *Collected Poems:* 'I have tried to establish a chronological order, because many of the poems are so personal that, in their fragmentary fashion, they make up a biography of an emotional and inner life.' There precisely is the difference: the theme of both the novels and the poems is fulfilment, the spiritual maturity achieved between man and woman. But in the novels the fulfilment is acted out; the forces, like the morality, are 'passionate, implicit'. By contrast, the poems present nakedly the inner flow that runs below the actions, the forces before they are externalized in drama. It is as though they presented not the body that acts but the blood itself, the lifeline of experience and feeling that feeds and supports the novels.

Here, for example, is a passage from a novel which develops much the same theme as 'End of Another Home Holiday':

No man was beyond woman. But in his one quality of ultimate maker and breaker, he was womanless. Harriet denied this, bitterly. She wanted to share, to join in, not to be left out lonely. He looked at her in distress, and did not answer. It is a knot that can never be untied; it can only, like a navel string, be broken or cut.

For the moment, however, he said nothing. But Somers knew from his dreams what she was feeling: his dreams of a woman, a woman he loved, something like Harriet, something like his mother, and yet unlike either, a woman sullen and obstinate against him, repudiating him. Bitter the woman was, grieved beyond words, grieved till her face was swollen and puffy and almost mad or imbecile, because she had loved him so much, and now she must see him betray her love. That was how the dream woman put it: he had betrayed her great love, and she must go down desolate into an everlasting hell, denied, and denying him absolutely in return, a sullen, awful soul. The face reminded him of Harriet, and of his mother, and of his sister, and of girls he had known when he was younger – strange glimpses of all of them, each glimpse excluding the last. And at the same time in the terrible face some of the look of that bloated face of a madwoman which hung over Jane Eyre in the night in Mr Rochester's house.

The Somers of the dream was terribly upset. He cried tears from his very bowels, and laid his hand on the woman's arm saying:

'But I love you. Don't you *believe* in me? Don't you *believe* in me?' But the woman, she seemed almost old now – only shed a few bitter tears, bitter as vitriol, from her distorted face, and bitterly, hideously turned away, dragging her arm from the touch of his fingers; turned, as it seemed to the dream-Somers, away to the sullen and dreary, everlasting hell of repudiation.

He woke at this, and listened to the thunder of the sea with horror. With horror. Two women in his life he had loved down to the quick of life and death: his mother and Harriet. And the woman in the dream was so awfully his mother, risen from the dead, and at the same time Harriet as it were departing from this life that he stared at the night-paleness between the window-curtains in horror.

'They neither of them believed in me' he said to himself. Still in the spell of the dream, he put it into the past tense, though Harriet lay sleeping in the next bed. He could not get over it.

This is from *Kangaroo*, where Somers is no less Lawrence than the much younger man who wrote the poem. And the same demon is at work in both, the same crucifixion between guilt and love, between independent male activity and unanswerable emotional ties; and, in the end, the same sense of inevitable betrayal. Yet although the dream-form allows Lawrence to use emotional shorthand and a bare directness of presentation, the novel and the poem only converge from opposite directions. In the verse the feelings *are happening* to the poet in all their conflict. In the novel they are embodied in action. They are given sides and the complexity is left to flower in the spaces between.

The whole of Lawrence's power and originality as a poet depends on the way he keeps close to his feelings. This is why he had to rid himself of conventional forms. The poems take even their shape from the feelings. And so it is a long way off the mark to think of them as jotted-down talk. The span of the lines is not that of the talking voice. The tone is: that is, it is direct and without self-consciousness. But the poems, for instance, use more repetitions than talk. Yet this is a matter of fullness, not of rhetorical elaboration. It is part of the purpose-fulness with which the poems explore the emotions in their entirety. And with the same sureness he can let them go: when he is writing from no more than an impulse or an irritation, short and transient, the poetry is equally brief and to the point – *Pansies*, for example; but when the feelings are profound and sustained, so is the verse-form – as in, say, 'Bavarian Gentians', one of his master-pieces. The dependence of the form on the subject means that the poems find it very hard to rarify themselves into mere words and device.

The lines themselves contribute to the accuracy and delicacy of expression. They are a means of emphasis rather than a pause for breath:

> He drank enough
> And lifted his head, dreamily, as one who has drunken,
> And flickered his tongue like a forked night on the air, so black,
> Seeming to lick his lips,
> And looked around like a god, unseeing, into the air . . .

> 'Snake'

Again, it is a question of movement, or rather of two movements, one playing against the other. There are actions, the ordinary, recognizable sanity of things happening in a human, or almost human way; these get the short matter-of-fact lines: 'He drank enough', 'Seeming to lick his lips'. And then, in subtle contrast, is the running, disturbed movement of the longer lines in which the poet catches up the factual description into his own excitement. The known merges with the unknown: 'as one who has drunken' becomes 'like a forked night on the air', and ends 'like a god'. And so, within the framework of a description, the interchange between these two creatures takes on the dignity of a strange visitation. The poet is unloosing, in fact, the reserves of power of two earlier lines in the poem:

> Someone was before me at my water-trough,
> And I, like a second comer, waiting.

For all the overtones, there is nothing 'other-worldly' about this. The stuff of Lawrence's poetry, the 'lifeline', are those essential experiences in which he registers his full humanity. His poems are the inner flow of a man in the act of becoming aware – aware not only of his feelings and their cause, but of their full implications. By the flexibility of his verse-forms he can catch this flow in all its immediacy and with peculiarly little fuss. For fuss has no part in what he has to say. Lawrence is not a mystic; his poetry has to do with recognitions, not with revelations. It should be read not against the cant of 'dark gods' and the stridency of *The Plumed Serpent*, but against the sanity of the 'creed' with which he answered Benjamin Franklin:

That I am I.

That my soul is a dark forest.

That my known self will never be more than a little clearing in the forest.

That gods, strange gods, come forth from the forest into the clearing of my known self, and then go back.

That I must have the courage to let them come and go.

That I will never let mankind put anything over me, but that I will always try to recognize and submit to the gods in me and the gods in other men and women.

There is only reverence, attention, awareness and an unprejudiced, independent intelligence at the bottom of this; no other-worldliness, nothing in the least of overblown pretension. It is the imaginative strength with which Lawrence voiced the fullness of his humanity that has got him the name of mystic and prophet, as it did for Blake. Lawrence does not have second sight, he has only a piercingly clear first sight. His genius is in expressing that, rather than waiting until his perceptions have gathered about them a decent abstraction, as the warm-blooded body of a whale is enclosed in protective blubber. Lawrence's mysticism is merely his first-handness, his distance from convention.

Earlier, I remarked that the controlling force in the verse is neither any formal metrical guide nor a set of preordained principles; it is the working intelligence. On this his most genuine and effective poetry relies and it appears primarily in the honesty with which he acknowledges his feelings and recognizes his motives with neither shuffling nor abstraction. But it is there, too, in the wit, the endless liveliness of his verse:

> How beastly the bourgeois is
> especially the male of the species –
>
> Presentable, eminently presentable –
> shall I make you a present of him?

Or

> It is a fearful thing to fall into the hands of the living God.
> But it is a much more fearful thing to fall out of them . . .

Or

> You tell me I am wrong.
> Who are you, who is anybody to tell me I am wrong?
> I am not wrong.

The closeness of this last to 'For Godsake hold your tongue, and let me love' seems to me to be apparent enough. Yet Lawrence's verse, for all its wit and swing, has never been resurrected in the craze for Donne. The reason is simply that the twentieth-century Metaphysical style has been used as an excuse for obliqueness. The canons of irony invoked to display its excellence are merely ways of avoiding commitment, a technical sleight of mind by which the poet can seem to take many sides while settling, in fact, for none. Lawrence, clearly, does not suffer from this – neither, I believe, did Donne. The wit of both is not a sparkle on top of indifference; it is a manifestation of the subtlety and breadth of their understanding.

Imagine that any mind ever *thought* a red geranium!
As if the redness of a red geranium could be anything but a sensual experience
and as if sensual experience could take place before there were any senses.
We know that even God could not imagine the redness of a red geranium
nor the smell of mignonette
when geraniums were not, and mignonette neither.
And even when they were, even God would have to have a nose to smell at the
    mignonette.

You can't imagine the Holy Ghost sniffing at cherry-pie heliotrope.
Or the Most High, during the coal age, cudgelling his mighty brains
even if he had any brains: straining his mighty mind
to think, among the moss and mud of lizards and mastodons
to think out, in the abstract, when all was twilit green and muddy:
'Now there shall be tum-tiddly-um, and tum-tiddly-um, hey presto! scarlet geranium!'
We know it couldn't be done.
But imagine, among the mud and the mastodons
god sighing and yearning with tremendous creative yearning, in that dark green mess
oh, for some other beauty, some other beauty
that blossomed at last, red geranium, and mignonette.

It is hard to know whether to emphasize more the ease and originality of the piece, or its tact. There is neither a jot of pretentiousness in the poem, nor of vulgarity, though the opportunity for both certainly offered. Lawrence uses his wit not in the modern fashion, to save his face, but to strengthen the seriousness of what he has to say. There is no disproportion between the colloquial liveliness of the opening and the equally alive tenderness of the close. The wit is not a flourish; it is one of the poetic means; it preserves the seriousness from sentimentality and overstatement, as the seriousness keeps the wit from flippancy.

Lawrence wrote too many poems. Their standard is not uniformly high; some of them are frankly bad. In this count I am leaving out *Pansies* and *Nettles*. Though some of these are good, they were intended primarily as squibs; and even if they have a serious enough edge to their satire, few are particularly memorable as poetry. Nor is he to be held responsible for the faults of his early verse; they are the faults of a poet who is still trying to find his own voice. The bad poems are those which have a complete originality, yet still fail. For example, the sequence 'Wedlock' in the transitional volume *Look! We Have Come Through!* Like his best poems, they go down to the pith of the feelings and present that in its singleness. But they fail because they are too naked. It is as though the feelings were overwhelming beyond speech, yet still the poet insisted on nothing less than their full force, muffled by no sort of poetic device. In 'Burnt Norton' Eliot justifies a long series of images which suggest an intense experience without stating it, by the comment: 'Human kind Cannot bear very much reality'. In these poems Lawrence is insisting on nothing short of the emotional reality, and the poetry cannot quite bear it. They are not private as the *Pisan Cantos* are private; they have no references which remain in the poet's keeping. They are private in the other sense: they make the reader feel he is listening in where he shouldn't be. It is for this reason that *Look!*, although it contains some excellent poems, is more successful as a series than in any one piece. Lawrence himself said, 'They are intended as an essential story, or history, or confession', and Amy Lowell thought they made up 'a greater novel even than *Sons and Lovers*'. That is an overstatement which was worth making. The impact of the book seems to me as direct and painful as anything since Clare. Yet it would be hard to localize this power in any one poem. If some of the pieces fail because of their nakedness, it is because they are approaching the vanishing-point of poetry, where expression itself is some sort of intrusion. It took genius and great courage even to fail in that way. When Lawrence's poems are bad they are victims of that peculiar honesty which, at other times, made for their strength.

Lawrence was honest about the emotions without being absorbed in them for their own sakes. He is not taken up in himself. The life-line of his poems is something more active, harder and more delicate. 'But it's no good,' he wrote to Murry, 'Either you go on wheeling a wheelbarrow and lecturing at Cambridge and going softer and softer inside, or you make a hard fight with yourself, pull yourself up, harden yourself, throw your feelings down the drain and face the world as a fighter. – You won't though.' Lawrence's poems are about that 'hard fight'. He never relished his feelings, nor played with them in front of the mirror; hence he never simplified them. But he always kept extraordinarily close to them; and so he never fell into oversubtlety, the intellectual counterpart of emotional looseness. The language of the poems, lucid, witty, vivid, often a bit slangy, preserved the balance. It made any kind of overstatement or evasion very hard.

The question why Lawrence's poetry has had so little recognition, despite its originality, delicacy, wit and, above all, its honesty and intelligence, is answered in that word 'carelessness'. Our modern poetry began with a vigorous attack on outworn conventions of feeling and expression. But the emphasis has gradually gone so much on the craft and technicality of writing that the original wholeness and freshness is again lost. One sort of academic nullity has been replaced by another: the English 'gentleman-of-letters' conceit, which prevailed at least until the end of the Georgians, has gone under. In its place is a Germanic *ponderismuskeit*, a deadening technical thoroughness. Lawrence's demon is as out of place in that as it was in the old port-and-tweed tradition.

I used to think that one of the troubles with the poetry we have now was that, despite the stress Eliot has laid on the intelligence, no one seemed capable of thinking. I was wrong – not about the inability to think, but in expecting it at all; or at least in expecting thinking to be carried on with something of the precision of the seventeenth century. Of course, no one is trained in the syllogism; nowadays that sort of logical clarity is impossible, or it is forced. In place of the old patterns the modern poet has to rely far more heavily on his own native intelligence, on his ability to feel accurately, without conceit or indulgence; to feel, that is, when he has 'thrown his feelings down the drain'. He is left then not with a vague blur of emotions or a precise, empty dialectic, but with the essential thread that runs beneath the confusion, with 'the instant; the quick'. This, I believe, is the real material of poetry, material which could not take any other form. This inner logic is quite as difficult as its older formal counterpart. It depends on getting close to the real feelings and presenting them without formulae and without avoidance, in all their newness, disturbance and ugliness. If a poet does that he will not find himself writing in Lawrence's style; but, like Lawrence, he may speak out in his own voice, single and undisguised.[3]

The Poetry of D. H. Lawrence – With a Glance at Shelley
Edward Lucie-Smith

The poetry of D. H. Lawrence has been the last part of his oeuvre to be systematically examined and revalued. The chief reason for this is obvious: as a poet, Lawrence had a high rate of failure. Nevertheless, the extraordinary merits of some of his poems have not escaped notice. 'Snake' appears over and over again in school anthologies. Dylan Thomas made 'The Ship of Death' into a spectacular performance piece. What was lacking, at least until recently, was a sense of how those poems by Lawrence which really counted should be placed in relation to the development of the English poetic tradition. It is not too much to say that, as a poet even more than as a novelist, Lawrence had to wait until events caught up with him.

Lawrence seems to me (I am not the first to make this claim) the only English-born modernist poet of real importance to survive the First World War. His two rivals, or potential rivals, Wilfred Owen and Isaac Rosenberg, were both killed. In the twenties, the field was left open to the traditionalist Georgians on the one hand, and to the party of Eliot and Pound on the other. The Sitwells, who fit into neither of these categories, were to my mind too limited as poets (even Edith) to provide a viable alternative.

If we compare the poetry that Lawrence was producing, during the war years and just after them, to the poetry that Eliot was writing, we encounter a very marked difference in both method and sensibility. The difference is never more marked than at moments when they both seem to be doing the same thing – for example, when they appeal to the authority of the past against the degenerate present. Eliot's appeal is by means of an elaborate network of allusion:

> There I saw one I knew, and stopped him, crying: 'Stetson!
> 'You who were with me in the ships at Mylae!
> 'That corpse you planted last year in your garden,
> 'Has it begun to sprout? Will it bloom this year?

> 'Or has the sudden frost disturbed its bed?
> 'O keep the Dog far hence, that's friend to men,
> 'Or with his nails he'll dig it up again!
> 'You! hypocrite lecteur! – mon semblable, – mon frère!'
>
> *The Waste Land*

Lawrence prefers a dramatic recreation:

> So now they come back! Hark!
> Hark! the low and shattering laughter of bearded men
> with the slim waists of warriors, and the long feet
> of moon-lit dancers.
>
> Oh, and their faces scarlet, like the dolphin's blood!
> Lo! the loveliest is red all over, rippling vermilion
> as he ripples upwards!
> laughing in his black beard!
>
> 'For the Heroes are Dipped in Scarlet'

It is not too much to say that Eliot and Lawrence have diametrically opposite views about the way in which the poetic mind conducts its operations. With Eliot, we are presented with an elaborately wrought, polished surface. Darting across this surface are brilliant discharges of intellectual energy, and the routes whereby these discharges travel are the allusions. Immediately before the war, Eliot had been associated with the Vorticist group, through Pound and Wyndham Lewis. The Vorticists, in turn, were influenced by the doctrine of simultaneity, as proclaimed by F. T. Marinetti and the Italian Futurists. In *The Waste Land* we find Eliot practising a version of simultaneity which is at once much refined from the original, and greatly elaborated. The sequential progression of the poem, despite the fact that it is broken into sections, is almost lost, and we can think of the whole – all its words and phrases, the experience of the works of literature that Eliot cites, the life-experience intermingled with this – as existing simultaneously in the poet's mind.

Lawrence, on the other hand, often seems too concerned to dramatize the way in which the mind encounters and apprehends experience. The most successful poems in *Birds, Beasts and Flowers* are about a gradual process of permeation. The self becomes suffused by what is being looked at:

> You contract yourself,
> You arch yourself as an archer's bow
> Which quivers indrawn as you clench your spine
> Until your veiled head almost touches backward
> To the root-rising of your erected tail.

225

And the intense and backward-curving frisson
Seizes you as you clench yourself together
Like some fierce magnet bringing its poles together.
Burning, pale positive of your wattled head!
And from the darkness of the opposite one
The upstart of your round-barred, sun-round tail!

'Turkey-Cock'

What is notable here is the way in which the metaphorical energy in the last four lines quoted helps to validate the descriptive style of the previous seven. As soon as the image of the magnet is introduced, we get the sensation that Lawrence's perceptions have found the track they were seeking – the track which leads directly to the inner nature of the subject.

When I said that Lawrence the poet had to wait for events to catch up with him, I was thinking, in particular, of the British poetry written in the 1960s. An obvious comparison is with the work of Ted Hughes, who has clearly been much influenced by Lawrence – by the prose, one suspects, as well as by the poetry. It is interesting to set some of Hughes's beast poems side by side with Lawrence's. We immediately notice that the strategies adopted are very similar:

Then, slowly, as onto the mind's eye –
The brow like masonry, the deep-keeled neck:
Something come up there on to the brink of the gulf,
Hadn't heard the world, too deep in itself to be called to;
Stood in sleep. He would swing his muzzle at a fly
But the square of sky where I hung, shouting, waving,
Was nothing to him; nothing of our light
Found any reflection in him.

Ted Hughes, 'The Bull Moses'

He drank enough
And lifted his head, dreamily, as one who has drunken,
And flickered his tongue like a forked night on the air, so black,
Seeming to lick his lips,
And looked around like a god, unseeing, into the air,
And slowly turned his head,
And slowly, very slowly, as if thrice adream,
Proceeded to draw his slow length curving round
And climb again the broken bank of my wall-face.

D. H. Lawrence, 'Snake'

It is not merely that the poetic method is the same in both extracts – a slow, almost groping progression, a *feeling into* the life of the creature – but there is,

226

in addition, an insistence on the mystery and darkness to be found at the heart of the experience which is being described. Lawrence and Hughes discover a godhead in animals, but it is a godhead 'deliberately going into the blackness' like the snake, something which gives no light back to the light of human reason.

From another point of view, Hughes and Lawrence are also closely comparable: the kind of form they try to make is an expressive form. Lawrence's eloquent letter to Edward Marsh, written at the end of 1913, with nearly all the best of his poetry still to come, has long been recognized as a key document when it comes to gauging his intentions as a poet, and it is worth quoting some sentences from it here. 'I think,' says Lawrence, 'more of a bird with 'road wings flying and lapsing through the air, than anything, when I think of metre.' Trying to define his attitudes further, he continues (and the italics are his):

It all depends on the *pause* – the natural pause, the natural *lingering* of the voice according to the feeling – it is the hidden *emotional* pattern that makes poetry, not the obvious form. . . . It is the lapse of feeling, something as indefinite as expression in the voice carrying emotion. It doesn't depend on the ear, particularly, but on the sensitive soul.

Collected Letters, Vol. I, p. 243

The first part of this quotation might perhaps be used to make Lawrence look like a forerunner of Charles Olson, an advocate of a kind of projective verse. But the second part of it corrects this impression. It is the development of emotion which the poet's writing must strive both to mime and to mirror, and the ear is subordinate to the spirit within. So eloquent an advocacy of expressive form leads one to think of Lawrence as being in some respects like the German Expressionist poets who were his contemporaries, though he never indulges in the dislocations which are characteristic of their work. This comparison is reinforced when we consider pictures which Lawrence was to paint towards the end of his life. They have a kinship with the kind of painting which German artists, such as Kirchner, had produced a little earlier.

If we are looking for one word with which to sum up Lawrence's poetic ideal, however, that word must surely be 'naturalness'. Edward Thomas had already hit on it long before Lawrence had really discovered his true poetic capacities. Reviewing the early volume *Love Poems and Others*, he described its contents as being 'as near as possible natural poetry'. A definition of the qualities Lawrence himself instinctively looked for in poetry can be found in a letter of June 1914, in which he discusses his reactions to a big anthology of Italian Futurist verse which he had recently read. 'I like it,' he says, 'because it is the applying to emotions of the purging of old forms and sentimentalities. I like it for its saying –

enough of this sickly cant, let us be honest and stick by what is in us.' But in the long run he finds that poetry of this kind has not got enough to give him:

The one thing about their art is that it *isn't* art, but ultra-scientific attempts to make diagrams of certain physical or mental states. It is ultra-ultra intellectual, going beyond Maeterlinck and the Symbolistes, who are intellectual. There isn't a trace of naïveté in their works – though there's plenty of naïveté in the authors. It's the most self-conscious, intentional, pseudo-scientific stuff on the face of the earth.

Collected Letters, Vol. I, p. 280

But it is at this point, I think, that we reach a really interesting crux. If Lawrence's commitment to the idea of naturalness and natural expression is one of the things that makes him truly original and memorable as a poet, it is also the thing which links him most closely to the nineteenth-century Romantic tradition. In searching for Lawrence's poetic ancestry, critics usually tend to find that his most important roots are in Whitman. Certainly there are passages in his later work where he uses Whitman's accumulative technique with great skill:

I remember the scream of a rabbit as I went through a wood at midnight;
I remember the heifer in her heat, blorting and blorting through the hours, persistent and irrepressible;
I remember my first terror hearing the howl of weird, amorous cats;
I remember the scream of a terrified, injured horse, the sheet-lightning,
And running away from the sound of a woman in labour, something like an owl whooing,
And listening inwardly to the first bleat of a lamb,
The first wail of an infant,
And my mother singing to herself,
And the first tenor singing of the passionate throat of a young collier, who has long since drunk himself to death,
The first elements of foreign speech
On wild dark lips.

'Tortoise Shout'

In addition, we find a generous appreciation of Whitman in *Studies in Classic American Literature*: 'Whitman, the great poet, has meant so much to me. Whitman, the one man breaking a way ahead. Whitman, the one pioneer. And only Whitman. No English pioneers, no French.' Trying to localize Whitman's unique importance, Lawrence declares: 'Whitman was the first to break the mental allegiance. He was the first to smash the old moral conception that the soul of man is something "superior" and "above" the flesh. . . . Whitman was the first heroic seer to seize the soul by the scruff of her neck and plant her down among the potsherds.'

Nevertheless, anyone who is at all familiar with Lawrence's work and attitudes would expect praise to be balanced by condemnation. In a letter written at the end of 1913, we find him assessing Whitman rather differently:

Whitman is like a human document, or a wonderful treatise in human self-revelation. It is neither art nor religion nor truth: Just a self-revelation of a man who could not live, and so had to write himself. But writing should come from a strong root of life: like a battle song after a battle. – And Whitman did this, more or less. But his battle was not a real battle: he never gave his individual self unto the fight: he was too much aware of it. He never fought with another person – he was like a wrestler who only wrestles with his own shadow – he never came to grips. He chucked his body into the fight, and stood apart saying 'Look how I am living'. He is really false as hell. – But he is fine too.

Collected Letters, Vol. I, p. 258

I have quoted this passage from the letters at some length because it serves as a reminder that, though Lawrence is a great critic, he cannot entirely be trusted in this role. Any evidence from outside that we bring to the poems, in the hope of understanding them better, must be treated with a degree of reserve.

Let us look at a case which is seldom, if ever, cited – not Lawrence's relationship to Whitman, but Lawrence's relationship to Shelley. There is, I think, a general feeling that a taste for Lawrence's poetry is incompatible with a taste for Shelley's. Dr F. R. Leavis, Lawrence's most important contemporary advocate, has also been responsible for the severe downgrading of Shelley's poetic reputation. The essay on Shelley in *Revaluation* is intensely hostile. Again, if we are searching for evidence of rather a different sort, we can turn to Aldous Huxley's novel *Point Counter Point*. Rampion, one of the characters in the book, is generally acknowledged to be a portrait of Lawrence, whom Huxley knew well. Into Rampion's mouth, Huxley puts a tremendous diatribe against Shelley and his poetry: 'There's something very dreadful about Shelley. Not human, not a man. A mixture between a fairy and a white slug.'

Lawrence himself reverts to the subject of Shelley more than once in his letters and criticism. The most complete and formal judgement is to be found in the essay on Thomas Hardy which was published posthumously in *Phoenix*. Shelley, Lawrence declares, is the type of the one-sided artist: 'I can think of no being in the world so transcendently male as Shelley. He is phenomenal. The rest of us have bodies which contain the male and the female. If we were so singled out as Shelley, we should not belong to life, as he did not belong to life.' Nevertheless, so Lawrence declares, there is a necessary and beautiful dichotomy in Shelley's 'To a Skylark'. He comments as follows upon the first stanza of the poem:

Shelley wishes to say, the skylark is a pure, untrammelled spirit, a pure motion. But the very 'Bird thou never wert' admits that the skylark *is* in very fact a bird, a concrete, momentary thing. If the line rang 'Bird thou never art', that would spoil it all. Shelley wishes to say, the song is poured out of heaven: but 'or near it', he admits. There is the perfect relation between heaven and earth. And the last line is the tumbling sound of a lark's singing, the real Two-in-One.

Lawrence's letters, too, contain a number of important references to Shelley and his work. In 1913, for instance, he tells Marsh that he thinks Shelley 'a million thousand times more beautiful than Milton'. In another letter, written three years later, he expresses an admiration for Swinburne, saying: 'I put him with Shelley as our greatest poet'.

In fact, I only labour the point – Lawrence's instinctive sympathy for Shelley – because critics have since tried to consign them to opposite ends of the poetic spectrum. On the face of it, many things would lead us to suppose that Shelley would interest Lawrence. There are, for example, the biographical links, despite the fact that one was of working-class and the other of aristocratic origin. Both men exiled themselves from an England which seemed irremediably hostile. Lawrence even lived for a period at Lerici. In both men, the spirit of opposition to the England they knew was directed against, not merely philistinism and sexual intolerance, but specific social evils. Compare the conclusion of Shelley's 'Song to the Men of England', with the concluding lines of Lawrence's poem 'Wages'. The form may be very different, but the content is more or less identical:

> With plough and spade, and hoe and loom,
> Trace your grave, and build your tomb,
> And weave your winding-sheet, till fair
> England be your sepulchre.
>
> Shelley

> Living on our income is strolling grandly outside the prison
> in terror lest you have to go in. And since the work-prison covers
> almost every scrap of the living earth, you stroll up and down
> on a narrow beat, about the same as a prisoner taking exercise.
> This is called universal freedom.
>
> Lawrence

It may perhaps be objected that Shelley's celebrated essay 'A Defence of Poetry', represents, in its Platonic and idealizing tendency, much of what Lawrence was concerned to oppose. And this is indeed true. But there are many passages which nevertheless seem to anticipate Lawrence's actual practice as a poet. Take, for example, Shelley's remarks upon form:

An observation of the regular mode of the recurrence of harmony in the language of poetical minds, together with its relation to music, produced metre, or a certain system of traditional forms of harmony and language. Yet it is by no means essential that a poet should accommodate his language to this traditional form, so that the harmony, which is its spirit, be observed. The practice is indeed convenient and popular, and to be preferred, especially in such composition as includes much action: but every great poet must inevitably innovate upon the example of his predecessors in the exact structure of his peculiar versification. The distinction between poets and prose-writers is a vulgar error.

The notion of 'naturalness', which I have already cited as a key concept if we are to understand Lawrence's attitudes towards the writing of poetry, has its roots in the tradition which Shelley, both as poet and critic, may be taken to represent. For Shelley, the forces of nature play upon the instrument which is man, and produce harmony 'like the alternations of an ever-changing wind over an Aeolian lyre'. Savages and children already have the fundamental elements of poetry within them: 'A child at play by itself will express its delight by its voice and motions. . . . In relation to the objects which delight a child, these expressions are what poetry is to higher objects'. Naturalness, in Lawrence, must be related to that whole complex of ideas about Nature herself which lies at the very centre of the Romantic Movement in the arts.

It would be sophistry, however, to ignore what seems to be a very real difference between the poetry of Shelley and that of Lawrence: the one (so present-day critics assert) is chronically unspecific; while Lawrence, upon the other hand, is marvellously concrete, with an unequalled gift for conveying the detail of physical sensations and observations.

As a view of Shelley, this is an oversimplification. For example, the 'Ode to the West Wind' (*pace* Dr Leavis, who roundly condemns this poem in particular for what he takes to be its vagueness and imprecision) contains much which seems to be based upon Shelley's scientific studies: his wind brings with it cloud effects which meteorologists, at any rate, find credible. Yet if we put Shelley's 'The Sensitive Plant', sometimes acclaimed as one of his best works, side by side with a 'plant' poem of Lawrence's, such as 'Sicilian Cyclamens', we see at once that there is not much to be gained from the comparison. Whenever Lawrence uses a metaphor or a simile, it is incomparably fresher and more unexpected than anything Shelley can find:

> Cyclamens, young cyclamens
> Arching

Waking, pricking their ears
Like delicate, very-young greyhound bitches . . .

However, this does not settle the matter. Certain important questions remain. Upon them, and the answers to them, hinges our real estimate of Lawrence's stature as a poet. Do we believe that the best of Lawrence is to be found in poems like 'Sicilian Cyclamens', 'Turkey-Cock' and 'Snake'? Or are there other, equally beautiful poems, of a different sort, which must also be taken into account?

Poetry after the Second World War in Britain has mostly been unambitious poetry. When confronted with large issues, it has often sought to deal with them obliquely. Concreteness, vividness and concision have been amongst its principal virtues, in theory if not in fact. The poems which Lawrence brought together in *Birds, Beasts and Flowers* therefore represent something which is easily assimilable to current practice. They seem absolutely contemporary, where Eliot, for example, no longer seems contemporary in quite the sense in which I am now using the word. But, granted that Lawrence's poetry needs rigorous selection, do we not maim his achievement if we concentrate on the poems I have designated, and others that resemble them, and those alone?

One poem of a different sort which has nevertheless forced itself upon the attention of those who read Lawrence's poetry is 'The Ship of Death'. This is perhaps Lawrence's most successful attempt to achieve a reconciliation with the idea of his own imminent dissolution. When he wrote it, he knew that he had not long to live. The poem is what a psychoanalyst might term an act of self-mourning. The fact of death, and feelings about death, are ritually purged of their power to damage the psyche. Another ambitious poem of purgation, which also tries to deal with the fact of death, is Shelley's 'Adonais'. What do comparisons yield here?

There is no port, there is nowhere to go
only the deepening blackness darkening still
blacker upon the soundless, ungurgling flood
darkness at one with darkness, up and down
and sideways utterly dark, so there is no direction any more
And the little ship is there; yet she is gone.
She is not seen, for there is nothing to see her by.
She is gone! gone! and yet
somewhere she is there.

'The Ship of Death'

The splendours of the firmament of time
May be eclipsed, but are extinguished not;

232

> Like stars to their appointed height they climb,
> And death is a low mist which cannot blot
> The brightness it may veil. When lofty thought
> Lifts a young heart above its mortal lair,
> And love and life contend in it, for what
> Shall be its earthly doom, the dead live there
> And move like winds of light on dark and stormy air.
>
> 'Adonais'

Images of darkness and light are almost inevitable in poems of this genre, whether they be works of genius or pedestrian rubbish, and it is not for superficial resemblances of this kind that I cite the two passages above. What I find in them, and hope that other readers may find too, is a more ambitious feeling of responsibility towards one's own humanity and the condition of being human than I am accustomed to find in the poetry written by my contemporaries.

What I have chiefly wanted to suggest, in drawing parallels between Lawrence and Shelley, is that we can only make a judgement of Lawrence's poetry if we admit that in this, as in many other respects, he is one of the bridges between the great writers of the Romantic Movement and the poetry of our own epoch. Despite his rebellion against many of the things which the nineteenth-century stood for, and despite his concern to be recognized as an innovator, he is himself closely linked to his Romantic predecessors by an all-embracing moral concern. The 'naturalness' I have spoken of is at its deepest level a moral virtue, and Lawrence recognized it as such. Indeed, his feeling that he had a firm footing in a morality he understood was what enabled him to revolt, and, more important, to re-invent. In this, too, he resembled his predecessors of the generation of Shelley. Pound and Eliot were the heirs of Browning: Lawrence, on the other hand, seems to have been the residuary legatee not merely of Whitman and Shelley, but of Wordsworth. He makes the true and uncontaminated spirit of Romanticism viable for a later and more complex epoch. His best poems have, even now, a casual and unpolished look which is deceptive. The shock to the heart which they give us does not spring from observation alone, nor even from a delicate sympathy for other existences (though both of these are present). It comes, too, from the courage to dare as the Romantics dared, and to speak out as they spoke out.

D. H. Lawrence
and Painting
John Russell

The paintings for which D. H. Lawrence became notorious in 1929 are not very good. He had almost no natural gift, his acquired skills were few and insufficient, and his subject-matter was simplistic to the point of absurdity. It is difficult to believe that if they were not by him, and if they had not been the object of a particularly ridiculous court action, the paintings in question would be ranked higher than curiosities. What keeps them alive, in the context of Lawrence's career as a whole, is the intensity of his commitment to painting.

That commitment began early, and it was of a kind now rarely met with. Lawrence grew up in a place, and at a time, in which culture did not come ready-made but was the result of sustained effort, most often with materials which would now seem to us paltry and incomplete. The quality of the response was what counted, in the Nottinghamshire of the 1890s, and no one was more true to himself, in his responses, than Lawrence. He found wonder in what was to hand. 'The hymns which I learned as a child, and never forgot, mean to me almost more than the finest poetry, and they have for me a more permanent value, somehow or other. They live and glisten in the depths of a man's consciousness in undimmed wonder . . .' Something of the same sort happened when Lawrence began to respond to painting. He did not address himself to a conscious choice among the old masters; he *participated*. He took what was to hand – a friend's album, or a reproduction of whatever picture was being talked about at the time – and he did the best he could, in the way of a copy or a free embellishment. It was a social act: one that brought him nearer to his friends, and nearer to a completely developed idea of himself as a social being.

He is known to have been contributing to his friends' albums as early as 1902, when he was seventeen; and on his twenty-first birthday he was given something that he always remembered with gratitude and excitement – six issues of the 'English Watercolour' series which had been edited by Charles Holme and published in 1902 by *The Studio*.

I copied them with the greatest joy, [he wrote] and found some of them extremely difficult. Surely I put as much labour into copying from those watercolour
reproductions as most modern art students put into all their years of study. And I
had enormous profit from it. I not only acquired a considerable technical skill in the
handling of watercolour – let any man try copying the English watercolour artists
from Paul Sandby and Peter de Wint and Girtin, up to Frank Brangyn and the
Impressionists like Brabazon, and he will see how much skill he requires – but also I
developed my my visionary awareness.

Lawrence wrote these lines in April 1929, at a time when painting was much
on his mind and his exhibition at the Warren Gallery in London was imminent.
But the crucial experience which he refers to must have been above all between
11 September 1906, the date of his twenty-first birthday, and October 1908
when he went to London and began to teach in the Davidson Road School in
Croydon. This was a time of intense and accelerated development for Lawrence;
and he became aware of art as what he later called 'a form of supremely delicate
awareness and atonement – meaning at-one-ness, the state of being at one with
the object.' Quite clearly his excitement was contagious; May Chambers
Holbrook, Jessie Chambers's elder sister, suggested this when she described
the Lawrences' kitchen

the table littered with watercolours and autograph albums, and Bert in his shirt sleeves
painting furiously, surrounded by an admiring group of half a dozen girls and one
boy, who had presented each other with albums for Christmas. Bert painted a child
with a watering-can over the flower-bed and an umbrella over her own head in a
heavy shower on a page of my album from himself, and wrote:

> His 'prentice han' he tried on man
> And then he made the lasses 'O'.
>   (Burns).

Each one of us wanted a painting done for every one in the group, and Bert ran his
fingers through his hair excitedly. 'I tell you what, you'll have to have them, and
I'll do them one by one. You won't mind what I choose, will you?'

He was assured his choice would satisfy everyone.

'Just so long as there's a bit of colour will suit me', said several, all of us accepting his
kindness with out any sense of obligation. Bert was the centre of the gay crowd, and
we took it for granted that he liked to do us such favours.

After so lively an account it is discouraging to have to say – on the evidence of
the drawings which were shown as part of the 'Young Bert', an exhibition
held in 1972 at the Castle Museum in Nottingham – that the vivacity in question
resided more in the human contacts which were involved than in anything
that Lawrence got down on paper; a more cheerless group of pictures can
rarely have been put on view. It is almost poignant that these stiff little daubs

should be the work of a man who as early as July 1908 could write like this in a letter to a friend:

From morning till night I have worked in the fields, when the willows have glittered like hammered steel in the morning; till evening when the yellow atmosphere seemed thick and palpable with dense sunshine. You might have found me crawling from side to side on the horse rake, bending, then a jingle as the tines fell behind the winrow; you might have heard the whirr of the file as I sharpen the bristling machine-knife under the hornbeam; you could have seen me high on the load, or higher on the stack, like a long mushroom in my felt hat, sweating, with my shirt neck open.

Nothing of this immediacy, this full realization of detail, came through in the paintings. But then landscape came second best to figure-painting, in Lawrence's canon; and when he found a figure-painting that he really liked he got from it precisely that 'visionary awareness' of which he wrote in 1929. 'One can only develop one's visionary awareness,' he went on, 'by close contact with the vision itself; that is, by knowing pictures, real vision pictures, and by dwelling on them, and really dwelling in them. It is a great delight, to dwell in a picture.'

A picture in which Lawrence undeniably dwelt over and over again is Maurice Greiffenhagen's *An Idyll*, which is now in the Walker Art Gallery, Liverpool. This had been a popular painting ever since it was first shown in 1891; and by comparison with such earlier memorials of physical attraction as Millais's *The Black Brunswicker* of 1860 it could be called outspoken. I owe to Dr C. E. Baron, along with much else that appears here, the fact that a contributor to the *Art Journal* of 1892 said that 'seldom, if ever, had the passionate embrace been pictorially attempted' and the fascination of *The Embrace* for its large audience was undoubtedly related to its having broken a taboo. Greiffenhagen was of Baltic German descent, and there is about his *Idyll* something weighty and something explicit which appealed directly to Lawrence.

But if the painting had an altogether exceptional hold upon the young Lawrence it was because kisses and kissing were very much on his mind during the winter of 1908–9, when he seems to have made his first attempts to copy *An Idyll*. This was the period of his most revelatory correspondence with Blanche Jennings, the feminist and Post Office worker. On 15 December 1908, Lawrence wrote to Miss Jennings:

I have kissed dozens of girls – on the cheek – never on the mouth – I could not. Such a touch is the vigorous connection between the vigorous flow of two lives. Like a positive electricity, the current of creative life runs through two persons, and they are instinct with the same life force – the same vitality – the same I know not what – when they kiss on the mouth – they kiss as lovers do.

D. H. LAWRENCE AND PAINTING

Given this state of mind, it is not surprising that Lawrence, with his belief in the virtues of copying, should have tried over and over again to capture the quintessence of *An Idyll*. ('I know we were all very tired of it,' said one candid friend; 'there is no doubt that his figures were awful.') The picture drove him in December 1908 to temerities which he might not otherwise have attempted; under the effect of it he kissed 'a certain girl till she hid her head in my shoulder'. Questions of a more general order were also raised: 'In love, or at least in love-making', he wrote to Miss Jennings, 'do you think the woman is always passive, like the girl in the "Idyll" – enjoying the man's demonstration, a wee bit frit – not active? I prefer a little devil – a Carmen – I like nothing passive. The girls I have known are mostly so; men always declare them so, and like them so; I do not.'

That particular problem was solved when Lawrence ran away with Frieda Weekley in May 1912; but Dr Baron points out that as late as December 1912 Lawrence was writing from Italy in search of yet another reproduction of *An Idyll* from which to make yet another copy. Perhaps by then he was bringing more of himself to the work: his friend George Henry Neville said of one copy that 'Lawrence had the woody background and the poppy-spangled foreground with wonderful effect, the colours brighter and possibly better contrasted even than Greiffenhagen's own. Lawrence was always like that: he saw colours always about three shades brighter than the rest of us . . .'

During Lawrence's years in Croydon (1908–12) he could have seen great painting at first hand: and not by the Old Masters only. But the magic of dwelling seems to have been originated most often in black and white photographs which left Lawrence free to invent his own colour: this was, at any rate, the basis on which Lawrence copied what he called Lorenzetti's 'great picture of the Thebaid' and an unnamed Carpaccio (probably *The Dream of St Ursula*) from Venice. The strongest first-hand experience to which he referred in his letters was that of the Winter Exhibition at Burlington House in February 1909, where he saw among the visitors 'women such as I have never seen before, beautiful, flowing women, with a pride and grace you never meet in the provinces'. From our point of view the exhibition that year – modern paintings and sculpture from the collection of George McCulloch was mediocre even by the standard of the long Presidency (1896–1918) of Sir Edward Poynter; but Lawrence identified strongly, even so, with Bastien-Lepage's *Pauvre Fauvette* ('a terrible picture of a peasant girl wrapped in a lump of sacking'). Of another painting from the same hand he said 'The peasant woman is magnificent – above all things, capable: to work, to suffer, to endure, to love – not, oh Bastien Lepage, Oh Wells! Oh the God that there isn't – to enjoy.' Lawrence liked pictures for what he got out of them and not for their status in the hierarchies.

237

His notions of living art could have changed radically from the summer of 1912 onwards. The year 1912 was fundamental, for instance, to the development of the modern movement, and nowhere more so than in Munich, where the 'Blue Rider' group opened its first exhibition in December 1911 and Kandinsky had just published *On the Spiritual in Art*. But the effect of all this on Lawrence was to make him 'think with kindliness of England, whose artists so often suck their sadness like a lollipop, mournfully and comfortably'. To those who are familiar with the 'Blue Rider' group and regard Kandinsky, August Macke and Franz Marc as people of perpetual consequence it may seem a sign of provinciality that Lawrence did not even respond to Kandinsky's Murnau landscapes or to Franz Marc's vision of the animal world: in the one, as in the other, Nature is so freshly seen and so convincingly re-interpreted that we may well think of them as akin to the great set-pieces of landscape-painting in Lawrence's letters and novels and to the acute, succinct characterization of animals and insects in his poems. Lawrence might have seen in Kandinsky's Murnau landscapes the fulfilment of the ideas which he attributes to Paul Morel in *Sons and Lovers*. (Morel painted pine trees towards sunset and challenged Miriam to say if they were pine trees or 'red coals, standing-up pieces of fire in that darkness? There's God's burning bush for you, that burned not away.'). But Lawrence was neither curator nor historian, and when he went to an exhibition he swallowed what he needed, whole, and spat the rest out.

Lawrence did better with the Italian Futurists. 'There isn't one trace of naïveté in the works,' he wrote in June 1914, 'though there's plenty of naïveté in the authors. It's the most self-conscious, intentional, pseudo-scientific stuff on the face of the earth.' His opinion was based on 'a book of their poetry – a very fat book too – and a book of pictures – and I read Marinetti's and Piero Buzzi's manifestations and essays and Soffici's essays on cubism and futurism'. 'I like it,' he went on, 'because it is the applying to emotions of the purging of the old forms and sentimentalities. I like it for its saying – enough of this sickly cant, let us be honest and stick by what is in us.' Lawrence at that time knew very little of Italy – he had lived there for less than a year – but he put his finger on the particular thinness of spirit which is the mark of Futurism when he said that the Futurists 'will progress down the purely male or intellectual or scientific line. They will even use their intuition for intellectual and scientific purpose. The one thing about their art is that it *isn't* art, but ultra scientific attempts to make diagrams of certain physic or mental states.' Coming from someone whose allegiances had been on the side of Victorian story-telling in paint there is something very impressive about Lawrence's instinctive summing-up (in his 'Study of Thomas Hardy') of the merits and shortcomings of Boccioni's sculpture. But then the experience of Futurism bore directly on an idea that he was preoccupying him at the time: that 'the only re-sourcing of art, revivifying it, is to make it more the joint work of man and woman'. Futurism seemed to him to be man-oriented, exclusively; as such, it was unacceptable to him.

Altogether, therefore, he returned to England in June 1914 as someone who had seen more, in matters of art, but who had not loved more. Of course he could be very good about things he disliked: 'Think of the malice, the sheer malice of a Beardsley drawing,' he wrote in 1922, 'the wit and venom of the mockery.' But fundamentally he still demanded of art that it should nourish him with the assurance of a cultural nearness of the kind that he had got from the English watercolourists as *The Studio* had presented them. (It is difficult to read *The Rainbow* and not be struck by the assonance of Brangwen and Brang-wyn when Will Brangwen and his paintings are under discussion). Lawrence had never known any of the painters whom he admired during his years in Nottingham; but when he and Frieda returned to England they soon got to know people who took it for granted that first-hand acquaintance with painters and their work was a necessary element in life. Sometimes this worked well for Lawrence, sometimes it didn't. But what mattered most was that in *Women in Love* he had new material for the dialogue with the idea of being an artist which he had begun in *The White Peacock* and continued in *Sons and Lovers* and *The Rainbow*.

'Every true artist is the salvation of every other,' says Birkin in *Women in Love*. Lawrence himself did not find many true artists, in this sense, in the course of his forays, from 1914 onwards, into the English art world. There were several reasons for this. He found it easier, for one thing, to come to terms with imagi-nary painters, or with North Country amateurs, than with real live professionals. For another thing, many of his contacts during the First World War were poisoned, whether or not he was directly aware of it, by awareness of class. In particular, Duncan Grant and his friends had a natural assurance in life that Lawrence never attained to. They made him feel uneasy, and his uneasiness led him to tell them just how inadequate they were, both as human beings and, necessarily, as writers and artists and philosophers. The only painter in England with whom Lawrence struck up a lasting friendship was Mark Gertler; and Gertler, like Lawrence, did not *belong*, in a now-obsolete but none the less mortifying and exasperating sense, to the world of the Grants of Rothiemurchus.

Lawrences's fallings-out with Bloomsbury are too numerous and too well-documented to need investigation here. He tried to find in Lady Ottoline Morrell an ideal protectress, tried to work closely with Bertrand Russell, tried to like Duncan Grant: but the antitheses were too fundamental. Among literary persons it has been mostly been taken for granted that the fault in this lay with Bloomsbury and that Lawrence was wholly in the right when he spoke of an atmosphere of 'horrible little frowsty people, men lovers of men', who gave him 'such a sense of corruption, almost of putrescence, that I dream of beetles'. Perhaps this should be set against Bertrand Russell's belief that Lawrence's ideas 'led straight to Auschwitz' and Virginia Woolf's entry about Lawrence in her diary: 'It's the preaching that rasps me. Like a person delivering judgment when only half the facts are there; and clinging to the rails and beating the cushion.' All of these points of view can be disputed; but where painting is concerned there is no doubt that the intelligent, reflective and widely-aware procedures of Grant were at the farthest possible remove from Lawrence's. If Lawrence spoke harshly of Grant's work in January 1915, it was because he had hoped to find a kindred spirit ('We liked Duncan Grant very much. I *really* liked him') and was therefore all the more sensitive to what he regarded as further evidence of his rejection by England and the English. Once again, he spoke not as a historian, or as a curator, but as a living creature who had one skin too few; and it is for us, not for him, to acknowledge that what he called Grant's 'silly experiments in the futuristic line' were among the most radical English paintings of their date.

It was in the autumn of 1926, and with no previous warning, that Lawrence for the first time began to paint in oils, out of his own head and on quite a large scale. Maria Huxley had chanced to come over to the Lawrences' villa near Florence with four stretched canvases which had been left behind in her house. The Lawrences had paints and brushes lying around, Frieda Lawrence said 'Let's have some pictures!', and Lawrence plunged straight in and finished the first one – *A Holy Family* – in a couple of hours. In no time at all he was hooked, and by the spring he was telling visitors that he had had enough of writing and was going to devote himself to painting, full-time. In March 1928 he asked to have an exhibition of his work at the Dorothy Warren Gallery in London; the Mandrake Press announced the publication of a book on his paintings; and in 1929 he wrote one of the most remarkable of all his essays, 'An Introduction to These Paintings'.

All this may astonish, in that it came from a man who for many years seems hardly to have touched a brush. That it certainly did not result from any wish to break into the modern-art scene as it then existed we can infer from his account of a visit in January 1927 to the Italian painter Alberto Magnelli. 'He didn't care for me: nor I for him. And when I think over his pictures they seem to me pretentious rubbish, and about as formless as a paper-chase.' It would seem most likely that Lawrence turned to oil-painting for love of its immediate, instinctual quality. (Visitors were often told, for instance, how he had applied the paint in certain areas with his thumb, or with the palm of his hand.) Not only was it a complete change of activity, but it assuaged the feelings of which he wrote to Earl Brewster in February 1927:

You and I are at the *age dangereuse* for men: when the whole rhythm of the psyche changes: when one no longer has an easy flow outwards: one rebels at a great many things. It is as well to know the thing is pysiological: though that doesn't nullify the psychological reality. One resents bitterly a certain swindle about modern life, and especially a sex swindle. The only thing is to wait: and to take the next wave as it rises.

It was, as I see it, to keep such feelings at bay that Lawrence sought 'an easy flow outwards' in the paintings which came, one after another, in the winter of 1926–7. 'I simply *can't* stand people at close quarters', he wrote to Earl Brewster at that time; and the period during which he first produced his paintings and then saw to it that they got through to the public was for Lawrence one of almost continual harassment – much of it of a kind which can only be called barbaric. There was trouble, from the spring of 1927 onwards, about *Lady Chatterley's Lover*. There was the tapping of Lawrence's mail from Bandol to London in the winter of 1928–9, and the interception of the manuscript of *Pansies*. In the summer of 1929 there was the exhibition of Lawrence's paintings in London and the subsequent seizure of many of them by the police. There was trouble of a cognate sort about the Mandrake Press book of reproductions. Even the **most** robust and secure of natures would have felt violated by such a series of events.

Lawrence seems, in point of fact, to have used his painting as a means of bringing about a new and final stage in his relations with his friends, with England in general, and with English officialdom in particular. There was from the first an element of provocation in all this. A painter, unlike a novelist, can put his work before his friends and get an instantaneous impression of what they feel, or fail to feel, in the presence of it. Lawrence was quick to find this out: 'I feel', he wrote to Dorothy Brett in March 1927, 'that people *can't even look* at them. They glance, and look quickly away. I wish I could paint a picture that would just *kill* every cowardly and ill-minded person that looked at it. My word, what a slaughter!'

Lawrence need have not shown the paintings in London, and he need not have allowed their publication in book-form. There is no doubt that he deliberately set up a definitive confrontation, on new ground of his own choosing, with the authorities who had treated him as a common criminal. In the hierarchy of his achievements the paintings do not stand high; but in the context of what he had to endure in the last years of his life they are of fundamental importance. The resentments of a lifetime come out in them, also: Lawrence had it in mind, beyond a doubt, to manifest his contempt for Bloomsbury in a domain – that of the modern-art galleries of the West End – where Bloomsbury's influence was then very strong. In his 'Introduction to These Paintings' he spoke of 'the dear highbrows who gaze in a sort of ecstasy and get a correct mental thrill! Their poor highbrow bodies stand there as dead as dustbins, and can no more feel the sway of complete imagery upon them than can feel any other real sway.' Here and elsewhere the 'Introduction' quite clearly refers to Roger Fry and his friends; and Fry was not among those who protested against the seizure by the police of twelve of Lawrence's paintings.

Judged as polemical instruments, the oil-paintings of D. H. Lawrence were undeniably effective, in the short term. To judge them as works of art is not so easy, since most of them are several thousand miles away. Lawrence was critical of the then-existing reproductions in a detailed way (see his *Collected Letters*, pp. 1145–6, 1149–51) which not only carries conviction in itself but suggests that he had a much more conscious idea of what he was doing than is conveyed by the letters which he wrote at the time the pictures were painted. The paintings have a combination of bombast and inner vulnerability which will be familiar to all readers of Lawrence; but even if we allow for the betrayals of reproduction (and these may be presumed to be fewer and smaller in the later volume of *Paintings of D. H. Lawrence* of 1964) there still remains an awkwardness, and an obviousness, for which 'amateurish' is the kindest world. Lawrence is here relying on literal statement of a kind, and of a quality, which he would never have countenanced on the printed page. 'If you try to nail anything down in the novel,' he had written in 1925, 'either it kills the novel, or the novel gets up and walks away with the nail.' The nail, in this sense, killed the pictures.

It should be remembered that Lawrence was, as Aldous Huxley put it, 'a slowly dying man' when he painted the oil-paintings and wrote his 'Introduction' to them. It was in that condition, and in part because of it, that he found Aldous Huxley 'a weed', and derided Maria Huxley as someone who had been taken up by Lady Ottoline Morell and never got over it, and dismissed Chekhov – *Chekhov*! – as 'a second-rate writer and a willy wet-leg'. But, as Lawrence also wrote at that same time, 'There are many men in a man'; and the Lawrence of the last years whom we shall read for ever is the author of the 'Introduction to his Paintings'.

It is characteristic of Lawrence that his own paintings play virtually no part in this 'Introduction'. (A more direct preface to them is the essay of April 1929 called 'Making Pictures'). The long and idiosyncratic exordium on the history of English art will not commend itself to art-historians, though Matthew Smith, for one, used to say 'It's all there! It's all there!' when anyone asked him if the essay was worth reading. The attack on Roger Fry and his disciples has still some life in it, but it needs an effort of the historical imagination for younger readers to understand to what an extent Fry had a monopoly of influence at the time the 'Introduction' was written. Where the essay has an indestructible relevance both to Lawrence himself and to the predicament of the artist in no matter what medium is in the long section on Cézanne, and on Cézanne's lifelong struggle to re-invent the language of art. Lawrence had spent the whole of his short life in that same 'fight with the cliché'. When Lawrence says of Cézanne that 'he *never* got over the cliché denominator, the intrusion and interference of the ready-made concept, when it came to people, to men and women', he was not making a contribution to art-history. He was making common cause with someone who, like himself, had 'uttered the foreword to the collapse of our whole way of consciousness, and the substitution of another way'. A little later, Lawrence went on to say that 'We can see what a fight it means, the escape from the domination of the ready-made mental concept, the mental consciousness stuffed full of clichés that intervene like a complete screen between us and life. It means a long, long fight, that will probably last for ever. But Cézanne did at least get as far as the apple. I can think of nobody else who has done anything.'

On this level, Lawrence's paintings simply do not merit discussion. But a gravity of a completely different order attaches to his realization that Cézanne, like himself, had literally worked himself to death in the effort to describe the world as it really is, and as it had never been described before. That is why it is worth while to think about D. H. Lawrence in the context of painting, and to think about painting in the context of D. H. Lawrence.

Notes

WOMEN IN D. H. LAWRENCE'S WORKS

1 *Yale University Library Gazette*, no. 46, April 1972, p. 264.
2 *Ibid.*
3 *Ibid.*
4 *D. H. Lawrence: The Croydon Years* (Austin, Texas 1965).
5 Almost as good as an abortion. An interesting earlier case of symbolic miscarriage, not approved by her author but perhaps less unsympathetic now, is Rosamond Vincy's in *Middlemarch.*
6 Derek Hudson, *Munby, Man of Two Worlds* (London 1972).

D. H. LAWRENCE AND HOMOSEXUALITY

1 D. H. Lawrence, *David*, in *Complete Plays* (London 1965), p. 106. The covenant is sworn in I Samuel 20. But see also Leviticus 20:13: 'If a man also lieth with mankind, as he lieth with a woman, both of them shall have committed an abomination: they shall surely be put to death; their blood shall be upon them.'
2 See the chapter, 'Sexual Pathology' in my book, *The Wounded Spirit: A Study of "Seven Pillars of Wisdom"*, to be published in London by Martin, Brian & O'Keeffe in May 1973.
3 D. H. Lawrence, *Collected Letters*, ed. Harry T. Moore (London 1962), p. 251.
4 Quoted in H. Montgomery Hyde, *The Other Love* (London 1970), p. 1:

'The love that dare not speak its name' in this century is such a great affection of an elder for a younger man as there was between David and Jonathan, such as Plato made the very basis of his philosophy, and such as you find in the sonnets of Michaelangelo and Shakespeare. It is that deep, spiritual affection that is as pure as it is perfect.

5 To Godwin Baynes, quoted in Edward Nehls, *D. H. Lawrence: A Composite Biography* (Madison 1957), I, 500–1.
6 D. H. Lawrence, *Studies in Classic American Literature* (London 1924), pp. 167–8. Lawrence wrote the first version of this book, later published as *The Symbolic Meaning*, during 1916–19.
7 Quoted in Knud Merrild, *A Poet and Two Painters* (London 1938), p. 92.
8 To Katherine Mansfield, ?21 November 1918, in *Letters*, p. 565.
9 Letter of 19 April 1915, quoted in David Garnett, *Flowers of the Forest* (London 1955), pp. 53–4. See also Lawrence's letter to S. S. Koteliansky, ?20 April 1915, in *Letters*, p. 333:

I like David, but Birrell I have come to detest. These horrible little frowsty people, men lovers of men, they give me such a sense of corruption, almost putrescence, that I dream of beetles. It is abominable.

Beetles are a symbol of corruption in *Women in Love*.

10 Letter to Bertrand Russell, 13 February 1915, in *Letters*, p. 320.

11 'The Noble Englishman', *The Complete Poems of D. H. Lawrence*, eds. Vivian de Sala Pinto and Warren Roberts, I (London 1964) pp. 446–7.

12 'Tortoise Shout', *Complete Poems*, I, 366.

13 John Middleton Murry, *Son of Women* (London 1931), p. 119.

14 Compton Mackenzie, *My Life and Times, Octave Five: 1915–1923* (London 1966), pp. 167–8.

15 See Emile Delavenay, *D. H. Lawrence: The Man and His Work* (London 1972), p. 226.

16 Cecil Gray, *Musical Chairs* (London 1942), p. 138.

17 Merrild, p. 104.

18 John Middleton Murry, *Between Two Worlds: An Autobiography* (London 1936), pp. 262, 332.

19 *Ibid.*, p. 334. It is not clear what 'solidarity with men' Lawrence experienced as a child. This could refer to the 'perfect love' he shared with a miner when he was sixteen.

20 *Ibid.*, p. 337.

21 Quoted in F. A. Lea, *The Life of John Middleton Murry* (London 1959), p. 41.

22 Murry, *Between Two Worlds*, p. 413.

23 Quoted in Lea, p. 53. See the letter about Lawrence from Katherine Mansfield to Gordon Campbell, May 1916, quoted in Anthony Alpers, *Katherine Mansfield* (London 1954), p. 225:

> once you start talking, I cannot describe the frenzy that comes over him. He simply *raves*, roars, beats the table, abuses everybody. But that's not such great matter. What makes these attacks insupportable is the feeling one has at the back of one's mind that he is completely out of control, swallowed up in an acute, *insane*, irritation. After one of these attacks he's ill with fever, haggard and broken.

24 See Delavenay, p. 279:

> Lawrence specifically denied to Catherine Carswell any suggestion of pederasty with William Henry. The denial is noteworthy: together with the description in the Prologue to *Women in Love*, of the attraction exercised on Birkin by the dark-eyed 'Cornish' types of men, it contains an element of admission.

25 D. H. Lawrence, *Phoenix II* (London 1968), p. 104. *The Sisters* was the original title for what became *The Rainbow* and *Women in Love*.

26 *Ibid.*, p. 107

27 D. H. Lawrence, *Women in Love* (London: Penguin 1972), p. 37.

28 Murry, *Between Two Worlds*, pp. 409, 412.

29 But see Birkin's allusion to Genesis 19:24–25: Well, if mankind is destroyed, if our race is destroyed like Sodom . . . I am satisfied' (p. 65).

30 For an interesting contemporary analogue to 'Snowed Up', see the 'Snow' chapter in Mann's *The Magic Mountain* (1924), which brilliantly describes what is omitted from *Women in Love*: the quest for death in the Alps.

31 See the ironic fatherly concern of Mr Brangwen (speaking to Birkin): 'she's had everything that's right for a girl to have . . . and I don't want to see her going back on it all' (p. 290).

32 Mark Spilka, *The Love Ethic of D. H. Lawrence* (Bloomington 1955), p. 153.

33 Mark Spilka, 'Lawrence Up-Tight, or the Anal Phase Once Over', *Novel* (1971), IV, p. 257.

34 Eugene Goodheart, *The Utopian Vision of D. H. Lawrence* (Chicago 1963), pp. 121–2.

35 H. M. Daleski, *The Forked Flame* (London 1965), p. 185.

36 Spilka, 'Lawrence Up-Tight', p. 259. The quoted phrase is Ursula's, not Lawrence's, interpretation of Birkin's feelings. See also G. Wilson Knight, 'Lawrence, Joyce and Powys', *Essays in Criticism* (1961), XI, pp. 403–17; and Ford, Kermode, Clarke and Spilka, 'Critical Exchange on "Lawrence Up-Tight," ' *Novel* (1971), V, pp. 54–70.

37 Both doctors and homosexuals agree that the first experience of anal penetration is extremely painful. There is an old homosexual pun: 'Rectum? I nearly killed him!'
    Norman Mailer's superb story, 'The Time of Her Time', describes a battle of sexual wills that climaxes in comical anality.

38 D. H. Lawrence, *Phoenix*, ed. Edward McDonald (London 1936), p. 693.

39 For a fascinating, though somewhat simplistic theory of how incestuous desires are transformed into anal love, see Clifford Allen, *Homosexuality: Its Nature, Causation and Treatment* (London 1958), pp. 49–50:

> In homosexuality not only does the patient identify himself with the mother (and turns away from the father) in most cases, but it is not generally realised that he tends to regard other men as symbolising the mother in some manner. Various parts of the mother become metamorphosed into the male. . . . The vagina becomes symbolised by the anus or mouth. Anal intercourse is only unconscious incestuous behaviour although it has undergone considerable transformation.

> For other useful works on the theory of homosexuality see: Sigmund Freud, 'Character and Anal Eroticism' and 'On the Transformation of Instincts, with Special Reference to Anal Eroticism', *Collected Papers*, trans. Joan Riviere (London 1950), II, pp. 45–50, 164–71; Charles Socarides, *The Overt Homosexual* (London 1968); and Clifford Allen, *A Textbook of Psychosexual Disorders* (London 1969).

BIBLIOGRAPHICAL NOTE ON
D. H. LAWRENCE AND AMERICA

The quotations from Lawrence come from the following volumes:
Phoenix (London 1961).
Phoenix II (London 1968).
The Letters of D. H. Lawrence edited by Aldous Huxley (London 1956).
The Collected Letters of D. H. Lawrence edited by Harry T. Moore (London 1962), Vols. 1 & 2.
D. H. Lawrence, *Mornings in Mexico and Etruscan Places* (London 1965).
D. H. Lawrence, *The Short Novels* (London 1956), Vol. 2.
D. H. Lawrence, *The Complete Short Stories* (London 1955), Vol. 2.
D. H. Lawrence, *Studies in Classic American Literature* (London 1964).
The Symbolic Meaning, edited by Armin Arnold (London 1962).
The biographical material is taken from:
Mabel Dodge Luhan, *Lorenzo in Taos* (London 1933).
Knut Merrild, *With D. H. Lawrence in New Mexico* (London 1964).

Inevitably, there has been a good deal written of the subject of Lawrence and America. The following three books all contain interesting and valuable observations:

David Cavitch, *D. H. Lawrence and the New World* (Oxford 1969).
James C. Cowan, *D. H. Lawrence's American Journey*, The Press of Case Western Reserve University 1970.
Richard Swigg, *Lawrence, Hardy, and American Literature* (Oxford 1972).

1 Due to the limits of the available space I have had to exclude all considerations of Lawrence's writing on American literature and his important non-fiction writing about America contained in *Mornings in Mexico*.

NOTES

LAWRENCE'S POETRY: THE SINGLE STATE OF MAN

1 Robert Graves, whose poetry I admire, does not seem to me to have survived the war. For all his debonairness he has remained essentially a war poet. That is, he has created a drawing-room art out of anything but drawing-room feelings. His moments of savagery and tenderness appear like crevasses in a snowfield, unexpected and disconcerting. Lawrence himself summed it up in *Aaron's Rod*: 'In this officer, of course, there was a lightness and an appearance of bright diffidence and humour. But underneath it was all the same as in the common men of all combatant nations: the hot, seared burn of unbearable experience, which did not heal nor cool, and whose irritation was not to be relieved. The experience gradually cooled on top: but only with a surface crust. The soul did not heal, did not recover.'

2 This essay was originally written in 1956 and published two years later in my first book, *The Shaping Spirit*. I mention this not as an excuse but simply to explain the rather nagging, polemical tone. The poetical fashions of that drab time were unusually tight-lipped and narrow-minded, favouring elegant verse essays with moral endings. They made the qualities of Lawrence's poetry which now seem most admirable, its freedom and fluency, appear downright eccentric. Perhaps that is why almost nothing had been written about his verse at that time, although in every other area the Lawrence industry was already in full production. So it seemed necessary to make – and keep repeating in different ways – a number of rather basic points which may now appear tiresomely obvious. Later, after the book was published, I saw that if I was right about what Lawrence was doing in his poetry, then I was pulling the plug on many of the careful judgments on which several of the other chapters were based. But knowing now how poetry has changed and developed over the last seventeen years, those careful judgments seem less important than my emphasis on Lawrence's very different and unfashionable originality as a poet.

3 Since writing this it has occurred to me that the clue to the technical originality of Lawrence's mature verse may be that it has a different metrical norm from most other English poetry. Its point of departure is not the iambic pentameter; instead, it is the terser movement of his narrative *prose*. I can see no other way of explaining the extraordinarily wide and subtle variation of rhythmical period within the span of a single line of free verse.

Index

INDEX

SOURCES OF ILLUSTRATIONS

Alinari 181; *Ferdinand Anton* 176*t*; *Lord Astor
Collection* (by courtesy of L. E. Pollinger) 149*t*;
Australia News and Information Bureau 153*t*; *Bassano
& Vandyke Studios* 102*r*, 110*l*; *G. Bunzel* 177;
Mansell Collection 103*tl*, 103*tr*, 104, 148, 149*b*, 152;
Nottingham Public Library, D. H. Lawrence Collec-
tion 12*t*, 13*b*, 15*t*, 16, 17*t*, 54*b*, 55*t*, 55*b*, 56*t* 57*tl*,
57*tr*, 57*b*, 58, 62–3, 64, 65 (from *Young Lorenzo*),
100*b*, 101, 108*b*, 109*t* (from *Sussex Life*), 110*r*
(Mrs L. Vinogradoff), 111 (Mrs L. Vinogradoff),
112, 114*t*, 114*b* (Mrs Roberts), 147 (from Secker,
Calendar of Letters), 180*t*, 185*b*, 186; *The Open
University* 11, 14, 18, 106, 107, 108*t*; *Paul Popper*
100*t*, 109*b*, 150, 154*b*, 178–9, 184; *Radio Times
Hulton Picture Library* 102*l*, 113; *H. Roger Viollet*
176*b*; *Bertam Rota Collection* (by courtesy of L. E.
Pollinger) 175; *University of Nottingham Library*
12*b*, 13*t*, 15*b* (Mr G. L. Lazarus), 51 (Mr H. F.

Gunns), 53, 54*t*, 56*b* (Mr P. C. Barnet), 59
(Prof. J. T. Boulton), 60, 61, (Croydon Public
Library), 66 (by courtesy of L. E. Pollinger), 99
(Montagu Weekley), 103*b* (by courtesy of L. E.
Pollinger, 105 (by courtesy of L. E. Pollinger),
151 (Miss F. G. Wilkinson), 153*b* (Mrs M. E.
Needham), 154*t* (Witter Bynner), 155 (Witter
Bynner), 156*t* & *b* (Witter Bynner), 157 (Witter
Bynner), 182 (Mr Clarke), 183*t*, 183*b* (Mrs M. E.
Needham), 185*t*; *University of Texas*, Collection
of the Humanities Research Center (by courtesy
of L. E. Pollinger), 158, 180*b*.

The photographs kindly lent by the Open University were specially commissioned to illustrate
a correspondence text written by Mr Graham
Martin, Reader in Literature at the Open
University.

Due 28 Days From Latest Date

OCT 27 1977			
MAY 10 1980			
APR 16 1981			
MAY 2 1981			
FEB 16 1990	WITHDRAWN		
JUN 21 1990			